The Conflict Revisited

NEW COMPARATIVE CRITICISM

PETER LANG
Oxford • Bern • Berlin • Bruxelles • New York • Wien

The Conflict Revisited

The Second World War in Post-Postmodern Fiction

Marco Malvestio

PETER LANG
Oxford • Bern • Berlin • Bruxelles • New York • Wien

Bibliographic information published by Die Deutsche Bibliothek
Die Deutsche Nationalbibliothek lists this publication in the Deutsche Nationalbibliografie; detailed bibliographic data is available on the Internet at http://dnb.ddb.de.

A catalogue record for this book is available at the British Library.

Library of Congress Cataloging-in-Publication Data

Names: Malvestio, Marco, author.
Title: The conflict revisited : the Second World War in post-postmodern fiction / Marco Malvestio.
Description: London ; New York : Peter Lang, 2021. | Series: New comparative criticism, 2235-1809 ; volume 10 | Includes bibliographical references and index.
Identifiers: LCCN 2020019920 (print) | LCCN 2020019921 (ebook) | ISBN 9781789972092 (paperback) | ISBN 9781789972108 (ebook) | ISBN 9781789972115 (epub) | ISBN 9781789972122 (mobi)
Subjects: LCSH: Fiction--21st century--History and criticism. | Post-postmodernism (Literature) | World War, 1939-1945--Literature and the war.
Classification: LCC PN3504 .M35 2020 (print) | LCC PN3504 (ebook) | DDC 809.3/051--dc23
LC record available at https://lccn.loc.gov/2020019920
LC ebook record available at https://lccn.loc.gov/2020019921

Volume pubblicato con il contributo del Dipartimento di Studi Linguistici e Letterari dell'Università degli Studi di Padova.

Cover image: *It was not a blank space* by Ophelia Borghesan. Collage created from images in the public domain or available for free use.

ISSN 2235-1809
ISBN 978-1-78997-209-2 (print) • ISBN 978-1-78997-210-8 (ePDF)
ISBN 978-1-78997-211-5 (ePub) • ISBN 978-1-78997-212-2 (mobi)

Published by Peter Lang Ltd, International Academic Publishers,
52 St Giles, Oxford, OX1 3LU, United Kingdom
oxford@peterlang.com, www.peterlang.com

This publication has been peer reviewed.

Contents

He asked him to tell them how and where he got his wound. This pleased Rostov and he began talking about it, and as he went on became more and more animated. He told them of his Schöngrabern affair, just as those who have taken part in a battle generally do describe it, that is, as they would like it to have been, as they have heard it described by others, and as sounds well, but not at all as it really was. Rostov was a truthful young man and would on no account have told a deliberate lie. He began his story meaning to tell everything just as it happened, but imperceptibly, involuntarily, and inevitably he lapsed into falsehood.

Leo Tolstoy, *War and Peace*

Acknowledgements

This work started in 2015 as a doctoral thesis conducted at the Department of Linguistic and Literary Studies of the University of Padua under the supervision of Emanuele Zinato. At the department, I received the constant support of professors, colleagues and friends. I am thankful to Alvaro Barbieri for inviting me to the *XLVII Convegno Interuniversitario di Bressanone* and for all the discussions on the 'Western way of war' we had through the years; to Gabriele Bizzarri for reading my chapter on Roberto Bolaño; to Alessandro Metlica for reading parts of this work and to Annalisa Oboe for providing useful suggestions on Sarah Waters and Andrea Levy. My colleagues Stefania Santoni and Valentina Sturli made a hard and challenging path if not enjoyable, at least more than bearable.

During the course of this research, I had the opportunity to spend two long periods as a visiting graduate student at the University of Cambridge and at Royal Holloway, University of London (RHUL). I am thankful to those who supervised my work there and read it: Pierpaolo Antonello and Robert Gordon in Cambridge and Stefano Jossa at RHUL.

Both the members of my thesis committee and the external reviewers of the thesis provided precious feedback on my work. I am especially thankful to Alessandro Cinquegrani, Daniele Giglioli and Pia Masiero.

Christopher Coffman, Françoise Palleau-Papin and Filippo Pennacchio read a first draft of this book and provided me with countless suggestions on how to improve my work (and, in Christopher's case, my English). I am also thankful to Giuseppe Carrara and Daniel Lukes for the interesting and enriching exchanges we had about Vollmann.

I completed this book while I was a postdoctoral fellow at the Department of Italian Studies at the University of Toronto and my gratitude goes to this institution. I am especially thankful to Eloisa Morra, who read the conclusion of this work, and to Konrad Eisenbichler and his 'Halfway House for Wayward Scholars'.

Finally, I am deeply in debt with my friends of the 'Accademia'. They know who they are, but, most importantly, they know why I own them my gratitude.

I already discussed some of the ideas contained at pp. 82-94 in '*Europe Central* tra raccolta di racconti e romanzo massimalista', *Nuova prosa*, 67 (2017), 99-122. Some earlier reflections on mythology in contemporary fiction can be found in 'Mito e romanzo negli anni Zero: Littell, Roth, Vollmann', *Classicocontemporaneo*, 3 (2017), 14-30. An earlier and shorter version of the discussion of *The Third Reich* and *2666* in Chapter 2 can be found in '*Wargames*, etica e responsabilità: la Seconda Guerra Mondiale in *El Tercer Reich e 2666*', *Orillas*, 6 (2017), 85-97.

Preface
Global War, Global Literature

Considerations on the Choice of Texts

The primary aim of this book is to connect the interpretation and treatment of a prevalent literary theme in twenty-first-century global literature, the Second World War, with the evolution of post-postmodern poetics. I contend that the increasing popularity of the Second World War as the subject of many important post-postmodern literary works signals growing anxieties over derealization and a lack of agency and purpose, which manifest in several aspects of contemporary everyday life, digital technologies, and warfare. The specific mobilization of the Second World War to counterbalance these anxieties can be attributed both to its historical importance and the peculiarity of its memorialization.

Expanding on current conceptions of the period that followed postmodernism, I argue that post-postmodernism is characterized by a renewed preoccupation with the relationship between reality and fiction and a non-parodying reprise of the narrative techniques of the traditional novel (such as plot, characters, temporality, mimetic effort), together with features of postmodernism (metafiction, autofiction, the reprise of genre literature). I elucidate how post-postmodern poetics treats history in a radically different way to postmodern deconstructivism and historiographic metafiction. Specifically, I contend that post-postmodernism recovers the materiality of history, whereas postmodernism reduces history to the textual.

My analysis focuses mainly on three authors. Chapter 1 discusses Roberto Bolaño's *El Tercer Reich* [*The Third Reich*] (1989/2010), *La literatura nazi en América* [*Nazi Literature in the Americas*] (1996), *Estrella distante* [*Distant Star*] (1996) and *2666* (2004), Chapter 2 explores William T. Vollmann's *Europe Central* (2005) and Chapter 3 examines Jonathan

Littell's *Les Bienveillantes* [*The Kindly Ones*] (2006). These authors are compared with several others: Ian McEwan (*Atonement*, 2001) in Chapter 1; Sarah Waters (*The Night Watch*, 2006) and Rachel Seiffert (*The Dark Room*, 2001) in Chapter 2; and Laurent Binet (*HHhH*, 2010) and Giorgio Falco (*La gemella H* [*The H Twin*], 2014) in Chapter 3. With the exception of Bolaño's first books, all the novels I consider were written in the new millennium and the authors belong to the postwar generations. Authors like Norman Mailer, who was alive during the Second World War but wrote novels about it in the 2000s (*The Castle in the Forest*, 2007), were excluded. This distinction is not arbitrary. My enquiry analyses the Second World War as a literary theme and not as a personal experience. Although Mailer's *The Castle in the Forest* can hardly be considered a memoir (it explores the devil's corruption of Adolf Hitler's childhood), I restrict my enquiry to the generations born after the war that have no personal involvement with it. As such involvement can be memorial or postmemorial, I also exclude books that focus on the experiences of the parents or the families of the author, such as Jonathan Safran Foer's *Everything Is Illuminated* (2002) and *Extremely Loud and Incredibly Close* (2005). In sum, this book focuses solely on novels that thematize the Second World War without drawing upon personal experience, however mediated.

My choice to focus on Bolaño, Vollmann and Littell is motivated by the critical acclaim their novels have received and the pre-eminence that these authors accord the theme of the Second World War. In the cases of Bolaño and Littell, the reputation of their novels among critics and the debate they generated made them a somewhat obligatory choice. This is also true of Vollmann, though to a lesser degree; I chose him primarily because of the originality in his representations of the Second World War. I devote less space to the other authors I consider due to the marginal place war occupies in their works (e.g. Falco and McEwan) or their lack of stylistic complexity in comparison with the three authors I focus on. Moreover, this selection is international and offers an account of different national literatures (Chilean, American, French) and the interrelations between them. The same can be said of the authors I compare: Binet is French, Falco is Italian, McEwan and Waters are British and Seiffert is of Australian and German heritage. My selection of texts aims to facilitate as wide an exploration as possible of the processes of memorialization of the Second World War and of post-postmodern poetics.

That said, I am painfully aware of the two main risks of literary criticism when the analysis involves contemporary writers: abstractness and imprecision. I believe that the content of a book should be explained and its coordinates extensively charted. For instance, those who wish to critique Philip K. Dick's *The Man in the High Castle* ought to provide an explanation not only of the theory of alternate history, but also of what the I Ching is and what function it performs in the novel – no matter what their approach to the text is. Therefore, the reader of this book will find digressions on board games, Kabbalistic parables and Norse epics, because these subjects are contained in the novels I discuss and are intertwined with the role that the Second World War plays in my literary corpus. At the same time, I understand that the risks of this rigorous approach are that I could devote *too much* individual attention to the novels and, consequently, neglect the general framework in which they are inserted. In order to avoid these risks and combine the two approaches, which we can characterize as close and distant readings, in the monographic chapters I try to balance the close readings of the novels by making wider comparisons between the novels, especially in relation to their stylistic features.

Global War, Global Literature

When we refer to the Second World War, it seems clear what we mean: the conflict fought between the Axis powers (Germany, Italy, Japan and their allied and satellite countries) and the Allies (mainly the United States, the Soviet Union, China, France, the United Kingdom and members of the Commonwealth) from 1 September 1939 to 8 May 1945 (in Europe) and 2 September 1945 (in Asia). From a strictly formal perspective, this is correct; however, the reality is much more complex. More than any other war, the Second World War was not an isolated conflict that occurred between two precise dates. It was composed of several distinct parts. In fact, as Chris Bellamy suggests (2009: 3–4), the Second World

War appears to be the sum of at least four separate wars: the 'cabinet war' that followed Germany's invasion of Poland on 1 September 1939; the war in the Mediterranean and North Africa; the war on the Eastern Front, which can be backdated to the 1939–1940 Soviet–Finnish War; and the war in Eastern Asia, which started with Japan's invasion of China in 1937 and attained global proportions in 1941. The dates of these wars reach beyond the chronological limits of the established narrative of the Second World War. The hostilities in Asia, for instance, can be backdated to 1931 (Calvocoressi, Wint and Pritchard 1989: 618); indeed, in Japan, the Second World War is called 'the Fifteen Years War'. Although German aggressions and annexations started in 1938, the soldiers of the Axis powers had already fought the Allies during the Spanish Civil War (1936–1939). The date of the end of the war is similarly controversial, not only because it ended on two different dates in Europe and in Asia (as Germany surrendered on 7 May and Japan on 2 September). The series of conflicts that we call the Second World War could be considered to have terminated in the year 1947, which marked the beginning of the Cold War, or perhaps 1948, when the economic restrictions in Germany came to an end, or even 1989, when the Cold War ended (Rousso 2010: 5).

Bearing in mind the spatio-temporal scale of the Second World War and the diversity of opinion regarding when the war started and ended, it is unsurprising that literature about the Second World War includes a vast number of different narratives. Tales set on the Russian front, in Japan after the nuclear attack, in the Appennines where the Italian Resistance occurred, during the London or Dresden bombings, on the Thai 'Railway of Death', in Berlin surrounded by the Red Army, in Iwo Jima or Pearl Harbor, in Manchuria, in Alsace, in Spain, in Norway, in Greece or in Stalingrad all belong to the category of 'novels about the Second World War', despite their experiential and narrative heterogeneity.

At this early point, I want to clarify that I am not concerned with *war literature*, but with the Second World War *in* literature. In other words, I do not limit my analysis exclusively to texts that narrate the experience of soldiers fighting. I also include texts in which the Second World War merely appears and is thematized as a structural element of the plot and a precise historical fact (rather than through metaphors or symbols). By way of example, this book considers novels that narrate the active war (such as *Les Bienveillantes* by Jonathan Littell and *Europe Central* by William T. Vollmann) and novels in which there are almost no depictions of actual conflict, but in which the presence of the war is essential to the plot and its meaning (for example, Sarah Waters's *The Night Watch* or Giorgio Falco's *The H Twin*).

With the exceptions of military history accounts and board games created for entertainment purposes, the Second World War cannot be conceived without engaging with totalitarianism and the Holocaust.[1] Many of the powers that fought in the war were totalitarian dictatorships at the time (Germany, Italy, the Soviet Union and, in certain respects, Japan). Moreover, both the motivation and the implementation of the Axis aggressions were based on ethnic and racial discrimination (Fritz 2011: 4).[2] That is to say, the events of the Second World War are bound up with the notion of a totalitarian state ruled on ethnic grounds or the fight against such a state. As Enzo Traverso argues, the German aggression of 1941 aimed to fulfil two ideological premises of Nazi ideology: the fight against communism and the conquest of *Lebensraum*, a 'living space' similar in scope to the colonial dominions of France and England (Traverso 2003: 68). Therefore, the extermination of Jewish people continued until the very last days of the Reich, despite being at odds with economic and practical considerations (Traverso 1998: 308), because it represented one of the central aims of the Nazi war.

1 I deliberately use the word 'Holocaust' rather than 'Shoah'. I do not intend to ignore the polemics surrounding the sacral dimension of the term 'Holocaust', which views the extermination of Jews from a teleological perspective. It is worth noting that the term 'Shoah' is similarly associated with religious meanings, as Agamben (1998: 29) and Benbassa (2007: 156–157) argue. Because of its history, I agree with Weissman, who considers the term 'Holocaust' the most appropriate to express both the historical event and its subsequent reception, transmission, representation, trivialization and Americanization (2004: 25–26).

2 See also Hartmann 2013: 3. It is significant, as Christian Hartmann points out (2–33), that Hitler was unwilling to exploit Slavic collaborators in his war against the Russians. For further information regarding the racial premise of the war in the Pacific, see Dower 1986.

Whilst there would have been no Second World War without totalitarianism, totalitarianism exists, of course, in many forms outside of this war. It is possible to discuss fascist and communist dictatorships, their totalitarian dimensions and their crimes without mentioning the involvement of these dictatorships in the conflict because totalitarian states existed before this war and, in the cases of Russia and Spain, survived it. Likewise, it is possible discuss the Holocaust without necessarily invoking the Second World War. As we will see, it is true, as Bauman writes, that war is the necessary condition for the development of the Holocaust (Bauman 1989: 94), but it is more productive to analyse it in relation to the Nazi bureaucratic machine than it is to analyse it in relation to the German army.

I appreciate that these observations may seem quite schematic when considered in the abstract, but their significance will become clear when we take a closer look at examples of literary production. We would never qualify Primo Levi's *Se questo è un uomo* [*If This Is a Man*] or Thomas Keneally's *Schindler's List*, two rather different novels, as novels about the Second World War: they are about the Holocaust, imprisonment and factory-like extermination. On the other hand, the Holocaust plays a relevant role in novels such as *2666* by Roberto Bolaño, *Europe Central* by William T. Vollmann or *The Kindly Ones* by Jonathan Littell, all of which take the Second World War as their subject.

In conformity with the global nature of the conflict represented in the novels I explore, this book is written in the context of an international literary landscape. My approach is comparative, not in the sense that I compare two or more national literatures, but rather in that I compare several novels in different languages in the context of the broader global literary sphere. In the last two decades, the discipline of comparative literature has been reinvigorated by debates about World Literature. World Literature is not a canon of texts; it rather represents a network of exchanges or a system. As Franco Moretti writes in his influential essay 'Conjectures on World Literature', the initial hypothesis for his conception of World Literature comes from 'the world-systems school of economic history, for which international capitalism is a system that is simultaneously one, and unequal: with a core, and a periphery (and a semi-periphery) that are bound together in a relationship of growing inequality' (Moretti 2013: 46; see also Casanova 2004: XII). In this sense, an international approach to literature is more productive than a national approach because it enables us to understand that the hierarchies of literature, its balances of power and even its historical progression do not arise in a self-sustaining national space. Rather, they exist *because* of their interactions with other national literatures and, therefore, national and linguistic boundaries are not a sufficiently useful lens through which to interpret literary inequality and domination (Casanova 2014: 198–199).

The assumption that literature appears as a transcultural phenomenon, rather than a national one, is particularly relevant in relation to the contemporary novel. The literary texts (or 'objects') I consider in this book belong to the category of the global novel (or the 'cosmopolitan global novel', Levin 2014: 478, or the 'international novel', Patterson 2014: 3). They are novels conceived and composed in a global literary landscape, which makes comparisons between them possible and significant. It is important to underline that the global novel emerges as a distinct cultural product in the post-1989 era as a result of the typically postmodern tendencies to merge so-called 'low-' and 'highbrow' culture and to compare 'centres' of literary geographies to their 'peripheries'. While World Literature is a network of relations between texts, the global novel is an object, the product of a global literary market – as opposed to the national novel, which is conceived for a national market (Casanova 2014: 169). Not only does the global novel belong to a world-system (a characteristic of all literature); it is *conceived* in this system (Ganguly 2016: 2).

Both World Literature and the global novel represent useful concepts with which to understand literature, rather than necessarily having a set of precise characteristics. Discussing the contemporary novel as a global product invites us to look beyond its national aspects and focus on its interpretation in a global literary landscape. In this book, I refer to the global novel as a market category, rather than using the term to imply generic 'exoticness' based on the commodification of national traditions and sceneries for foreign markets. Further, I adopt the term 'global novel' critically and recognize that such categorization risks denying the differences that exist between the novels I am considering and the literary spaces in which they were written. In other words, as Emily Apter puts it, I keep in mind the risks of translatability assumption (Apter 2013: 3). In my analysis, I do not ignore that Bolaño, for example, is a Chilean writer whose career is deeply influenced by the political history of his country and the Chilean literary environment. I, of course, acknowledge that Vollmann's work is influenced by American postmodernism and that Littell has a strong relationship with the French literary tradition. At the same time, however, I stress the importance of understanding these authors in a broader international context, because their work contains themes involving international politics and is influenced by an international literary canon. William T. Vollmann claims that his main influences are Japanese, Serbian and Italian writers like Yukio Mishima, Yasunari Kawabata, Danilo Kiš and Elsa Morante (Vollmann 2004b: 35–38). *Europe Central*, which I analyse in this book, has German and Russian protagonists. Roberto Bolaño's literary world is international both in terms of characters and space and Bolaño himself spent his life in several countries, across two continents. Jonathan Littell, of French heritage but raised in the US, explicitly proclaims the end of national literature as a critical concept (Littell and Millet 2007: 16–17). Needless to say, this international dimension of contemporary literature is of great importance to this book, which focuses on the Second *World* War – a phenomenon that was lived, and continues to be represented, at national, international and transnational levels (Echternkamp and Martens 2010: 249). It is thus singular and plural, global and local, at the same time.

As the Second World War was a global phenomenon and, partly in consequence, literature registers the war in global terms, a comparative approach influenced by world literature studies is paramount. An adequately global outlook on cultural production necessitates breadth. As Moretti tells us, 'distance is a condition of knowledge' (Moretti 2013: 48); it is for this reason that he advocates that literary criticism adopt the approach of biology (Moretti 2007). Moretti's methodology of distant reading is framed as the opportunity to study a broad array of texts and schematize their relationships. Certainly, it is important to consider his approach in relation to literature written and published in the past because it enables us to avoid depending on a limited range of transmitted canonical texts. But is it applicable when we study contemporary literature? Moretti shares Fernand Braudel's disregard for the 'histoire événementielle' [history of events][3] in favour of a history of profound structure and 'longue durée' [long duration] (Braudel 1958). I believe, however, that when we consider the post-1989 contemporary period, in which human (and indeed literary) events are unfolding faster than ever before, Moretti's approach becomes problematic. Mayer argues that short-term history has to be reconsidered in light of an event like the Holocaust, since it took the Nazis just three and a half years (1941–1944) to almost wipe out 'a community that had been part of the history of Europe for two thousand years' (quoted in Traverso 2003: 4). Similarly, we should reconsider the usefulness of distant reading in such a fast-moving and hyper-connected period. Thus, I offer an in-depth examination of a number of texts selected on the basis of their national and linguistic diversity and critical approval as part of a still in formation post-postmodern canon, rather than discussing a large amount of texts in brief.

3 All translations are my own, except for texts whose translator is credited in the bibliography.

Introduction

Post-Postmodernism and the Second World War

The Historical Singularity of the Second World War

The peculiar role that the Second World War plays in contemporary narratives can be attributed to two closely related factors: the intrinsically exceptional nature of the conflict and the omnipresence of its memory. In order to illustrate the incomparability of the Second World War, I refer to the three components that, as I have previously explained, are evoked in its memory: the war itself, the Holocaust and totalitarianism.

The exceptional status of the Second World War is not simply a truism. It stems from the reality of the war itself. Chris Bellamy, in his important study of the war on the Eastern Front, defines the Russian campaign as

> the greatest and most hideous land-air conflict in history. A war that was total, because it was fought by all elements of society. And a war that was absolute, because both sides aimed 'to exterminate the opponents, to destroy his political existence', and in doing so perpetrated extremes of heinous violence and cruelty, shedding almost all of the customary restraints that had traditionally applied in wars between 'civilized' nations. (Bellamy 2009: xix)

Despite the fact that Bellamy only refers to the war in Eastern Europe, an analogy can also be made with the war in the Pacific, which, while 'inevitably overshadowed by Hitler's war in Europe', was also 'interdependent with it, and its events crisscrossed with those of the western conflict' (Calvocoressi, Wint and Pritchard 1989: 617). Looking only at the war's scale, then, a self-evident truth is reaffirmed: it was a conflict of such geographical proportions, in which so many people and economic resources were involved, with such a high death toll and number of casualties and a similar level of violence affecting civilians, that no event before or since is comparable to it. The Second World War is a total war because, like the First World War, it was a conflict in which the whole productive capacity of a country was mobilized since the development of air technologies extended the front line to every part of the hostile countries. As Mary Kaldor writes (2012: 27), in a total war, the whole society is incorporated into the public sphere and the borders between public and private, military and civil, combatants and non-combatants tend to blur.

The way in which I characterize the Second World War for its range and its unprecedented dimensions is, of course, also valid for my consideration of the Holocaust. Critics tend to agree that 'the destruction of the European Jews between 1933 and 1945 appears to us now as an unprecedented event in history', owing to its chronological extent, the number of victims (6 million people) and the means by which this destruction was carried out (Hilberg 2003: 8). Despite the fact that the Holocaust was the culmination of 2,000 years of European anti-Semitism, nothing of its scale had previously been attempted, either in numerical terms or in scientific and systemic terms. While the thesis of the uniqueness of the Holocaust is in various ways a trivialization of the event, its singularly paradigmatic value is undeniable.

I conceive the Holocaust as an act of state violence against its subjects and not as an act of war between two powers. In other words, it must be examined as a form of violence carried out by means of a repressive bureaucracy rather than a military invasion. Nazism can be understood in a similar manner to the way Bauman understands the Holocaust, which I will analyse in greater depth in the chapter focusing on Jonathan Littell. According to Bauman, the Holocaust does not represent an eclipse of reason, but rather adheres perfectly to the logic of industrial modernity and the Enlightenment. Indeed, Nazism, although it made similar use of propaganda, police and militarization, is distinguished from all other totalitarian regimes by the extent of its crimes and the radicalness of its politics, which make Nazism a kind of totalitarian paradigm and the most extreme case of political violence in the twentieth century (Naimark 2010: 122).

According to Enzo Traverso (2003: 150–151), Nazism is an ideology that is perfectly coherent with European thought generated by the Enlightenment era, in much the same way as the Holocaust is the product of the logic and the dynamics of modernity. The Enlightenment resulted in colonial violence, reclusion as a solution to social problems, mass wars and assembly lines. Just as the extermination camp applies Fordist dynamics to the elimination of human beings (44–45), so the racial ideology of Nazism constitutes a brutal application of the colonial policies of European countries. In this sense, Nazism, like the Holocaust, has a paradigmatic value that makes it, more than any other form of totalitarianism, a vehicle for a variety of meanings and interpretations that are still relevant to the modern day. These characteristics give the fight against Nazism a dimension that other wars lack. This fight offers, and indeed offered to those who fought it, a binary ideology suggestive of a fight between Good and Evil.[1]

Finally, the uniqueness of the Second World War is even more striking when compared to contemporary warfare. While this will be discussed in greater detail in the final section of this introduction, it is worth noting that the Second World War was in many respects the last *total* war. In the second half of the twentieth century, and particularly after the Vietnam war, war morphed into low-intensity, globally projected, highly technological, depersonalized and spectacularized conflicts. This explains the popularity of the Second World War among contemporary writers. Confronted with the unreachability and the hyperreality of contemporary wars, some authors turn to the representation of the conflict that, more than any other, represents war in all its terrible totality.

1 However, we should not forget that although the nature of the crimes of Japan and the USSR may have been different, they are comparable in magnitude to the crimes of the Nazis and some argue that they may even exceed them. Although the Japanese campaign did not specifically aim for total annihilation, as the German one did, the Japanese occupation in China led to the deaths of 11–15 million Chinese people and 4 million Europeans and members of other Asian ethnic groups (Philippine, Indonesian, Korean and Malayan) by the most deplorable means possible (Dower 1986: 295–296). Moreover, political repression in the USSR led to the deaths of some 20 million people, which is comparable to the number of victims of Nazi Germany (as verifiable in Werth 1999). From a purely numerical point of view, the memory of Russian and Japanese totalitarianism is as important as the memory of Nazism, just as the war in the Pacific was equally as violent as that in Europe.

The Memory of the Second World War

The exceptional status of the Second World War has resulted in an equally exceptional treatment of its memory. The relationship between history and memory is complex. We could draw a clear line between historical facts and the scientific precision of historiographical discourse, on the one hand, and the emotiveness of individual and public memory on the other. However, the interaction between these two poles is ambiguous, owing to the way in which the past is reconsidered and the conditions in which this happens. Facts are never free from interpretation. In this sense, the war not only involves national propaganda, but is also bound up with the self-representation of soldiers and their relatives (Connelly 2004: 4).

Much like individual memory, public memory changes over time. It is forced to assume narratable forms and structures and has a performative dimension because it aims not only to document, but also to educate and control. Taking all this into consideration, given the fallacy of memorial discourse, we could say that it is in opposition to the methodological rigidity and the precision of history. But history and memory are interconnected rather than rigidly separated; they do not constitute opposite conceptual poles of a discourse. History and memory are two different attitudes towards the real, but they are bound together and both flawed in terms of their accuracy. As John Foot notes, despite the existence of prejudice (even among historians) towards memory, which is perceived as unreliable, as opposed to the attitude towards history, which is perceived as more scientific and truthful, such a distinction between memory and history is no longer acceptable. Indeed, 'memory is part of history' (2011: 5).

The interaction between history and memory generates what can be termed collective or cultural memory – and the numerous synonyms for this expression testify to the expansion of the field of memory studies in the second half of the twentieth century ('public memory', 'collective memory', 'social memory', 'popular memory', 'mass memory', 'vectors of memory', 'transactive memory', 'prosthetic memory' and 'multidirectional memory'; Noakes and Pattinson 2014: 6). The weight of the Second World War as a historical fact must be considered in conjunction with the role of witnesses (and their heirs) in the second half of the last century. Further, both factors must be understood in relation to the large space that the Second World War occupies in public debates and nation-building processes. The identity of the individual must confront the identity of the collective. Collective identity is determined by memory – that is, the way in which memory is received and transmitted (Eaglestone 2004: 76). Collective memory later becomes cultural memory, a set of ideas that are passed from generation to generation and form the personality and conceptions of those they influence (Crownshaw 2010: 1–3). Collective and cultural memory are influenced by the way the community that produces them changes over time, the stylization of past events and the use of these events for propagandistic purposes.

Let us consider as an emblematic example the most paradigmatic process of memorialization associated with the Second World War: the memorialization of the Holocaust. Although the postwar generation of American Jews was far more integrated than previous generations, its identity was shaped by a memory of suffering and discrimination that had never been personally experienced (Benbassa 2007: 52–53). Even for those who did not live through it or those who experienced it only through the tales of their parents or relatives, the Holocaust becomes the lens through which Jewish history at large is read. The perception of history – the Holocaust in this case – comprises both the historical events and the transmission of these events. Additionally, the circumstances in which these events take place are no less important than the events themselves (Young 2000: 2). The exceptional dimension of the memory of the Holocaust has haunted and influenced the generations that followed. Marianne Hirsch coined the concept of 'postmemory' to describe this phenomenon, which 'is distinguished from memory by generational distance and from history by deep personal connection'. Her definition is concise: 'postmemory is a powerful and very particular form of memory precisely because its connection to its object or source is mediated not through recollection but through an imaginative investment and creation' (Hirsch 2002: 22).

Although this book does not focus on novels that are strictly considered postmemorial, postmemory nevertheless represents a crucial concept in the understanding of the way in which postwar generations dealt with the memory of the war and the Holocaust. It is especially useful for thinking about the Second World War and the Holocaust because it communicates the prevalence and pervasiveness of generational memory and narrativization (Hirsch 2002: 22). It denotes how events are represented and transmitted for those who did not experience them as a sort of 'real memory' (5–6). Those who have never experienced the Holocaust find themselves in a cultural atmosphere that has been shaped by its memory (Young 2000: 1). Having not directly experienced it, the historical facts are, for such people, as real as, and less attainable than, their representations.

Immediately after the war, the Holocaust was not at the centre of public debate for historical and political reasons (Novick 2000: 92 ff.).[2] It wasn't until 1961 that the Holocaust began to be perceived as a distinct and coherent set of events as a result of the Adolf Eichmann trial and its extensive media coverage. Indeed, in the United States, it was during that trial that the extermination of the Jews started to be widely referred to using the term 'Holocaust' (Novick 2000: 133). The spectacularization of witnessing, however, leads to the spectacularization of memory. The beginning of a public discourse about the Holocaust after the Eichmann trial led to a huge mediatization of Holocaust memory in television, theatrical and cinematographic shows, from the TV series *Holocaust* (1979) to Steven Spielberg's *Schindler's List* (1993) and the inauguration of the US Holocaust Memorial Museum in Washington in 1993 (Langford 2013: 113). Rather than being perceived as a clearly defined historical event, the Holocaust became 'a multi-layered sedimentation of images and discourses that reach from documentary to soap opera, survivor testimony to narrative fiction, concentration camp to memorial painting' (Huyssen 1993: 258).[3]

2 The historical reason is that it was difficult to comprehend and reconstruct the series of events that is now referred to as the Holocaust. The political reasons mainly relate to the American authorities not wanting to put too much blame on Germany, now a precious ally against the Soviets, and not wanting American war crimes to be recalled as a rebuttal. Additionally, in the McCarthyism years, Jewish authorities did not wish to strengthen the stereotype of the antifascist (and therefore communist) Jew.

3 A different yet complementary approach is the popular rhetorical idea that the Holocaust represents not only something peculiar and worthy of attention, but also something unique in a mystical, even religious way. Many writers and survivors have, in the postwar era, expressed the idea that the Holocaust cannot be understood by

I have chosen to explain the peculiar dimension of Holocaust memory for two reasons. Firstly, as we have established, the Second World War and the Holocaust are inseparable; secondly, similar memorial processes have shaped the memory of the Second World War. The presence of the Second World War in public discourse has, for the generations that followed, had the same effects as those generated by the mass-mediatization of the Holocaust. The memory of the war is not univocal; it is, rather, a continuously remade fiction consisting of a multitude of accusations and redefinitions, since all of the countries involved in the war employ representations of the war as part of their nation-building processes (Hall 1995: 613). In Italy, for instance, the 'myth' of the Resistance has been promoted for decades as a purifying moment for the Italian people after twenty years of fascist dictatorship, while the history of the Italian Social Republic (the puppet state in Northern Italy controlled by the Germans) has been neglected as a shameful moment in national history (Foot 2011: 157–158). In the United Kingdom, the war against the Nazis has gained the status of an 'ethnic myth' (Gilroy 2004: 95–104), while its most humiliating aspects, such as the defeats in the Pacific Ocean, have been obscured (Noakes and Pattinson 2014: 15).[4]

those who did not experience it personally and that its meaning cannot be communicated in words (Eaglestone 2004: 18). This claim, just like the objections of those historians who refused to consider the Holocaust alongside other political massacres without underlining its magnitude and its singularity (Katz 1996: 19–39), has been trivialized by public opinion, which privileges the view of the Holocaust as an event that somehow does not belong to human history. This turn in Holocaust memory can be linked to the cultural currency of the Holocaust as a sort of civic religion in countries like the United States and Israel. However, such approaches preclude serious attempts to comprehend the extermination of the Jews by placing it in a historical context and take away something more than a metaphysical and moralistic lesson regarding human nature. Such ideas reinforce the *absolute* dimension of the Holocaust, which represents a manifestation of *absolute*, *pure* evil (Nazism). This simplification strengthens the role of the Holocaust, and therefore of Nazism and Second World War, as a sort of 'gold standard' of abjection.

4 Paula Hamilton notes that in Australia the opposite has occurred and that the war in the Pacific is commonly considered 'the Battle for Australia' (2015: 50).

Given the pervasive presence of war memory in public discourse, it is not surprising that it is also prevalent in popular culture. I have already mentioned the proliferation of high- and lowbrow cultural products concerning the Holocaust since the 1970s (including the theatrical and filmic versions of Anne Frank's *Diary* in 1955 and 1959), which has continued up to the present.[5] The same could be said more generally about the Second World War and Nazi imagery. As Alvin Rosenfeld points out (2011: 5), this proliferation of cultural products concerning the Holocaust can be traced back to the early postwar years and linked to the exceptional status of the Nazi Holocaust amongst the other genocides of the twentieth century (14–16).

According to Sabina Hake, fascism is restaged in the postwar period as the postmodern equivalent of evil – meaning that 'moral categories have been displaced into aesthetic ones' (2012: 162). This idealized process, culminating in the great *Nazisploitation* cinematic era of the 1970s, further contributes to the large amount of humour employed in relation to the Nazi legacy and the Holocaust – humour that finds its natural place on the internet, thanks to the intrinsically communicative nature of the web. As Gavriel Rosenfeld writes, the underlying motivations behind the 'memefication' of Hitler are, once again, 'to subvert and ultimately reverse the symbolism that has traditionally surrounded the Nazi dictator'. He continues: 'as an internet icon, Hitler has acquired dual semiotic significance. He has become both a symbol of evil *and* a symbol of humour. Indeed, he has become a symbol of humour precisely *because* he is a symbol of evil' (Rosenfeld 2015: 307). Nevertheless, this often insensitive humour risks aestheticizing, relativizing and normalizing Nazism.

Rosenfeld argues that the process of normalization is necessary in order for us to be able to appreciate our relationship with the memory of the Nazi legacy (2015: 7–14). In fact, all of the processes we have underlined in this

5 Langford (2013) provides examples of Holocaust trivialization in blockbuster films, including *Chicken Run* (2000), *Captain America – The First Avenger* (2011), the *X-Men* franchise (2000–2011, updated in 2016 with the release of *X-Men Apocalypse*, in which the mutant Magneto destroys the Auschwitz camp whilst furiously remembering his imprisonment there) and horror movies like *The Exorcist – Dominion* (2004), *Hostel* (2005) and *The Unborn* (2009).

chapter – the temporal distance from the events allowing us to use them as a political tool, the abuse of memory in artistic products, the universalization of the Holocaust – lead to a normalization, and sometimes trivialization, sanitization and universalization (Weissman 2014: 12), of the Nazi legacy, be it organic or aesthetic. The normalization of the memory of the Second World War does not refute the importance of its memory in our culture; it takes place precisely because of the hypertrophy of memory in public discourse. There is a complementarity between the opposite processes of mythization and trivialization. A certain event becomes mythic because of its extremely significant meaning and place in the history of a people and because of the processes of public memory involved in its representation. At the same time, an event's status as mythic means that it becomes, over time, trivialized – an object of humour or a vessel for banal metaphors and comparisons. Conversely, the diffusion of this trivialization reinforces an event's status as a myth. This is what has happened to the memory of the Second World War: its centrality in public memory has led, over the decades, to its centrality in popular culture. I argue that art responding to the Second World War, be it written, visual or cinematic, serves to overcome the sense of inauthenticity that characterizes both the mythization and the trivialization of the memory of the war.

The Ethics and Poetics of Post-Postmodernism

This book outlines the key features of literature after postmodernism by exploring the common theme of the Second World War. My analysis reveals a series of peculiar stylistic features and ethical postures of post-postmodernism. The exceptional treatment of the war, in terms of its historical and symbolic importance, constitutes fertile ground for my analysis of a literary poetics concerned with narration, empathy, realism and commitment. Whilst postmodern fictions about the war were more concerned with its transmission, reception and memorialization, post-postmodern features of the representation of the Second World War allow its singularity and totality to emerge.

It is generally agreed by literary critics that the phenomenon of postmodernism has ended. The moment of its death is vague: it is traced back to somewhere between 1989, after the epoch-making changes caused by the fall of the Soviet Union (Eshel 2014: 170), 1993, a symbolic date for popular media's appropriation of postmodern poetics,[6] and 11 September 2001, when terrorists attacked the World Trade Center (Eshel 2014: 177). Whatever the precise date, important critics of postmodernism agree that postmodernism lost its function as an avant-garde style in the early 1990s. In the 2002 reprint of her landmark book, *The Politics of Postmodernism*, Linda Hutcheon argues that not only have we witnessed the institutionalization of the postmodern, but also 'its transformation into a kind of generic counter-discourse' (Hutcheon 1989: 166; Hutcheon 2007: 16; Hassan 2003: 199–212). She indicates that the subversive power of postmodern poetics has been diminished by its entry into common critical parlance, with the effect that postmodern poetics no longer has a transformative effect on reality and, therefore, its invocation can represent complicity.

It is important to highlight that total agreement has not been reached amongst critics regarding a clear definition of postmodernism. With this in mind, and considering postmodernism's variety of forms, we ought to consider it in the plural: postmodernism*s* rather than *a* postmodernism (Stierstorfer 2003: 3). Garry Potter and José Loperz agree, suggesting that 'given postmodernism's celebratory orientation to diversity, difference, ambiguity and contradiction, it is not surprising that wildly conflicting theory, practices and alleged knowledges, might all fly under the same designation or be labelled as doing so' (Potter and Loperz 2001: 5). As Linda Hutcheon suggests, terminological confusion results from the overlap between the notion of postmodernism as a literary style and postmodernity as a historical period or cultural condition, which is 'determined by universal, diffuse cynicism, by a panic sense of the hyperreal and the simulacrum' (Hutcheon 2007: 23). When referring to postmodernism, it is therefore necessary to differentiate between postmodernism as an artistic product (but not as a

6 Andrew Hoberek (2007: 233–234) echoes Minsoo Kang's judgement on John McTiernan's *Last Action Hero* (1993), starring Arnold Schwarzenegger. This blockbuster is a metafictional satire of the action movie genre.

coherent movement), postmodernity as a historical period (note that this definition is mostly used by sociologists, rather than historians) and postmodern as a cultural attitude. However, as Raffaele Donnarumma notes (2014: 25–26), this distinction is misleading when we consider the extent and interrelation of these phenomena and their impact.

Nevertheless, the phenomena variously called postmodernism are united by certain common denominators. Postmodernism refers both to philosophical and literary issues. As far as philosophical and sociological issues are concerned, postmodernism refers to the incredulity towards meta-narratives, as Jean-François Lyotard famously put it (1979: 7), owing to the increasing diversity of, and contact between, languages and cultures. A postmodern relationship with reality is defined by hyperreality, that is, the indistinguishability of reality and its simulation (Baudrillard 1980). The cultural dynamics of postmodernism are those of late capitalism, whereby life is dominated by market laws and economic value (Jameson 1991; Zima 2003: 22–23; Rudrum and Stavris 2015: xii).

The sociological traits of postmodernism are one thing, but postmodern poetics are quite another. From a literary perspective, postmodernism refers to literature published after the Second World War and, most importantly, after modernism, as Ihab Assan's famous spelling 'POSTmodernISM' suggests. To quote Brian McHale:

> This ISM (to begin at the end) does double duty. It announces that the referent here is not merely a chronological division but an organized system – a poetics, in fact – while at the same time properly identifying what exactly it is that postmodernism is *post*. Postmodernism is not postmodern, whatever that might mean, but post modernism; it does not come *after the present* (a solecism), but after the *modernist movement*. [...] As for the prefix POST, here I want to emphasize the element of logical and historical *consequence* rather than sheer temporal *posteriority*. Postmodernism follows *from* modernism, in some sense, more than it follows *after* modernism. (McHale 2003: 5)

Postmodernism is therefore not so much a radical break from modernism (as either a literary movement or a set of cultural sensibilities) as a reaction against modernism and is therefore intimately related to it. As we will see later in this chapter, literary postmodernism's main features include irony in the form of parody and pastiche, the crisis of the subject and therefore of the character, the death of the author and the great self-reflexiveness of the narrative structures (hence the importance of the prefix 'meta-').

Just as the word 'postmodernism' has been used to label several manifestations of postmodernism, the period after postmodernism, in which we are currently living, has been given many names.[7] This terminological diversity can be attributed to the ambition of many critics to vindicate the salience of particular expressions. While not all labels are equally useful, and though they differ in emphasis, they all share certain features. Among these possible expressions, I choose to employ the term 'post-postmodernism', as described in Jeffrey T. Nealon's book *Post-Postmodernism or, The Cultural Logic of Just in Time Capitalism*, even though the author writes of socio-political issues rather than literature. There are two main reasons for this choice. The first is the sense of continuity that 'post-postmodernism' conveys with both postmodernism itself and McHale's definition of postmodernism. 'Post-postmodernism' signals that something has changed, but also that postmodernism remains an important part of this new poetics (Nealon 2012: ix–x).

The second reason for my choice is the relative neutrality of the term, which communicates a sense of evolution and continuity without forcing strict interpretative patterns. I appreciate that sometimes neutrality is used to avoid adopting a position in relation to a certain matter, but it is also true that other labels used to describe post-postmodernism are part of a manifesto, which means that they not only *describe* the current literary landscape, but also try to *prescribe* its contextual and formal emphases. Terms that are not part of a manifesto and more usefully attempt to describe reality, moreover – such as 'digimodernism', 'hypermodernism' and 'automodernism' – foreground a single aspect of contemporaneity and only describe its sociological aspects. By contrast, post-postmodernism, as I conceive of it, is highly interdisciplinary in terms of its connotations and practices; like postmodernism itself, it focuses on both sociological and literary aspects. Although it is not the aim of this book to show how society has changed in the last twenty to twenty-five years, some sociological

7 The volume *Supplanting the Postmodern*, edited by David Rudrum and Nicholas Stavris, pointed me towards several of the works I mention in this section.

considerations are undeniably useful for understanding why the Second World War is such a popular theme in contemporary fiction and why literature has been used as a medium through which to represent a return to (a form of) realism.

As I explained at the beginning of this section, it is not easy to neatly delineate the periodization of the passage from postmodernism to post-postmodernism because cultural transitions tend to be porous and irregular. Although critics are in agreement that it was in the 1990s that postmodernism ceased to be an avant-garde style and became diffused in mainstream culture, several important postmodern novels were published in that decade, including Antonia S. Byatt's *Possession* (1990) and Philip Roth's *Operation Shylock* (1993). On the other hand, the main works of markedly post-postmodern authors such as Bolaño and Vollmann were composed and published in the same decade. I focus decisively on the twenty-first century in this book because the vast majority of the novels I discuss were published in the new millennium and, most importantly, because I believe that, irrespective of its origins and precursors, post-postmodernism is a literary style of the present.

Fields such as hypermodernism, automodernism and digimodernism are concerned with the end of postmodernism, or, rather, postmodernity, from a political and sociological point of view rather than a literary one. They focus on the continuity between postmodernity and the processes that characterize the age in which we are living. 'Hypermodernism', a term coined by Gilles Lipovetsky, is one of the most incisive labels attributed to (post)postmodernity so far. Automodernism and digimodernism, which I focus on later in this section, insist on the importance of changes in public and private life resulting from the development of the World Wide Web and portable devices. As the word suggests, hypermodernism implies the continued processes of modernity rather than their substitution with something else (whereas postmodernism, intentionally and unintentionally, signalled the end of modernity and modernism). These processes, however, occur at a level of intensity never experienced during the postmodern period and are much more pervasive in everyday life. The mechanics of modernity create a society of excess and individualism – or, better, hyperindividualism, which coincides with the interiorization of the logics of profit and the dissolution of traditional forms of social structures and behaviours (Lipovetsky and Charles 2004: 76–77; see also Donnarumma 2014: 99 ff.). In this hypermodern world, the dissolution of traditional institutions and ideologies, which began with modernity and continued with postmodernity, no longer encounters any obstacle. Individualism in private life and technocracy in public life are the consequences of these processes.

This sense of continuity with postmodernism, however, is more difficult to detect when we consider literary production. As Timotheus Vermeulen and Robin van den Akker note in their definition of the concept of metamodernism, which is characterized by 'a typically modern commitment and a markedly postmodern detachment' (Vermeulen and van den Akker 2010: 2):

> We do not wish to suggest that all postmodern tendencies are over and done with. But we do believe many of them are taking another shape, and, more importantly, a new *sense*, a new meaning and direction. [...] Most significantly perhaps, the cultural industry has responded in kind, increasingly abandoning tactics such as pastiche and parataxis for strategies like myth and metaxis, melancholy for hope, and exhibitionism for engagement. (Vermeulen and van den Akker 2010: 4)[8]

According to them, the very definition of *meta*-modernism signals an overcoming of postmodernism, together with a reprise of some of its stylistic features, for a different purpose. In Greek, 'meta' has three main meanings: with or among, between and after. Hence, metamodernism is situated with or among 'older and newer structures of feeling'. It 'is characterized by an oscillating in-betweenness, or, rather, a dialectical movement that identifies with and negates [...] conflicting positions, while never being congruent with these positions', and takes place historically after postmodernism (Vermeulen and van den Akker 2010: epub).

Raoul Eshelman's performatism and Josh Toth's renewalism, which together underline both the presence and the necessity of a new ethical

8 See also Holland 2014: 1–3 and 199–202. On metamodernism, see Vittorini 2017. Konstantinou's post-irony, 'a contribution to the critical project of naming what comes after post-modernism' (2016: 37), can be considered to be in a similar category to metamodernism because it focuses on how belief prevails over irony in contemporary fiction (2016: 167–266).

approach to literature in order to overcome postmodern nihilism, constitute two similar positions. Eshelman's performatism, which serves as a manifesto and a historical diagnosis, links the postmodern assault on metaphysics and the new presence of ethical values in art (2008: xi). In doing so, performatism, like renewalism and metamodernism, requires that the reader enact a kind of voluntary oscillation between naïveté and cynicism (3). One condition of this process is the instantiation of a monist *semiotic*, which 'requires that things or thingness be integrated into the concept of sign' (36). The world is no longer purely textual, made of language and idiolects, as postmodernism suggests. In post-postmodernism and related labels, words refer to things and this relationship is not up for debate. Something very similar is advocated by renewalism, which aims simultaneously to embrace and to defer the possibility of the referent and of mimesis (123). Toth's renewalism posits a return to 'neo-realism' or 'dirty-realism' (which is to say, a realism achieved by means of the language of postmodern literature; Toth and Brooks 2007: 1–9; Huber 2014: 24–40; see also Dalley 2014: 9).[9]

One of the main problems with post-postmodernism is that, as we have observed, reflections on post-postmodernism involve sociological and literary aspects, which tend to differ significantly. Sociologically, post-postmodernism is conceptualized as a continuation of the processes of de-realization that previously characterized postmodernity. In a wider sense, it also involves the dissolutive processes that can be dated back to modernity, which is now 'élevée à la puissance superlative' [enhanced to the nth level] (Lipovetsky and Charles 2004: 72). From a literary perspective, however, post-postmodernism is seen as an often intentional break with, and reaction against, the poetics of postmodernism, ushering in renewed attention to realism and an ethical approach to literature.

This sense of cultural continuity is extremely significant. Lipovetsky calls the time we are living in a 'seconde modernité' [second modernity], absolutely modern time since it is founded on three axiomatic constituents

9 Toth and Brooks 2007: 1–9. The expression 'dirty-realism' can be backdated to 1983, when *Granta* editor Bill Buford coined it to identify a new minimalist tendency in American literature. See Rebein 2011: 41–65.

of modernity: the market economy, technological efficiency and the individual (Lipovetsky and Charles 2004: 74). David Rudrum argues that, instead of focusing on the prefix 'post-' and its disappearance, greater emphasis should be placed on the persistence of the word 'modern'. This suggests that, contrary to what postmodernists argued, modernity has not ended, but has, rather, changed or intensified its previous characteristic features (Rudrum 2015: 334; see also Zima 2003: 26).

From a literary perspective, we face another problem when we consider post-postmodernism, one that I have already briefly noted. Just as the passage from modernism to postmodernism did not occur abruptly, so the passage from postmodernism to post-postmodernism cannot be precisely delineated. This is true in two senses. First, like postmodernism, post-postmodernism is a product of avant-garde (or at least highly cultured) authors. Diffusion of its poetics in a high-culture context does not correspond to diffusion in mass culture. Therefore, what we mean by the end of postmodernism is that postmodernism is no longer appealing to highly cultured and experimental writers. But its poetics are still present and deeply embedded in popular culture (for example, in superhero movies, cartoons and mainstream fiction).

Moreover, some of the formal qualities of postmodern poetics survive in post-postmodernism. As Hoberek writes, 'postmodern techniques – even if they no longer play quite the dominant role they once did – have hardly disappeared from contemporary fiction' (Hoberek 2004: 236). Post-postmodernism is different from postmodernism not because of a set of narrative techniques, but because of an ethical approach (Hoberek 2004: 238–239; Donnarumma 2014: 46). I have outlined this earlier in reference to performatism, renewalism and metamodernism. I will now describe how and why certain postmodern techniques survive in a different cultural environment.

The main features of the poetics of postmodernism were irony, the crisis of the subject, the death of the author and an emphasis on the self-reflexivity of literary texts. The importance of irony in postmodern literature is evident in the prevalence of pastiche and parody (Hutcheon 2007: 8 and 89), a form of imitation 'characterized by ironic inversion' and 'repetition with critical distance, which marks difference rather than similarity' (6;

see also Rose 1993: 195–274 and Dentith 2000: 154–185). This is relevant to the recovery of genre literature and to the contamination of high and low textualities. The crisis of the subject, already a modernist theme, resulted in fragmented and strange characters (Zima 2003: 24). Similarly, the death of the author, heralded by Roland Barthes, compromised the traditional notion of authorship (and readership) by allowing a text to be read as 'a multi-directional space in which a variety of writings, none of them original, blend and crash' (Barthes 1997: 146). The importance of self-reflexiveness in postmodern literature is evidenced by the importance of the prefix 'meta-', as it applies to generic metafiction and, more specifically, *historiographic* metafiction (which will be discussed later in this chapter; on postmodern metafiction, see McCaffery 1982). According to Patricia Waugh, metafictional novels pivot on an opposition: 'the construction of a fictional illusion (as in traditional realism) and the laying bare of that illusion. In other words, the lowest common denominator of metafiction is simultaneously to create a fiction and to make a statement about the creation of that fiction' (2001: 6). In texts in which such literary meta-techniques are central, the lines between reality and fiction are blurred in order to suggest that the world can be seen as a vast textuality.

Some of these features no longer belong to post-postmodernism. The death of the author is a concept more commonly encountered in literary criticism than in literature itself; it is difficult, for instance, to find authorial negation in contemporary novels, whose narrators have regained a sort of 'narrative authorship' (Pennacchio 2014: 9–28; see also Dawson 2013). We can suggest something similar about the death or fracturing of the subject, since post-postmodernist novels involve more developed and complex characters that are not intended to be ironic. However, other postmodernist devices continue to be used in post-postmodern fiction. For example, post-postmodern fiction consistently employs genre fiction (*The Kindly Ones*, *2666*), metafiction (Ian McEwan's *Atonement*) and autofiction (Roberto Bolaño's *Distant Star*). The crucial point here is that even features shared by postmodernism and post-postmodernism differ in their intentions. Irony, for example, no longer represents the foundation of the literary creation (Donnarumma 2014: 199). Post-postmodernism attempts to incorporate the double-coding poetics of postmodernism into a serious discourse about the world and displays renewed faith in the capability of literature to understand and influence the real.

The form of post-postmodernism has been variously described as 'critical realism', 'hybrid realism', as a continuation of 'magical realism'[10] or 'melancholical realism' (Ganguly 2016: 19). Mazzoni, reprising Auerbach, defines it as a 'serious realism of modern times' (2017: 340). This is a significant innovation compared to postmodernism. While it is true that postmodernism began as a committed poetics (despite its ambiguities)[11] and that postmodern literature sought to criticize the real world by providing a critical mimesis of it, it is also true that this genre has always been the least realistic form of poetics (Hutcheon 1989: 2). Postmodernism adopted realism in order to refract and distort it, presenting it through metafiction as a naïve possibility in which the contemporary novelist can no longer believe (Donnarumma 2014: 145–146).[12]

The gap between postmodernist metafiction and reality is particularly evident when we consider historiographic metafiction, the most common postmodern kind of historical representation. Historiographic metafiction is an eminently postmodern style and should be understood as a consequence of the 'postmodern challenge to history' (Singles 2013: 22) launched by the so-called 'linguistic turn' in historiography. With the publication of *Metahistory* in 1975, Hayden White forcefully underlined the eminently narrative (and thus fictional) nature of historiographical discourse, which is founded on sources that are continuously altered and re-elaborated through their transmission (White 1975: ix, 428). Historiographic metafiction differs from the traditional historical novel in that it focuses more acutely on the way history is transmitted to us, rather than on history itself, in order to expose the artificiality and non-objectivity of historical writing. As with

10 Potter and Lopez eloquently suggest that the difference between postmodernism and realism is 'the tone' (2001: 5).

11 Hutcheon mentions a 'complicitous form of critique' of postmodernism, highlighting 'its tendency to deconstruct cultural monoliths but never to reconstruct' (2007: 16). See also Hutcheon 1989: 4.

12 According to Alberto Casadei, postmodern poetics are not concerned with realism as they focus on ironic and parodic metanarration and on the reprise of existing textualities (2000: 33).

other features of postmodernism, this style was a response to the demand for political commitment (Hutcheon 1989: 48) and represents a form of deconstruction of dominant narratives. Historiographic metafiction represents an important paradigm of the postmodern approach to history and, consequently, to material reality. A main feature of historiographic metafiction is 'theoretical self-awareness of history and fiction as human constructs' (Hutcheon 1988: 5). Thus, it becomes a means of rethinking and reworking the traditional representations of the past. While it is true that historiographic metafiction does not question the existence of the past – it questions our capability to fully understand it – the outcome of this form of historical representation has often been hermeneutic pessimism because it suggests that history can be known only through texts that have previously been mediated and manipulated (16).

The term 'historiographic metafiction', however, no longer applies to post-postmodernist historical fiction, not because post-postmodernism has somehow dismissed Burke's and White's reflections on history being a product of representation rather than an objective discipline, but because the focus has moved again from the condition of representation to the represented object itself. I will elaborate on this distinction in Chapter 1, with reference to McEwan's metafictional *Atonement*, and in Chapter 3, in relation to Binet's *HHhH*. Such a distinction is especially productive when considering a novel like *The Kindly Ones*, in which the cultural dimension of historiographic representation is clearly signalled but does not interfere with the unequivocal message of the novel. Josh Toth has defined the post-postmodern form of historical writing as 'historioplastic metafiction' instead of historiographic. According to Toth, while Hutcheon's category 'emphasizes the inescapability of the graphic construct', historioplastic metafiction 'shifts our attention to the infinite yet bound pliability of the past' (Toth 2017: epub; see also Timmer 2010: 360 and Toth 2018).

Even postmodern historical novels that cannot be classified as historiographic metafiction are unrealistic in their style. Let us consider some of the most significant and innovative postmodern novels about the Second World War. Joseph Heller's *Catch-22* (1961) is structured circularly and non-chronologically, making it difficult for the reader to follow the action. Philip K. Dick's *The Man in the High Castle* (1962) is an alternate history, its plot pivoting on an event that never happened: the Nazi victory in the Second World War and the invasion of the United States by German and Japanese forces. Kurt Vonnegut's *Slaughterhouse 5* (1969) involves journeys through time and an alien race called Tralfamadorians. Thomas Pynchon's *Gravity's Rainbow* (1973), set in wartime London, has a male protagonist whose erections apparently foretell the explosions of the V rockets. In Martin Amis's *Time's Arrow* (1991), the soul of a deceased concentration camp doctor narrates his life in reverse chronology.[13]

Post-postmodernism, as we have described it thus far, does not ignore postmodernism's lessons of scepticism and doubt. Post-postmodernist realism constitutes an attempt to return to the characteristics of the modern novel without forgetting the lessons of postmodernism. The novels mentioned above, therefore, are more similar to the novelistic production of modernity than postmodernity (Calabrese 2005: viii). The post-postmodernist return to an open narratability signals the end of the double-coding poetics of postmodernism. All of the elements that were parodied or treated with disdain by postmodern writers, including plot, temporality and character (14), return and become the centre of the narrative. This sociological and literary shift is also the result of the influence of non-Western literatures and bestsellers – which may be closer to a kind of pure narration, free of metafictional and hyper-literary implications (14).

Writing War in the Age of Postmodern Warfare

At this juncture, another question arises: how is the cultural panorama in which this 'return to realism' takes place shaped? Is it different to postmodernity and, if so, how? I have signalled that post-postmodern times continue to be characterized by the 'crisis of experience' typical of modernism and postmodernism (Donnarumma 2014: 88). This crisis of experience results from both the gradual mediatization of life and a sense

13 On the topic of the Second World War in postmodernist narratives, see Crosthwaite 2009, Wyatt 2010 (135–162) and Brett 2016.

of a lack of agency. The postmodern age, from the late 1950s onwards, was marked by the invention and the diffusion of television, whereas the post-postmodern age, from the 1990s onwards, has been defined by the development of the World Wide Web. In the last fifty years, the world we live in has been characterized by the progressively more invasive presence of the media in everyday life. On the other hand, the development of atomic armaments and the transformation of work from the industrial to the post-industrial have resulted in a sense of alienation connected to the feeling of a lack of agency.

Postmodernist fiction has reacted to this technological, economic and psychological state of affairs by parodying reality and trying to deconstruct the main narrative that upholds our capitalist world. However, postmodernist fiction has proven incapable of proposing a counter-narrative that does not end in nihilism. Post-postmodernist fiction, on the other hand, reacts to the state of affairs in the context of which it is produced through a return to reality – specifically, a return to great narratives and great themes (Lipovetsky and Charles 2004: 143; see also Kirby 2009: epub). It is perhaps unsurprising, then, that the Second World War occupies a central position in post-postmodernist fiction.

Robert Samuels, in his description of automodernism, highlights that the internet experience is essentially postmodern (we could even say hypermodern) in that it involves open textualities and digital transpositions of the self. The internet allows for a recovery of agency that seemed lost in postmodern times through a kind of trade-off between the concrete self and the textual self. Indeed, the notion of personal freedom that is implied in interactions with machines and others and interactions through social media – despite being representative of a social and agential evolution when compared to the unidirectionality of pre-internet media – is partially misleading. Certainly, instruments such as smartphones offer their users a great range of choices and a sense of agency. But such devices also make users dependent on them. They generate, in other words, 'a paradoxical combination of individual autonomy and automated mechanics' (Samuels 2008: 229). Moreover, the diffusion of media exposes us to a variety of stimuli and images that do not fulfil the role of real experiences, but act as substitutes for them. Encounters and interactions on the web are 'visually boxed into the confines of the screen', which serves 'as a mental container for Otherness. Like a cage at a zoo or a picture frame at a museum, the structure of the framed screen provides a strong sense of limits and borders' (232). Virtual reality, as Slavoj Žižek argues, 'is experienced as reality without being so' (2002: 11).

The way in which digital technologies paradoxically foreclose experience for individuals and social groups is typical of the times we are living. Even wars, which, more than any other event, should be understood as traumatic, are consumed by Western viewers as anaesthetized and hyper-mediatized experiences. Let us consider as an example the perception and reception of one of the most traumatic and iconic events of post-postmodernity: the terrorist attacks on the World Trade Center on 11 September 2001. Far from representing an irruption of the real in the ironic and metafictional atmosphere of postmodernity, the 9/11 attacks resembled a blockbuster movie in media coverage (Žižek 2002: 16). Subsequently, the attacks were continuously and seemingly endlessly represented in world media, which contributed – as in the case of the Gulf War ten years before – to a perception of them as unreal. By absorbing fiction's energy, reality itself becomes fiction (Baudrillard 2002: 28).

It is no coincidence that the experiential absence of trauma in contemporary Western societies (the relative absence of famines, epidemics, wars and environmental disasters for the whole second half of the twentieth century) has been accompanied by the spectacularization of violence. Daniele Giglioli argues that, although contemporary Western society is perceived as one of the safest societies in human history and although human life has never been so protected and valued, trauma is *evoked* everywhere. He claims: 'Non vivendo traumi, li immaginiamo ovunque. È come se fossimo così traumatizzati dall'assenza di traumi reali da doverci costringere a inseguirli ansiosamente in ogni situazione immaginaria possibile' [Since we no longer experience trauma, we imagine it everywhere. It is almost as if we were so traumatized by the absence of real traumas that we are forced to look for them anxiously in every possible imaginary situation] (2011: 8–9). We perceive trauma mostly through an invasive and continuous series of media representations and we are constantly surrounded by cultural products that restage the trauma our life may lack. The prevalence of pulp movies, violent films and other extreme textualities that attempt to exorcize the crisis of individual experience can be attributed to the absence of trauma in Western life (7). The popularity of the Second World War (and other great epics) in contemporary literature, meanwhile, results from the un-narratability of contemporary wars and terrorist attacks.

Paradoxically, this absence of trauma arises from war itself, as traumatic distance and invisibility are central to the politics of contemporary warfare. In the first section of this introduction, I have briefly summarized the historical uniqueness of the Second World War and perceptions of the war, as well as the peculiarities characterizing its memory. My aim was to draw attention to the contrast between the trauma of the Second World War as a historical event and the comparatively less traumatic experience of life in the contemporary West. This contrast may partly explain the prevalence of the Second World War as a literary theme. Historiographers may debate the exceptionality of the Second World War or the Holocaust, but the exceptional status of the memory of these events cannot be denied. Memories and postmemories of the war are marked by different stylized traits. Nevertheless, contemporary renditions place significant emphasis on the uniqueness of the Second World War. One final contentious aspect of the memory of the Second World War amongst contemporary writers is the way in which warfare has changed in the last sixty years. This change mainly relates to two aspects: first, the form of warfare, which changed from totalizing (as in a total war) to low intensity, and second, the representation of the conflict (Ganguly 2016: 1). The changes in the ways in which wars are fought and depicted make contemporary warfare, in comparison, almost un-narratable, which in turn prevents contemporary wars from gaining a mythological status akin to that of the Second World War.

Since the earliest stages of Western literature, war as a literary theme has been characterized by several distinctive traits that have remained consistent despite the changes that have occurred in warfare and military life over the centuries. From Homer's *Iliad* to Leo Tolstoy's *War and Peace*, the representation of war is often characterized by an emphasis on open, direct, face-to-face combat and it is during such combat that the entire destinies of those involved are encapsulated and decided. This liminal nature of war makes it exceptional because the 'real' meanings of life, which are hidden during peacetime, can finally emerge and be more deeply understood during wartime.[14] However, the digitalized, asymmetric and unmanned forms of contemporary warfare do not possess these peculiar characteristics. In order to recover them, novelists must turn to the historic event that most embodies these features – the Second World War. As I have mentioned, this war was a total war. The fighting powers exploited all of their nations' labour power and economic resources in an effort to achieve the complete destruction of the enemy. The entire population was involved in the war effort and almost all civilians were at risk of becoming casualties (be it during land invasion or air bombing). Modern warfare is not characterized by the same degree of citizenry involvement or risk to civilians.

While some of the distinctive elements of the so-called postmodern wars (Hables Gray 1997: 21–23)[15] that we witness today can also be found in the Second World War (e.g. strategic bombing, system analysis and computers; 149), it should still be considered a modern war rather than a postmodern one since 'it continued modern war's quest for totality, up to and including Hiroshima' (128). The first example of postmodern war is the Vietnam War, described as 'the SA war, the electronic war, the computer war, the technological war' (158), which was the precursor to contemporary post-1989 wars.

Contemporary or postmodern warfare is characterized by four elements: low intensity, both geographically and economically; global scale; spectacularization; and depersonalization, as a result of high-technological development. Contemporary wars are 'high-tech, low density deadly conflicts' (Hables Gray 1997: 27), fought far from the national soil of Western nations, in countries of the so-called second or third worlds. They typically involve a small number of professional soldiers and the deployment of

14 For more on the representation of war through history, see Hanson 1989; Parker 2000; Scurati 2003 and 2006; Smith 2006 and Van Creveld 1991. The *XLVII Convegno Interuniversitario di Bressanone* and its organizers provided me with a rich and fruitful opportunity to discuss these topics and encounter the works of these scholars.

15 *Unrestricted Warfare* by Chinese Colonels Liang and Xiangsui, published in 1999, represents an early and insightful theorization of contemporary warfare as a system based on asymmetry and technological and digital specialization on a global scale.

technology and media. In contemporary wars fought by Western countries, physical battles are avoided in favour of violence that aims to intimidate rather than to resolve conflicts (Kaldor 2012: 9; see also Burke 2012). The low density of contemporary warfare also affects the war-economic system. While the total war needed a 'centralized, totalizing and autarchic' system, contemporary wars are globalized and mostly depend on predation and external financial support, rather than involving the entire economic life of the state, as was the case during the Second World War (94–95).

These low-intensity wars are global in scale, since the range of spectacular violence has widened, as 9/11 and subsequent terrorist attacks have proved (Kaldor 2012: 13). The contradiction lies in the fact that, despite this range being virtually infinite, war is never directly experienced by the majority of the population of Western countries, who are continually exposed to the virtual spectacle of the war without ever personally witnessing its effects (Ganguly 2016: 146–147). War itself is never present on the soil of Western countries, although it is continuously spectrally evoked through digital media and social networks (152–153). Notions such as the 'global war against terror' transform war into something that is indefinite in time, space and scope (Chamayou 2013: 53). That being said, and despite the fact that no serious act of warfare has taken place in the West in the last seventy years, the threat of terrorism creates a state of perpetual fear (although, like the fight against it, it is described as indefinite in time and in range). The 'ghostly enemy' represented by terrorism, as Baudrillard has argued, creates a situation in which 'the antagonism is everywhere, and in every one of us' (2002: 15). This fear is exacerbated by the perpetual representation of terrorism in the media.

Another notable element of contemporary wars is their mediatization. Propaganda has always been part of warfare, but it has had a new, macroscopic impact in the context of the post-1989 wars. While the beginning of this mediatization process can be traced back to the Vietnam War, it assumed new proportions during the Gulf War (Hables Gray 1997: 44–45; Ganguly 2016: 155–156) and the wars in Yugoslavia. Contemporary wars are represented in the media, which effectively 'sell' conflict to the public without filtering it or distinguishing it from war movies, as a result of which its reality is displaced. Jean Baudrillard wrote in 1991 that 'the media promote the war, the war promotes the media, and advertising competes with the war', in his well-known article 'The Gulf War: Is It Really Taking Place?', in which he satirically questions the very existence of the Gulf War (1995: 31).

Moreover, civilians now participate in the mediatization (and narration) of contemporary wars through social media, provided that they actively engage with images and videos posted and shared on Facebook or Twitter, for example. Civilians can have an influence on geographically and culturally distant wars through social media, as evidenced by the Kony 2012 campaign (Ganguly 2016: 138–141). However, as I have already explained, social media platforms provide their users with an augmented sense of agency whilst also exposing them to deceptive and manipulative marketing campaigns. Social media in general, and Facebook in particular, encourages an 'identity performance' (Marichal 2012: 7–9) consisting of the construction of a public image through the selection and sharing of content – including political content. At the same time, according to José Marichal, 'this voluntary and ubiquitous opportunity for capturing, storing and sharing personal data' can be considered a 'participatory panopticon' (76). This reprise of Michel Foucault's imagery of the panopticon underlines the ambivalence of the performativity inherent in the use of Facebook, particularly as the organization gathers personal data that societies can control, manipulate and share. As regards politics, and especially political activism, the use of social media is dubious and contradictory because it represents the use of 'a private-sector platform whose reason for being is not tied to movement activism' (114) for the purposes of political mobilization and public lobbying. Social media organizations, moreover, very rarely distinguish between the kinds of activism promoted on their platforms (which may range from right-wing agendas to veganism) and the proliferation of frauds, hoaxes and fake news testifies to their lack of control over content (Lee 2013: 103–119). On the one hand, it is true that in totalitarian societies citizens' access to social media can mitigate their state-enforced ignorance of local and global events and, further, can enable them to generate political participation (as in the case of the 'Arab Spring'; Marichal 2012: 122–126). In Western democracies, however, social media activism has tended to inspire more performative sharing of content amongst users, rather than a serious commitment to a cause (this has been labelled 'slacktivism', a mixture of oversimplification and virtue-signalling).

Finally, contemporary warfare is characterized by the increasing use of drones – which means, 'in the official vocabulary of the U.S. Army, [...] "a land, sea, or air vehicle that is remotely or automatically controlled"' (Chamayou 2013: 11). The use of drones as substitutes for human soldiers allows states to maximize the war effort, yet suffer virtually no losses. While it is true that certain aspects of the Second World War, such as mass bombings or the use of atomic weapons, represented an attempt to minimize human loss and reduce the risk of retaliation,[16] this technological shift in the way violence is carried out has changed the character of warfare. It has led to radical changes in military ethos, which is founded on notions of personal bravery, sacrifice and comradeship (17). These technologies have an alienating effect both on their victims (as they do not perceive that they are fighting against other human beings; 44–45) and on their users (as they are completely detached from the effects of their actions). Everything drone pilots do, indeed, 'is filtered through the interface' (117); they see without being seen (118). The distance between the drone and its pilot breaks the phenomenological unity of the act (106–113; see also Sparrow 2011: 118). The distancing effect of technology has now assumed unprecedented proportions (Žižek 2002: 35–36).

In light of recent changes in the ways wars are fought and the peculiar dynamics of contemporary warfare, the narrative appeal of the Second World War can be understood. Contemporary wars are detached from the material experiences of civilians and fighters. They involve a system of perpetual, globalized, low-density conflicts with ambiguous causes and motivations. The Second World War, on the other hand, offers a comparatively clearer panorama in which fighting can still take on a heroic dimension. The roles of the good and the bad, although problematized, are clear and that which is achieved is the result of individual and collective action. The Second World War therefore has a narratability that contemporary wars do not have (Eaglestone 2009: 365) because they are fragmented and continuously mediatized by old and new media. In sum, it offers some relief in

16 Bourke 1999: 7; Chamayou 2013: 17 and 53. See also Coker 2001: 11–15.

the search for materiality, teleology and authenticity that motivates contemporary literature. Similarly, it should be underlined that the abstractness and depersonalization that characterizes contemporary warfare has caused authors to (re)construe the Second World War and representations of warfare by returning to material reality and attempting to make it less inhuman and surreal. Contemporary literature responds to an increasingly cybernetic and virtual form of war-making by returning to realism.

CHAPTER 1

Board Games, Serial Killers and the Banality of Evil: The Part about Roberto Bolaño

Nazi imagery is present throughout Bolaño's oeuvre, including *The Third Reich* (*TR*), *2666* (*2666*), *Nazi Literature in the Americas* (*NLA*) and *Distant Star* (*DS*). As Federico Finchelstein argues, 'Bolaño's work frames fascism at the centre of politics and literature' (2016: 32). In *2666* specifically, an account of the Second World War occupies a central position in the fifth section, 'The Part about Archimboldi', which consists of Hans Reiter's Bildungsroman. In Bolaño's fiction, Nazism epitomizes political violence in the twentieth century, especially that characterizing Latin America dictatorships, as well as being a symbol for the unintelligibility of evil. This emphasis on violence is consistent with the endless list of femicides described in the fourth section of *2666*, 'The Part about the Crimes'. Rather than simply drawing a comparison between varieties of violence, it is precisely through an implicit confrontation with the violence of the Second World War that Bolaño stresses the continuity between the world we live in and the paradigm of absolute evil in our culture.

In this chapter, I analyse the presence of the Second World War in Bolaño's work. I begin by exploring the representation of the war in a board game in *The Third Reich*, discussing how the board game critiques the detachment and irony of postmodernism – which is opposed to the horrors of fascism, for which the Second World War and Nazi imagery are a metaphor. I then consider *Distant Star* and *2666* in order to highlight how Bolaño's realistic treatment of the conflict contradicts postmodern anti-realism. Thereafter, I explore in detail the characteristics of Bolaño's post-postmodern literary style, from mimetic realism to narratorial authorship to his non-ironic reprise of genre fiction. Finally, in the last section of this chapter, I compare Bolaño's and McEwan's deployment of metafiction for validatory purposes.

The Ethics of the Board Game

In *The Third Reich*, the protagonist Udo – a German wargames champion – travels to Spain with his girlfriend Ingeborg to prepare a new strategy for his favourite game, *Third Reich* (modelled on the hex-and-counter wargame *Rise and Decline of the Third Reich*). During his stay at the end of the tourist season, Udo finds himself in an increasingly hostile and ambiguous environment, which culminates in the death of another German tourist. After this event, Ingeborg leaves Udo and goes back to Germany. In the empty hotel, Udo plays *Third Reich* with El Quemado [The Burnt One], a hotel employee who is covered with burns. What was supposed to be an easy game between the champion and the beginner turns into a disaster for Udo, who is defeated. After his victory, El Quemado claims his prize and almost beats Udo to death.

In *The Third Reich*, the wargame is not only the thematic centre of the novel; it structures the narration, with several chapters dedicated exclusively to what happens in the game. Meanwhile, the development of the game parallels the changes in the relationship between Udo and El Quemado. The wargame represents a double criticism, both of the map as a knowable totality and of the game as a trivialization of the war, which establishes it as counterfactual entertainment technology. Postmodern literature nostalgically parodies the totalizing and 'complete' map, which is a symbol of modern, topographically organized theories of knowledge. As Peta Mitchell argues:

> This notion of the totalizing map is implicitly linked with classical and modern theories of knowledge. Traditional epistemology is consistently defined in geographical terms – knowledge is surveyed and divided into fields, topics (from *topos*, or place), provinces, domains, realms, spheres. (2008: 2; see also Farinelli 2009: 112–113)

The modern map is perceived as a tool of objective knowledge and serves as a structured and readable representation of a world without any interferences. It is also a representation and instrument of colonial conquest. However, such a model is made impossible by the lack of faith in great narrations that characterizes postmodernity (Mitchell 2008: 10–16). Since the map of the Enlightenment and the modern era was presented as an objective and scientific instrument and document – or at least was intended as such by its makers – its function is to unproblematically represent a territory (2). However, postmodern deconstructivism has made it impossible for a map to function in this way.

Bolaño's obsession with maps recalls Jorge Luis Borges, an author with whom he was very familiar, who satirizes 'exactitude in science' (Borges 1998: 325) through his paradox of the map of the empire that, to ensure accuracy, must necessarily be as wide as the empire it represents. It is also useful to remember Borges's irony, directed against the analytical language of John Wilkins. Borges presents the absurd divisions contained in a mysterious 'Chinese encyclopedia' as equally valid as such analytical language. The animals are divided into

> (a) those that belong to the emperor; (b) embalmed ones; (c) those that are trained; (d) suckling pigs; (e) mermaids; (f) fabulous ones; (g) stray dogs; (h) those that are included in this classification; (i) those that tremble as if they were mad; (j) innumerable ones; (k) those drawn with a very fine camel's-hair brush; (l) etcetera; (m) those that have just broken the flower vase; (n) those that at a distance resemble flies. (Borges 2001: 231)

This sarcastic itemization concludes that every classification of the universe is, by definition, arbitrary.[1] In the same way, in the wargame, Bolaño parodies the very possibility of comprehending the real. To permanently map the real would deprive it of its complexity.

Bolaño's work abounds with maps, lists and summaries. His novels sometimes adopt the form of a catalogue or, as has been suggested by Enrique Schmukler, an atlas (2013: 113–123). Examples of this include *Nazi Literature*

1 For further details on Borges's list, see Duszat 2012 and Wicks 2003.

in the Americas and, to a certain extent, *2666* (Grall 2013: 485),[2] in which the narrator can be described as a 'narrador-archivista' [narrator-archivist] (Blejer 2010: 273). Several 'authors' of *Nazi Literature in the Americas*, by which I mean Bolaño's invented right-wing writers and protagonists of the stories of the book, use maps in their work. Willy Schürolz, for example, writes map-poems that include verses and topographic plans which 'were untitled [and] unintelligible' (*NLA*: 104–105). Zach Sodenstern is the author of the absurd novel *Checking the Maps* (*NLA*: 106). Harry Sibelius wrote a counterfactual novel inspired 'by his reading of Norman Spinrad and Philip K. Dick, and perhaps also by reflecting on a story by Borges' (*NLA*: 120). Further, he ends his career writing *wargames*.

The very nature of the biographies in *Nazi Literature in the Americas*, however, suggests the futility of the catalogue as the biographies largely focus on small details that make no obvious sense, yet they are presented as complete portraits of the characters' lives. Likewise, the summaries of Archimboldi's novels in *Los sinsabores del verdadero policía* [*Woes of the True Policeman*] (posthumously published in 2011) represent a map that is simultaneously complete and entirely unreliable, since they lack the essential thing we need in order to understand the author's value – his writing.[3] In *2666*, Amalfitano ultimately draws a series of meaningless diagrams in an obscure attempt to map philosophical knowledge (Blejer 2010: 272; Patterson 2014: 209–210). None of these maps, however, reliably reproduce the infinite variety of the world. Every model is insufficient in the face of this variety. As Bolaño, influenced by Borges, writes knowingly in *Woes of the True Policeman*: 'the Whole is impossible … knowledge is the classification of fragments' (196). This being the case, in *The Third Reich*, Bolaño depicts his characters as invested in the veracity of maps. When Ingeborg

2 Examples of the use of the catalogue as a structural element ('a world made of objects without any narrative') in *2666* are, according to Grall (2013: 485), Seaman's recipes, Florita Almada's plants, Elvira Campos's list of phobias, the list of misogynistic jokes contained in 'The Part about the Crimes' and the genealogy of Lalo Cura.

3 Ríos Baeza notes that this approach is typical of Bolaño's fiction; for instance, we are also unaware of the content of Udo's strategic articles and the poems written by the protagonists of *The Savage Detectives* (2013: 243–244).

asks Udo why he likes the wargame so much, he answers that what attracts him is 'the clarity of it' (*TR*: 108).

In the introduction, I explained that parody and irony are two important features of postmodern literature. The consistent presence of a parodied belief in the objectivity of maps and the precise shape of the world in the first phase of Bolaño's work is an eminently postmodern trait. The mobilization of this ironic distance between the author and his characters serves to denounce a form of nostalgia for the object it derides (notwithstanding that, in a way, Udo's passion and ambition belong to Bolaño too). However, this critical posture toward the protagonist of *The Third Reich* signals that, in this phase of his work, the author is already attempting to overcome postmodern irony (Asensi Pérez 2010: 349). The wargame, therefore, is not simply a game for entertainment purposes; it is, rather, a counterfactual game in which every historical fact can be repeated and contradicted. Indeed, Udo, unlike the Wehrmacht, conquers Moscow and invades Spain and England in the game.

The genre of alternate history is strongly connected to the 'postmodern challenge to history' (Singles 2013: 26). As Gavriel Rosenfeld notes, it is beyond doubt that the success of alternate history depends on postmodernism (2005: 4–10) and a vision of history that is no longer univocal and monolithic, but dynamic and open to new readings and reframing. The very term 'historiographic metafiction' insists on the paradox of writing historiography in a self-reflexive and self-referential form that exhibits its own fictionality and in which fact and fiction have the same epistemological value. In a sense, alternate history can be understood as a form of historiographic metafiction. Historiographic metafiction refutes the natural or common-sense methods of distinguishing between historical fact and fiction. It challenges the view that only history can lay claim to truth by asserting that both history and fiction are discourses. They are human constructs that signify a system and derive their claim to truth from that identity (Hutcheon 1988: 93).

At the same time, paradoxically, alternate history simplifies reality and historiography. In order to rethink history, its mechanisms must be understood and its dynamics must be in line with the Rankean vision of 'great men' and historical moments (Singles 2013: 170). While the prevalence of alternate history is strongly connected to the postmodern tendency to rethink history, the rules that regulate uchronic writing remain (as in classic historiography) those of causality and contingency (187) and not those of cultural historiography or even Braudel's profound structures.

The authors of alternate history focus on the narrative, and therefore fictive, form of historiography. They consider alternative and minoritarian versions of truth and challenge the official public discourse. Moreover, they trace an equivalence between history and narrative and therefore between reality and fiction. Alternate history, then, signals a strong continuity between the present and the past through its polemic discussion of the univocality of history (as Bolaño, a great admirer of Philip K. Dick, well knows; see Ríos Baeza 2013: 122–136) and by equating what has happened with what might have happened. Yet, at the same time, it permits the avoidance of this past, which could easily have never happened or taken place differently. All of this is present in the wargame at the centre of *The Third Reich*.

In the wargame in *The Third Reich*, Bolaño attacks the ambition to attain a knowable totality and the vulgarization of history and its horrors, that make them a source of entertainment. Like the postmodernists, Bolaño satirizes the modern ambition of knowledge and, at the same time, refutes the playful and detached vision of history and the equation of facts and fiction typical of the works of postmodernist authors. Udo is so absorbed in the abstract coordinates of the game he is playing that he does not understand the implications of what happens around him ('Everyone's touched [Hanna] and here you were in this room with your war', *TR*: 109). Responsibility for the death of the German tourist probably lies with El Quemado, who feels an irrational and never fully explained hatred for Germany and ultimately brings Udo back to reality with his violence (Kurnick 2015: 113).[4] Rationality, represented by Udo's maniacal meticulousness, cannot hide

4 According to David Kurnick, El Quemado represents 'the omnipresent proximity of the political real' (2015: 116). Carolyn Wolfenson (2013: 207) suggests the existence of a metafictional dimension in *The Third Reich*. I strongly disagree with Wolfenson's interpretation. According to her, the novel stages the power of literature to modify reality, as the game Udo plays changes the landscape around him and leads to his destruction. I would argue the contrary: Udo's fall is not caused by the influence of the game, but by his presumption that the game and reality are separate. In other words, it is not Udo's obsession that changes the world around him; it is

the violence that permeates reality and is destined to fail in its attempt to bring this violence under control: 'When I tell El Quemado that the papers I'm reading are plans for beating him, all moves and countermoves foreseen, all expenses foreseen, all possible strategies invariably noted, a hideous smile crosses his face [...], and that is his only answer' (*TR*: 186). El Quemado's smile is a sardonic disparagement of Udo's characteristically modern attempt to categorize and order the world.

Udo is also unable to decipher the meaning of the war that only represents a game for him. El Quemado is Latin American and his burns seem related to the political struggles on the continent. This causes him to perceive in Germans a manifestation of the Nazi dictatorship, which is the emblematic culmination of totalitarianism.[5] Udo, on the contrary, never draws a parallel between the war in the game he plays and the horrors of Nazism, just as he is unable to relate his German origins to what is happening to him.[6] For him, the Second World War represents a game so lacking in consequences that he dares to draw a comparison between the generals of the Wehrmacht and German writers of the twentieth century. Indeed, he does not even suspect the monstrosity of the comparison he makes between Erich von Manstein and the prisoner of a labour camp, Paul Celan (*TR*: 216).

---

the world that changes *despite* his obsession. The protagonist's consistent inability to acknowledge the omens around him should be interpreted in this sense. Moreover, there is nothing explicitly metafictional in the novel. Udo's game does not produce the reality around him; it simply runs parallel to it in his mind until the moment when they intersect.

5 Gutiérrez-Mouat suggests that the tragedy of Rodrigo Rojas, a young photographer burned alive in 1986 after a protest against Pinochet's regime, could be an inspiration for El Quemado's story (2016: 53).

6 In his study on wargames, Van Creveld argues that, although there are games that incorporate political factors in their rules, war is presented with a degree of autonomy from politics that real war does not have. Moreover, wargames cannot reproduce, for practical reasons, the variety of factors and conditions that influence the course of real wars and, on the contrary, are forced to adapt to the limits of the equipment and the duration of the game (2013: 4).

Despite Udo's historical superficiality, together with his perception of the generals as 'sympathetic figures, despite everything' (*TR*: 217), his disastrous fate is closely bound to the Second World War played in the wargame and the memory of Latin American dictatorships. Spring 1942 marks the end of Udo's initiative in England and the beginning of his retreat and defeat. It comes after the 11 September entry in the novel (which is Udo's diary), the day of Pinochet's coup in Chile (Kurnick 2015: 114). To Udo, this date represents nothing more than 'Catalonia Day' (*TR*: 178).

A Distant Nazi

In Bolaño's *Nazi Literature in the Americas*, which is part novel and part collection of short stories (modelled on Borges's *Historia universal de la infamia* [*A Universal History of Iniquity*], 1953; O'Bryen 2015: 18), the author links the lives of fictitious American fascist writers with the memory of European fascism. The genre of the collection of fictional biographies, the first example of which is conventionally considered to be Marcel Schwob's *Imaginary Lives* (*Vies imaginaires*, 1896), has been widely adopted by postmodernism as a form of epistemological critique of traditional technologies of knowledge – in this case, the encyclopaedia. In addition to Borges, this theme has been excavated by authors including Rodolfo J. Wilcock (for example, in *La sinagoga de los iconoclastas* [*The Temple of Iconoclasts*], 1972, a personal favourite of Bolaño's) and Danilo Kiš (*Enciklopedija mrtvih* [*Encyclopedia of the Dead*], 1982).

These texts, and indeed Bolaño's too, qualify as biographical dictionaries or encyclopaedias. According to these models, the texts should aim to compile a complete and exhaustive sum of information composed of precise data. At the same time, however, the incompleteness, eccentricity and randomness of the content of these encyclopaedias focusing on minor characters and protagonists of forgotten events refute the possibility of organizing knowledge by insisting on partiality, relativity and heterodoxy. The parodying nature of these texts is already evident in their titles, which claim that the texts are scientific and exhaustive but contain a specification that contradicts this. For instance, *Nazi Literature in the Americas* appears to be an eccentric literary history in the sense that its characters would be marginal in the context of literary history (in most cases they have written just one or two obscure books, which have sometimes even been published posthumously) and because it is, generically, right-wing literature, not all of which is qualifiable as Nazi. The title, therefore, is hyperbolic rather than descriptive.

Seemingly, then, we are not so far from what we have observed above in *The Third Reich*, formally or where content is concerned: the encyclopaedic model is a variation on the wider theme of the critique of the map. However, what makes *Nazi Literature in the Americas* such a remarkable and peculiar text by comparison to other collections of fictional biographies is that it has an explicitly political purpose. Of course, it is true that there is some playfulness in the descriptions of the eccentric right-wing aristocrats, the young and bright war fanatics, the anti-modern thinkers, the anti-communist agitators, the reactionary writers of science fiction, the elitist magicians, the ordinary criminals, the Christian fundamentalists, the white supremacists, the hooligans and the bikers that crowd the book. However, the novel goes beyond humour and deconstruction. Underneath this seemingly humorous catalogue of characters, Bolaño highlights the extent of the diffusion of right-wing ideologies in Latin America (whose ghastly effects he personally experienced) and their survival in contemporary times. As Augusto Monterroso's epigraph eloquently (and, again, playfully) states: 'if the flow is slow enough and you have a good bicycle, or a horse, it *is* possible to bathe twice (or even three times, should your personal hygiene so require) in the same river'. Once again, Bolaño uses a postmodern form to convey a message with political undertones – hence the seriousness and playfulness of the title.

The final fictitious biography of *Nazi Literature in the Americas* is the novella 'The Infamous Ramírez Hoffman', whose narrator is revealed in the last sentence to be Bolaño himself. This novella, enriched with more details and the addition of several other episodes, later became a novel in its own right, *Distant Star*. The autofiction continues from the first page of the novel. Bolaño narrates the story of the mysterious experimental poet, collaborator of the Chilean regime and serial killer named Carlos Wieder – a pseudonym for Alberto Ruiz-Tagle, whom Bolaño meets before the coup and later follows from a distance through the testimonies of his friends.

Wieder is part of the same group of left-wing poets that has formed around the figure of Juan Stein, but, after Pinochet's coup, he murders two female members of the group in their sleep, his good friends the Garmendia sisters. After this proof of loyalty to the new regime, Wieder starts creating air poetry, which Bolaño models on the work of Raúl Zurita (Usandizaga 2005: 87–88; Quílez 2015). In these performances, Wieder paints in the sky sentences about death or quotations from Genesis, statements that come to represent 'the regime's attempt to whitewash its reputation and present itself as a supporter of the fine arts, as if the avant-garde artists and the military intervention shared the same understanding of that historical context' (Villalobos-Ruminott 2009: 196). In 1974, after one of these shows, Wieder inaugurates a personal exhibition in a private house, where he displays a series of photographs of mutilated and murdered women, including the Garmendia sisters and other *desaparecidas*.

Although Wieder is not officially persecuted by the regime for this exhibition, he is forced to leave Chile. The news of him that Bolaño receives is imprecise and filtered through the testimonies of their mutual friends. In the following years, Wieder continues to write for increasingly obscure magazines and fanzines and self-duplicates using a series of pseudonyms. In the mid-1990s, Bolaño is asked to identify Wieder (now living in northern Spain and working as a cameraman shooting low-quality pornographic movies) by Abel Romero, who was a police detective in the time of Allende and is now a contract killer on commission. Bolaño positively identifies Wieder and Romero kills Wieder on behalf of his client.

As Bolaño writes in *Nazi Literature in the Americas*, '[t]he Infamous Ramírez Hoffman' serves to 'counterbalance the preceding excursions into the literary grotesque, or perhaps to come as an anticlimax' (*DS*: 1). As in the previous short stories, the Second World War is never directly depicted, but Nazi heritage is implied through the comparison between Carlos Wieder (who, not by chance, chooses a German pseudonym) and Pinochet's dictatorship, with which he collaborates. Despite the absence of overt reflections on the war, however, *Distant Star* is an important text that should be considered alongside *The Third Reich* and *2666* for three reasons.

The first is that it draws a parallel between Nazism and Latin American totalitarianism, which is also present in *Nazi Literature in the Americas* and is openly illustrated in *The Third Reich*. The second is Carlos Wieder's sociopathy and detachment, which echo Udo's. The third is that it tells the story of Juan Stein, a military history aficionado and the descendent of a Russian general in the Second World War.

Wieder's obsession with death is evident both in his exhibition of photographs of corpses and in his last air show, during which he writes the following phrases: that death is friendship, Chile, responsibility, love, growth, communion, tidiness and finally that death is 'my heart' (*DS*: 82). This morbid infatuation with death is inseparable from his political faith, but it cannot simply be reduced to that. Wieder's homicidal mania finds its equivalent in the death cult of fascist ideology (epitomized in the Francoist motto 'Viva la muerte'), but also exceeds it. Chris Andrews defines Wieder as a monster and a sociopath rather than a political criminal (2014: 156–161). He is not simply a man who commits evil for personal advantage; on the contrary, he is personally damaged by the crimes he commits. Wieder, 'like the star of the book's title [...] remains distant' (Andrews 2014: 156) – physically, from the narrator (who meets him personally only in the first and the last pages, but for the rest of the novel follows him through the testimonies of his friends), and temperamentally. He is usually described as being in a state of almost unnatural calm, in stark contrast to the brutality of his crimes. After his exhibition of photos of mutilated women, Wieder is 'at the window, showing no sign of fatigue, with a glass of whisky in his perfectly steady hand, contemplating the dark cityscape' (*DS*: 93). When Bolaño meets him twenty years later, noting that he has aged disgracefully, he still cannot help but notice this very same sense of calm (*DS*: 153). These qualities highlight Wieder's detachment from normal people and at the same time are related to his political faith. Wieder commits his first crime 'like a sleepwalker, without hesitation' (*DS*: 22), an expression that, as Bolaño certainly knew, was famously used by Adolf Hitler. 'I follow my path', said Hitler at the time of the remilitarization of the Rhineland, 'with the precision and the self-confidence of a sleepwalker' ('Seguo il mio cammino con la precisione e la sicurezza di un sonnambulo'; in Galli 1989: 108–109).

The inspiration for Wieder's character is the protagonist of the short story 'Deutsches Requiem' in the collection *The Aleph and Other Stories* by Borges (*El Aleph*, 1949). In Borges's short story, the narrator Otto Dietrich zur Linde is the fanatic director of a death camp. Speaking the night before his execution, it is clear that he is, like Wieder, an educated and aristocratic Nazi with mannerisms comparable to those of Wieder. Both show contempt for the people around them, including their own comrades, but they also show a fanatical devotion to their cause – although, as I mentioned, Wieder's dedication seems more personal than political. Moreover, zur Linde's parable crosses over into the realm of art as he deliberately decides to drive a Jewish poet named David Jerusalem, a prisoner in his camp, mad. What unites these characters is their lack of feeling. Zur Linde conveys impassibility in the face of his own death, whilst Wieder is unperturbed by the consequences of his deeds. Despite receiving the death sentence, zur Linde is not afraid to die because he is convinced of the rightness of his actions. And, while we do not know whether or not Wieder is afraid of death, he certainly does not pay much attention to the punishment that may be meted out as a result of his actions.

There are certain similarities between Wieder and Udo. Wieder represents the macroscopic and monstrous expansion of the detachment from reality that Udo manifested in *The Third Reich*. It is no coincidence that Wieder himself is (or may be, considering our uncertainty regarding the truthfulness of the narrator's identifications) the author of a wargame about the 1876 war between Chile and the alliance of Peru and Bolivia. What in Udo manifested as thoughtlessness, a sort of incapacity to connect the real and the fictional, becomes in Wieder an erasure of the boundaries separating art and life, resulting in the lack of respect for human life that leads him to use corpses as works of art. Wieder is a symbol of evil, one of the incarnations of absolute evil that inhabit each of Bolaño's novels, as impenetrable and magnetic as black holes. For this reason, Wieder resembles El Quemado more than he does Udo and plays a role not so different to that played by the femicides and the Holocaust in *2666*, as we will see. The very name 'Wieder' belongs to the semantic field of menace and abjection and its variety of meanings (together with his pseudonyms) makes Carlos, literally, legion, revealing the alienation and intimidation evoked by the character (*DS*: 50–51).

Distant Star and *The Third Reich* have another thing in common: one character's obsession with the military history of the Second World War. Jean Stein, a poet and professor around whom Bolaño and his left-wing friends gather before the coup, is said to have at home more geographical charts than books (*DS*: 59), seemingly attracted by the realm of possibilities they represent. Moreover, hung on his wall is a photograph of Ivan Chernyakhovsky, the youngest general of the Red Army, whom Stein claims is a remote relative of his. Like Udo, Stein is obsessed with the military career of his hero and with his victories. Although motivated by political reasons, this passion takes the form of a list, in a way that closely resembles certain passages of *The Third Reich* (*DS*: 59 and *TR*: 283–284). However, as in the case of Udo, this passion never impacts on the real and remains an intellectual exercise. Interestingly, Stein disappears after the coup and, for years afterwards, is believed by Bolaño to be fighting fascism in several Latin American countries, though he has actually sought refuge at his mother's place in the south of the country (O'Bryen 2015: 29).

The story of Stein's character contrasts with that of his friend Diego Soto, another poet who leaves Chile after the coup. While Stein is proud and passionate about his political commitment to idolizing a Soviet general, Diego Soto is described as a serene and relatively selfish bourgeois character who is unconcerned by politics ('Soto was a socialist sympathizer, but that was all, he wasn't even a faithful socialist voter; I would have described him as a left-wing pessimist', *DS*: 66). Whereas the passionate and politically committed Stein behaves as a coward after the military coup, however, Soto dies an honourable death trying to prevent right-wing vandals from killing a homeless man. The meaning behind the double parable of Stein and Soto, together with Wieder's story, is clear: intellectual engagement does not preclude cowardice (Stein) or savage cruelty (Wieder) because commitment remains a way of behaving and requires practice, rather than merely intellectual statements. 'Now he wouldn't have to choose between Tel Quel and OuLiPo. For him, life had chosen the crime reports' (*DS*: 71); by comparing the prestigious highbrow intellectualism of the French avant-garde and the modesty of the crime reports of a newspaper, Bolaño is paradoxically highlighting how Soto's fate is actually more honourable and noble.

Once again, Bolaño appears to punish characters whose political fervour is only intellectual and not substantiated by a similar ethical commitment in practice. We have already noticed this paradigm as it relates to Udo in *The Third Reich* and it can be seen even more clearly in 'The Part about the Critics' in *2666*. The contrast between Stein and Soto and, from a wider perspective, Stein and Wieder, is significant. Wieder is distant, but he is also a star, as the title suggests. His magnetism is such that he draws the attention of the character Bolaño for decades. In other words, Bolaño seems to tolerate monstrosity better than hypocrisy, favouring insane passion over apathy. Wieder's magnetism, moreover, is important because it suggests the mediumistic dimension of fascism (the fascination, etymologically, of it), a trait that generates ambivalence in the narrator and that is also of great importance in the novels of Littell and Vollmann.

666 x 2

2666 is Bolaño's magnum opus. This book, published in 2004, is 1,000 pages long and composed of five parts that, in a sense, function like five independent novels. The apocalyptic title (which should be read as 'two/twice 666', a reference to the 'number of the beast' in Saint John's Revelation) immediately suggests the importance of the theme of evil in the novel. Indeed, the book's main concern is the disturbing mass femicides occurring in Ciudad Juárez (called Santa Teresa in the novel) between 1993 and 1997. *2666* is divided into five parts: 'The Part about the Critics', 'The Part about Amalfitano', 'The Part about Fate', 'The Part about the Crimes' and 'The Part about Archimboldi'. Although interrelated, the five parts of the novel can be read independently of one another, especially as the structure of the narration is circular, even when the parts are read in a different order.

'The Part about the Critics' describes the attempt of four European literary critics to find the German writer Benno von Archimboldi, a search that eventually leads them to Santa Teresa, a Mexican city in the Sonora desert. During their stay, they are unable to find clues or pieces of evidence attesting to the presence of Archimboldi and consequently abandon their task. 'The Part about Amalfitano' focuses on the everyday life of Oscar

Amalfitano, a professor of philosophy who has just arrived in Mexico with his daughter, Rosa. In 'The Part about Fate', the protagonist is Oscar Fate, an African-American journalist from New York who is sent to Santa Teresa to cover a boxing match for his newspaper. While there, he begins to investigate the femicides. 'The Part about the Crimes' is a disturbingly long, historically accurate and emotionally detached description of the 112 femicides that occurred in Santa Teresa between 1993 and 1997. It also documents the failed attempts of the police to solve the crimes. These attempts lead only to the arrest of Klaus Haas, a German albino giant, but it is doubtful whether he is guilty or not. It is, however, evident that, even if he is guilty, he could not possibly be guilty of *all* of the many murders, which were committed in different ways. The final section, 'The Part about Archimboldi', narrates the life of Archimboldi (whose real name is Hans Reiter) from his childhood. Reiter participates in the Second World War as a private, fighting in Poland, Ukraine and Romania. After the war, Reiter starts his career as a writer under the name of Benno von Archimboldi. In the last few pages of the book, through an account of the life of Archimboldi's sister, it is revealed that Klaus Haas (the man arrested on suspicion of femicide in 'The Part about the Crimes') is Archimboldi's nephew. The novel ends with Archimboldi, who intends on supporting his nephew during the trial, preparing for his departure to Mexico.

2666's approach to the Second World War represents an overturning of Udo's perspective. In *2666*, Bolaño's major accomplishment, the Second World War is no longer an abstraction nor a game, but a central part of the biography of Hans Reiter. On the Eastern Front, and in the pages of Boris Ansky's diary, Hans finds his pseudonym, Archimboldi. The Second World War appears in *2666* in two distinct but related forms: first, in the horrors of the war, culminating in the grotesque crucifixion of General Entrescu and, second, in the horrors of totalitarianism, represented by the story of Soviet writers Ivanov and Ansky and the confession of the Nazi administrator Leo Sammer.

The narrative involving the Romanian general, Eugenio Entrescu, is one of the parts of *2666* in which evil manifests most clearly (Candia 2006: 125). Entrescu – who, prior to his appearance in the 2004 novel, was a background character in *Nazi Literature in the Americas* – appears several times in 'The Part about Archimboldi'. Reiter meets Entrescu for the first time during the German army's stay at Dracula's castle. There, Entrescu dines with the young and erudite Paul Popescu, General Von Berenberg, the writer Hoensch, an SS officer and the baroness Von Zumpe (whose cousin was Reiter's friend and who later becomes the wife of Reiter's publisher). In this gothic parenthesis, the guests have a long conversation about Konrad Halder, a relative of the baroness and a painter of dead women (similar, in this sense, to Carlos Wieder; see Lainck 2014: 194). Later that evening, Reiter and two other soldiers spy on the passionately violent intercourse between the general and the baroness. Entrescu is described, as in *Nazi Literature in the Americas*, as having a 30-centimetre-long penis (perhaps, as Finchelstein suggests, an allusion to the fascist obsession with masculinity; 2016: 42–43).

Reiter never sees Entrescu alive again. During the retreat through Romania, in a rural castle (not Dracula's this time), Reiter's division meets a group of Romanian soldiers who killed their commander, Entrescu, and then crucified him. Reiter sees the general's corpse in what seems to be an absurd and grotesque parody of a sacred image, complete with a soldier praying before it (*2666*: 932). This crucifixion was senselessly carried out by the soldiers ('"We made it before we killed the general," said a Romanian. "I don't know why we made it, but we made it even before we got drunk"'; *2666*: 747) and does not seem to have a precise meaning in the novel. Like Bolaño's fascination with Entrescu's genitals, this crucifixion simply recalls the disturbing presence of the real. It is a manifestation of the bestial violence that underlies human history and, at the same time, the indiscriminate enactment of this violence.

Entrescu is not an ordinary character. During the conversation in the castle, his opinions about art and life are morbidly extreme (Lainck 2014: 196–197). Moreover, in a conversation between Popescu and a mutilated official of Entrescu's division that takes place decades after the end of the war, we come to learn that the general was adored by his soldiers almost as if he were a prophet (although, as usual, we do not know why). The place where he ordered that a trench be dug was a graveyard (or perhaps a potter's field) and the disturbing memory of bones emerging from the earth torments the official for decades after the war.

Finchelstein suggests that Entrescu is a prototype of the fascist, like Wieder in *Distant Star* (2016: 41–42). Entrescu displays apparent calm and detachment before the troops, in contrast to the brutality Reiter witnesses during Entrescu's intercourse with the baroness. Although it is true that Entrescu's opinions about art are similar, in a way, to Wieder's (*2666*: 854), I find it difficult to agree with the interpretation that straightforwardly aligns Entrescu and Wieder politically. First of all, Entrescu's detachment does not appear to be pathological, like Wieder's; rather, it is contingent on his position in the army. Further, it commands the respect, rather than the suspicion, of his comrades. Indeed, as the captain explains, the soldiers attribute almost supernatural powers to Entrescu. Entrescu's violence, too, cannot be seriously compared to Wieder's because his violent intercourse with the baroness was consensual. The sex scene does not appear Sadean, as Finchelstein suggests, because it lacks the elements of abuse and control that characterize sadistic relationships. It should also be noted that Entrescu's command that the soldiers dig in a field full of human bones at a moment when he seems to know that he is going to be killed can be interpreted as a denunciation of the crimes that his army, as a force of the Axis powers, has committed. He effectively makes the soldiers face the reality of their violence, with the potential consequence of evoking remorse. Finally, Entrescu's resignation in the face of death is very different to that of Borges's zur Linde. It does not signal fanatical faith, but, rather, repentance.

While Entrescu serves as a symbol for the horrors of the war, the Soviet writers Ansky and Ivanov[7] and the Nazi administrator Leo Sammer are manifestations of the intrinsic evilness of power. Reiter discovers Boris Abramovich Ansky's diary in Crimea in a rural house in which he hides. In the diary, Ansky narrates his youth as a Jew, his faith in the revolution, his career as a writer, the persecution under Stalin and his friendship and collaboration with Efrem Ivanov. Ivanov is a science-fiction writer who, according to Ansky, was successful in the 1920s and early 1930s, but, after 1935, experienced an inexplicable and unforeseen fall from favour before ultimately dying at the hands of the political police. The reasons for the

7 For further critique of the 'Russian' part of *2666*, especially in relation to Bolaño's encyclopaedic knowledge of the Soviet literary demi-monde, see Possamai 2017.

persecution of these two characters by the political police are never explained; for instance, while it is stated that Stalin finds Ivanov's novel *Twilight* suspicious, no reason is given to justify this judgement.

Leo Sammer, whom Reiter meets in prison after the fall of Berlin, is a Nazi civic administrator in occupied Poland who is asked, amidst the chaos of the general retreat, to organize the elimination of 500 Greek Jews. Sammer does not know how to complete this task. He first tries to use them as a labour force in a local factory and then sends them to the Chełmno extermination camp. He is torn between obedience to his superiors and the fear of retaliation, and the human sense of sympathy he feels for the Jews. He tries, in a confused and contradictory way, to take care of them, giving them food and ensuring that the citizens do not disrespect them. Despite this sense of pity, he ultimately obeys orders and has them all killed.

2666 could not be farther from what we have observed in *The Third Reich*. During the twenty pages in which Bolaño makes Sammer speak, since he is an Eichmannesque administrator rather than an anti-Semitic fanatic (Andrews 2014: 161–165), we are immersed in the bureaucratic and moral mire in which he is stuck, represented by his difficulty reconciling his pity and desire not to kill the Jews with his obligation to obey orders. In a strikingly similar manner to Jonathan Littell in *The Kindly Ones*, as we will see, Bolaño refuses to give the Holocaust a metaphysical dimension. He rehearses its sordid details as part of an everyday routine, for example, when Sammer discusses the 'problem' of the Greek Jews with the civil officers of the city during a serene work breakfast. Moreover, their fate is discussed in conjunction with other everyday problems, such as the changing of a border between two fields and the disappearance of a truck full of potatoes (*2666*: 759–760).

Sammer's crime is represented as the consequence not of his will, but of a bureaucratic logic that is, in the end, senseless. A few pages later, the order to exterminate the Greek Jews completely loses its importance and the priority becomes the evacuation of the Germans. The representation of the Holocaust is not abstract, but is bound to practical problems, like how the Greek Jews should be fed, where they should sleep and where and how to transport them. At the same time, Sammer's elimination of the Jews is not an act of sadism or sociopathy, as in the case of Wieder. Sammer does not think of himself as an evil man and blames the situation in which he was stuck: ' "Anyone else in my place," says Sammer to Reiter, "would have killed all those Jews with his own hands. I didn't. It isn't in my nature" ' (*2666*: 767).

Another element of realism in Sammer's story is the choice of the narrator – not the omniscient narrator of *2666*, but Sammer himself. This, as Bieke Willem notes, allows Bolaño to recreate the bureaucratic language of omissions and euphemisms that characterized official Nazi communications about the Holocaust (2013: 87). This can be observed in the communication between Sammer and his superiors and in Sammer's narration itself. In the pages dedicated to the extermination of the Jews (*2666*: 760–767), which is carried out in small groups, Sammer's voice becomes elusive and evasive. He prefers circumlocutions to exact words. For example, he tells us that 'the deed had been done' (*2666*: 761), that the Jews 'disappeared' (762) and that the children whom he forces to kill the Jews 'put their hearts into it' (764). In addition, when they dig around the potter's field, he does not name what they find, simply stating that 'there was something' (764). Everyone around Sammer seems nervous and uncomfortable, but he deliberately never explains why.

In *The Third Reich*, the Second World War represents, for Udo, an all-encompassing passion that gives form and meaning to the plot of the novel, but it is a passion that is completely detached from reality. It takes the form of fetishism rather than knowledge. In *2666*, Bolaño represents the Second World War, both in terms of the horrors of totalitarianism and the war itself, as a complex phenomenon with precise historical coordinates and problematic ethical choices, in stark contrast to the abstractness and imprecision of the wargame maps. Human history is not a board game through which to challenge our lucidity and dexterity, but an entangled series of unpredictable, cruel and degrading situations in which (to borrow examples from *2666*) the disappearance of a truck full of potatoes can be compared to the death of 500 people or, over the course of a day, a person can go from being successful to being imprisoned, as happens to Ivanov. None of Udo's commendable generals could be crucified in the wargame, like Entrescu. Bolaño depicts two antithetical ways of approaching history.

One is detached and abstract, postmodern in the worse sense of the term, whereas the other is ethically complex.

Once he has told his story, Sammer is killed in his sleep by Reiter. Sammer's complaint regarding the circumstances of his actions and his good faith are futile. As Chris Andrews writes, 'his compassion is soon extinguished, and his disobedience comes too late' (2014: 164). This death, however, is not depicted. We are laconically informed that Sammer is found dead (*2666*: 767) and, a few pages later, during a brief dialogue with his girlfriend Ingeborg, it is revealed that the killer is Reiter himself (*2666*: 775). It is an act that is not problematized and lacks nuance, as well as representation. There is a possible objection, then. If Bolaño is attempting to implicate the readers by making them ethically responsible, why is the narrator always silent, rather than providing moral judgement?

The memory of the Second World War and totalitarianism in *2666* parallels Latin American dictatorships and the atrocious femicides of Santa Teresa narrated in 'The Part about the Crimes'. I have already explained the importance of the parallel between Nazism and Latin American dictatorships in *The Third Reich*, *Nazi Literature in the Americas* and *Distant Star*. What is more significant in *2666* is the parallel between Nazism and 'The Part about the Crimes'. Like the Holocaust in Sammer's story, the long list of more than 100 femicides in the Sonora desert and the narration of the fruitless investigations into these murders are illustrated in a richly detailed manner and, at the same time, a sense of detachment in the narration recalls a journalistic chronicle or an autopsy.

The femicides are a catalogue – a list – as underlined by the sterile way in which they are narrated (Walker 2010: 201). As we have seen in relation to Bolaño's maps, no explanation is offered for the problem of evil and the femicides merely depict the incomprehensibility of evil in a monolithic manner (Donnarumma 2015: 224). Similarly, the representation of the Holocaust is deprived of metaphysical dimensions, in contradiction to the trivialization of the inexpressibility of the Shoah. We have already seen in *The Third Reich* (through the mysterious origins of El Quemado's hate for Udo) and in *Distant Star* (in relation to the reason behind Wieder's crimes) that Bolaño refuses to explain the causes and the nature of evil. Entrescu's and Ivanov's deaths, Ansky's persecution and Sammer's transformation into a mass murderer are all manifestations of the irrational and arbitrary course of human history, just like the femicides in the previous part.[8] We can also observe a similarity between the text's refusal to narrate the act of killing, as in 'The Part about the Crimes', in which only the discovery of the corpses is shown, and the euphemistic language adopted by Sammer to describe the extermination of Jews. Both the femicides and the Holocaust 'son fenómenos ininteligibles y por eso inefables' [are unintelligible, and thus ineffable, phenomena] (Willem 2013: 82). At the same time, the punishment for these crimes has no explicit motivation. Like Wieder, Sammer is killed, but his death is an act of revenge rather than justice, a personal and not a collective decision. Of course, he has committed a crime in the eyes of the reader and Reiter, but he is not put on trial for it because his crime is unspeakable. He faces only punishment. Similarly, the monstrous detective quest around which *2666* is constructed is left unsolved.

The judgement that is never explicitly made by the narrator of *2666* is palpable in the formal juxtaposition employed by Bolaño. The collocation of these narratives establishes a moral equivalence between the Holocaust and Latin American femicides, but also broader equivalences between Hitlerism and Stalinism and between European and Latin American fascism. The juxtaposition of these episodes, which, as is common in Bolaño's work, float in the river of narration without a clear explication of their meaning, establishes an equivalence and communicates an implicit judgement, but still refuses to name that which cannot be named: the nature of evil. This equivalence is not artificial. That is, it does not use the Holocaust as a measure of all crimes. Rather, it reconstructs the circumstances of the Holocaust and represents it as an everyday reality, generated in a specific situation. The Holocaust is represented as a consequence of the deliberate actions of certain people and the complicity and cowardice of others (Kurnick 2015: 128).

From this standpoint, the purpose of the relationships between the Mexican and the European parts of the novel and the two chronological

8 Barberán Reinares argues that 'the gruesome deaths of countless poor and racialized women become the Lacanian "real" of Bolaño's narrative – the ugly, traumatic, and ever-present junction where many different characters intersect' (2010: 55).

plains becomes clearer. As Sergio Villalobos-Ruminott argues, 'violence [i]s the synecdoche of contemporary history' (2009: 201) and 'what makes Latin American political history part of the European saga (and vice versa) is war and violence, which are not accidental to the plot but its main topic' (202). It is no coincidence that it is Archimboldi who serves as the bond that holds these two parts together. He is the only character that has a direct relationship to the Second World War *and* Santa Teresa and he is the reason the critics move from Europe to Mexico (Boe Birns 2015: 67–84). Archimboldi's given name, Benno, is symbolic of his role as a kind of spatial and thematic conjunction as it refers simultaneously to Benito Mussolini, Benito Juárez (after whom Mussolini was named) and Benedict of Nursia, patron saint of Europe (*2666*: 809).

The formidable variety of *2666*, which is not only thematic but spatial and chronological, creates another contrast with *The Third Reich*. The setting of the latter novel, a hotel on the coast of Spanish at the end of the tourist season, is a parody of the purgatorial theme of the sanatorium and derides the postmodern ambition to present a close space as a comfortable allegory of the world's chaos. Like this allegory, the world represented by the map of the wargame is a product of modern cartography. It is therefore abstract and emotionless and lacks human and subjective implications. But the irruption of the real destroys this illusion. On the contrary, in *2666*, the Second World War represents things that are neither explicable nor intelligible, like the senseless death of a science-fiction writer or the crucifixion of a Romanian general. It refutes the precise clarity of the wargame and its accompanying oppositions of good and evil, paradoxically illuminating a grey area that presents a challenge to individual responsibilities and ethics.

Bolaño's critique of purely intellectual passion, which is at the centre of *The Third Reich* and is also evident in Juan Stein's story in *Distant Star*, is present in *2666*. Despising intellectual poets and scholars in favour of their picaresque, self-educated and omnivorous counterparts, Bolaño establishes his distance from postmodern models by signalling an interest in the combination of life and literature, rather than literature as an abstract phenomenon that requires no practical elaboration (Donnarumma 2015: 226). From this point of view, the comparison between Sammer and Entrescu echoes the double comparison between Stein and Soto or Stein and Wieder in *Distant Star*. The Nazi administrator attempts to make excuses for his crimes, whereas Entrescu never apologizes, but admits his responsibility when, facing death, he orders his soldiers to dig in the graveyard. In *2666*, the opposition between morals and intellectual knowledge is clear in 'The Part about the Critics'. Pelletier and Espinoza's intellectual superiority does not prevent them from committing a racist aggression against a Pakistani taxi driver in London.[9] Moreover, their quest to find Archimboldi is presented as purely intellectual. It terminates when they find themselves stuck in Santa Teresa, where the mysterious and unspeakable nature of evil manifests itself.

In *The Third Reich*, the Second World War is fetishized and becomes the object of a professional, specialized interest because of its uniqueness and enormity. *2666*, by contrast, refuses a metaphysical or teleological vision of the conflict. The war is implicitly compared to other manifestations of evil. Bolaño refuses to explain or judge; however, by simply presenting the events in their complexity and dramatic strength, he underlines their incomprehensibility and their menacing and imponderable importance. As Oscar Fate argues, in reference to the femicides of Santa Teresa, 'no one pays attention to these killings, but the secret of the world is hidden in them' (*2666*: 348). Amalfitano, a scholar whose statelessness and apparent madness position him between intellectualism and real life, creates a readymade inspired by Marcel Duchamp.[10] This takes place after he has drawn the diagrams I previously mentioned, which are another symbol of the partiality of the map. He hangs a copy of a book he cannot recall receiving, *Testamento geométrico*, on the drying rack, exposed to the wind and the rain, 'to see if it learns something about real life' (*2666*: 195). We might say that Roberto Bolaño enacted something similar by exposing to reality, in *2666*, the postmodern detachment parodied in *The Third Reich*.

9 Martin Paul Eve (2016: 103–111) proposes a convincing reading of the university in *2666* as a space of complicity and collusion with the neoliberal dynamics of power.

10 On Duchamp in *2666*, see Piva 2017.

'The Increasingly Animated Ghost of Pierre Menard': Roberto Bolaño between Postmodernism and Post-Postmodernism

So far, I have demonstrated the importance of the Second World War as a literary theme in Bolaño's work, underlining how its pre-eminence is significant in the positioning of his work outside of the field of literary postmodernism. It is also important to understand, however, the extent to which Bolaño's style is an evolution of postmodernism.

As I stated in the introduction, the works of the authors I discuss belong to a globalized form of literature that has been variously defined, but that I refer to as the global novel. Among these authors, Bolaño, as a Latin American and not an Anglo-Saxon, is the author who best fits into this category (alongside Jonathan Littell). Although Bolaño's narrative is, of course, deeply rooted in the Chilean political experience and the trauma of Pinochet's coup, his personal history and the variety of his inspirations make him, as Sergio Villalobos-Ruminott asserts, a 'post-nationalist' (Villalobos-Ruminott 2009: 193). In other words, rather than conceiving of Bolaño simply as a nationally situated writer, his statelessness and autodidacticism allow us to understand him within a post-national and globalized framework. He occupies a nomadic position that is connected to contemporary warfare as a conflict that is virtually infinite in both time and space (Villalobos-Ruminott 2009: 193). Even those who contest the classification of Bolaño as a post-nationalist agree that the national aspects of his work deal with themes of marginality, liminality and postcolonial agency that must be understood in relation to other countries and in a globalized context (Kurnick 2015: 123–124).[11] Bolaño's global character is further reinforced by his identity as a Latin American writer, who is situated by his language in a super-national landscape.

It is almost self-evident that several features of Bolaño's work are strictly connected to postmodern poetics. Let us consider the author's

11 On this topic, see the volume *Roberto Bolaño as World Literature*. Nicholas Birns's chapter underlines the importance of American (and not just Latin American) heritage for Bolaño (2016: 220–243).

strong connection with genre literature and low-culture media or the use of meta- and auto-fictional devices. These features, though identical to those of postmodern poetics, have a different role and meaning than their postmodern origins might suggest. Moreover, in Bolaño, we find certain traits that are typical of post-postmodernism, such as narrative authorship and a general attention to realism.

In the first instance, Bolaño's use of genre literature aligns him with postmodern poetics, specifically to his inspirations Borges and Julio Cortázar (Ríos Baeza 2013: 122).[12] His work contains many references to genre literature (mostly, but not exclusively, the detective novel) and pop culture. I previously mentioned the author's mobilization of forms of low culture in relation to certain passages of the works analysed in this chapter, but *repetita iuvant*. Felipe A. Ríos Baeza (2013: 123–215) provides a rich and convincing analysis of the use of lowbrow literature and mass culture in Bolaño's work, be it in the form of science fiction (as in *Nazi Literature in the Americas*), pornography (as in the case of Wieder), the fantastic and supernatural novel (as in the episode of *2666* set in Dracula's castle), B-movies (for example, zombie movies are invoked by the surname

12 I appreciate that the concept of literary genre is vast and complex and that dealing with its entire theoretical premise would require more space and attention (see, for instance, Fowler 1982). When I refer to genre literature (e.g. crime fiction, horror, science fiction, etc.) as opposed to a more neutral category of mainstream or highbrow literature, I mean a set of texts produced for a precisely identifiable set of readers with a relatively fixed structure and a particular array of types and functions of characters. Following a structured pattern, genre literature provides the reader with a series of expectations 'concerning the kind of characters to appear, the situations they encounter, the themes they are likely to be confronted with, their conception as flat or round, or static or dynamic, and typical constellation with other characters' (Eder, Jannidis and Schneider 2010: 42–43). Genre literature has been understood mainly as popular fiction and its value has been undermined for a long time. Even its postmodern parodic reprises are motivated by the same lack of critical consideration. The very idea of merging highbrow culture and popular fiction, as Auster does in the *New York Trilogy*, is intended as a provocation and a comment on the end of fixed hierarchies in the postmodern world. On the contrary, as I explain here, post-postmodernism recognizes the literary value of genre literature and the incorporation of genre literature into post-postmodern models is not intended to be ironic.

of the detective in *Distant Star*, Romero, who appears also in *Los detectives salvajes* [*The Savage Detectives*], 1998) or television (as in the reference to David Lynch's *Fire Walk With Me*, the cinematic prequel of his TV series, *Twin Peaks*, in *2666*).[13]

The detective novel, in particular, recurs in Bolaño's works, thematically and structurally. In his early work, *The Third Reich*, it is evoked by the presence of the Florian Linden novel (a detective story Ingeborg reads) and also by Udo's behaviour when he investigates the mysterious events going on around him. His solitude in the desert hotel, for example, recalls the setting of Stephen King's novel and Stanley Kubrick's film *The Shining*. The same can be said of *Distant Star*, in which we find a real detective trying to identify Wieder, but in which we also find Bolaño himself as a detective who is both narrator and character, discussing how he collected information about Wieder in the previous years. In *2666*, this parallel assumes macroscopic proportions. The plot focuses on the critics' quest to find Archimboldi and then, most importantly, on the femicides occurring in Santa Teresa. Finally, in *The Savage Detectives*, the theme of investigation serves two functions: one detective strand relates to the three young 'detective' poets who look for Cesarea in the Sonora desert, whilst the other relates to the reader's own role as he/she is turned into a detective seeking the elusive characters of Ulises and Arturo through the endless interrogations in the central part of the book.

However, as we have seen, detective work in Bolaño's fiction always fails or, if successful, eventually leads to disaster, as in *The Savage Detectives*, in which the protagonists end up accidentally killing the woman they were looking for. *The Third Reich* ends with Udo's beating, while Wieder's discovery and death in *Distant Star* do not represent the recovery of a previous order, but rather represent a mysteriously motivated act, the execution of which the reader does not witness. In *2666*, the critics never find Archimboldi and the police never capture the party responsible for the many femicides. The man arrested for the murders, Klaus Haas, may be guilty of some of them, but certainly not of them all.

13 Carmen Fragero Guerra shows how close Bolaño is to the *feuilleton* novel (2012: 245–264). On Bolaño and science fiction, see Bizzarri 2017.

These events appear to suggest that the presence of the detective novel has a parodic function in Bolaño's novels, as it does in postmodern literature. Several postmodern authors, from Borges to Umberto Eco, adopt the genre of crime fiction in order to represent an impossible quest for truth in a world in which truth cannot be found. On the one hand, it is true that the detective novel as a genre can be seen 'as a paradigm and an implement of the hegemonic processes of the Western nation-state, tantalizing readers with aberrant, irrational criminality while assuring them that society ultimately coheres through a shared commitment to reason and law' (Pearson and Singer 2009: 1). However, it is worth noticing that Bolaño does not look to classic crime fiction, but rather to the less gratifying genre of realist crime fiction. This distinction is significant. Classic crime fiction (e.g. Agatha Christie's novels) depicts the disruption of order and then its recovery, in accordance with the cited definition of crime fiction as a socially reassuring genre. By contrast, realist crime novels (e.g. the works of Raymond Chandler) depict an already chaotic world in which there is no order to restore. While it is true that Bolaño's crime investigations do not lead anywhere, it is also true that this happens partly because of the very rules of this genre. It is possible, therefore, that postmodern parody is not taking place.

The contrast between these two types of crime writing is much more striking if we compare Bolaño's reprise of the crime fiction novel to its mobilization by postmodern authors such as Borges, Paul Auster or Eco. With the exception of *The Third Reich*, Bolaño's use of the crime fiction novel has nothing of the 'hermeneutic skepticism and generic self-reflexivity of the metaphysical detective stories' (Pearson and Singer 2009: 6) associated with postmodern writers. While Borges's metaphysical detective stories certainly inspire Bolaño, whose work is imbued with philosophical reflections, the reader will not find in Bolaño's novels the rarefied and paradoxical atmosphere of postmodern prose. Instead, his works attempt to engage reality as a material fact (and not as an abstract principle), using the means and the patterns of genre literature.

If we compare Bolaño's reprise of the detective novel with Auster's postmodern masterpiece *The New York Trilogy* (1985–1986), we can observe some similarities, but the differences are striking. Both Bolaño's and

Auster's characters belong to the category of the 'accidental detective' (Ciocia 2012: 198–199), meaning they are amateurs (most often literates or writers) who end up solving mysteries. They are, in other words, a contemporary version of the Decadent movement's 'art for art's sake' myth, which has infected the detective story from Edgar Allan Poe's C. Auguste Dupin onwards. However, in Auster's trilogy, the detective fiction genre is employed as an auto- and metafictional experiment that investigates the gnoseological limits of our language. In Bolaño's works, by contrast, detective fiction is a metaphor (albeit a structural one) for the lack of clarity in the world. Auster's triptych contains structuralist reflections on language and 'deconstructs the form of the novel, the canons of criticism, theory, and tradition, and it deconstructs itself, as it literally falls apart in its profession' (Lavender 2004: 78). At the thematic centre of *The New York Trilogy* is the blurring of individual identity in a world deprived of meaning and ruled by chaos, in which the very basis of communal life falls apart. As Enrico Testa argues, Auster's premise is the linguistic nihilism common in twentieth-century literature, according to which words hide, rather than reveal, the objects to which they refer, which makes communication between individuals impossible (Testa 2009: 28–29). This aim is pursued through the deployment of literary and intertextual references – most notably to Don Quixote, of which the first book of Auster's trilogy is a re-writing – and the continuous loss of identity experienced by Auster's characters, narrators and, to a certain extent, readers, as a result of all the characters also being readers of someone else's story and their own story. Even the author himself is doubled in the collection; he appears as a character and then another character adopts his name as a pseudonym.

The reprise of the detective story in Auster has a double purpose. First, it lends a metafictional framework, and therefore a sense of unreality, to the story. The characters increasingly become aware that they are being turned into characters in a novel as the plot proceeds. Second, it creates an even stronger sense of meaninglessness and unknowability through the contrast between the pointlessness of the story and the genre of crime fiction, which is typically characterized by clarity and conclusion. 'Everything is simple, if you arrange the facts methodically', Hercule Poirot states in Agatha Christie's excellent *The Murder of Roger Ackroyd* (2016: 73). This contrasts starkly with Auster's sabotage of the detective novel through meaningless clues and indecipherable behaviour.

Bolaño's broad deployment of the detective genre and his portrayal of criminal investigations signal that the detective novel has value beyond the literary. But what separates Bolaño's use of genre fiction from postmodern pastiches like Auster's? According to Andrea Torres Perdigón, Bolaño's style is parody, but cannot be reduced to pastiche (2015: 98–99; see also Asensi Perez 2010: 349–350). Perdigón argues that Bolaño never imitates the style of the detective novel; he simply appropriates the form in order to fill it with his own contents (Torres Perdigón 2015: 96). Bolaño's ironic, eccentric and chaotic investigations represent a tragic and violent vision of the world, rather than a metaphysical one, or, in Ríos Baeza's words, a kind of nihilistic intellectual experiment (Ríos Baeza 2013: 164). In other words, there is nothing in Bolaño's work that is akin to the deceptive, endless quest staged by Auster, for whom 'the detective novel [is] an allegory for novels in general' (Lavender 2004: 77). Bolaño's reappropriation of detective fiction is not intended as a labyrinthian exposition of the meaninglessness of life and the limits of human understanding. While it is true that Bolaño's detectives never find what they are looking for, they always find something else at the end of or during their quest. Incapable of finding *the* truth, they find a multiplicity of experiences, which, in the end, is what the truth consists of. The quest of García Madero, Ulises Lima and Arturo Belano in *The Savage Detectives* fails. When they meet the woman for whom they have been searching throughout the book, they accidentally kill her. However, this quest ends up being rather marginal in a book that is largely composed of interviews with the protagonists' friends, all of whom have their own story. In Auster's work, the detectives cannot find anything and are faced with the very absence of something to find; in that void, they find their own meaninglessness.

Another allegedly postmodern feature of Bolaño's fiction is the presence of meta- and sometimes autofictional devices. Although Bolaño rarely uses metafictional devices explicitly (unless we consider García Madero's and Ansky's diaries as such), the numerous writers and poets in his books (such as his alter ego, Arturo Belano), together with the centrality of the experience of Pinochet's coup, suggest that there is a continuity between

Bolaño's life and fiction. There are instances, moreover, in which Bolaño makes intertextual references to other novels that resemble the main novel in their style (such as Archimboldi's *Bifurcaria Bifurcata* in *2666*) or structure. In *Distant Star*, for example, mention is made of a book by Bibiano O'Ryan, *The Warlocks Return*, that resembles closely *Nazi Literature in the Americas* (*DS*: 117), except for the chronological delimitation and the focus on real rather than fictional people.

Distant Star is also the only book in which Bolaño explicitly exploits meta- and autofictional devices. Autofiction is defined as a text in which, like autobiography, author, narrator and protagonist are the same person (Lejeune 1975: 14), but in which the 'facts' narrated are understood by the reader to be false (Marchese 2014: 10).[14] Autofiction begins, thus, as a deliberate breaking of the autobiographic pact as a result of a hybridization of autobiography and the literary theories of the twentieth century (78). If autobiography has an ambiguous relationship with truth despite its professed interest in accurately representing a life, autofiction is premised on deliberate ambiguity. The author suggests that what happens to the character that bears his name is true, even though the events are actually false, through the use of paratexts such as the title, subtitle, notes, dedications and epigraphs (the classic warranties of truthfulness for autobiographical writing; Gasparini 2008: 72–84). Autofiction thereby offers a double opportunity. On the one hand, by staging the author as protagonist-narrator it assumes the properties of reality. We know, for instance, that the author really lived and so we expect the books to be faithful accounts provided by a real person. On the other hand, autofiction represents the widest disclosure of the mechanisms of narration. No other kind of writing is at once so personal and so artificial; in no other kind of writing are both the author and narrative artificiality (the gap between truth and fiction) so exposed. Indeed, although readers are advised by the author (or at least by the paratext) that what they are reading is a work of fantasy, the coincidence between the protagonist and the author prevents us from reading

14 This understanding can arise on the basis of internal elements, such as the presence of supernatural features in the story, or on the basis of a statement provided by the author – even, as here, the simple fact that the book is published under the name 'novel'.

autofiction without the feeling that its narrative is the *real* life of the writer. As we read in the introduction to *Distant Star*:

> In the final chapter of my novel *Nazi Literature in the Americas* I recounted, in less than twenty pages and perhaps too schematically, the story of Lieutenant Ramírez Hoffman of the Chilean Air Force, which I heard from a fellow Chilean, Arturo B., a veteran of Latin America's doomed revolutions, who tried to get himself killed in Africa. He was not satisfied with my version. It was meant to counterbalance the preceding excursions into the literary grotesque, or perhaps to come as an anti-climax, and Arturo would have preferred a longer story that, rather than mirror or explode others, would be, in itself, a mirror and an explosion. So we took that final chapter and shut ourselves up for a month and a half in my house in Blanes, where, guided by his dreams and nightmares, we composed the present novel. My role was limited to preparing refreshments, consulting a few books, and discussing the reuse of numerous paragraphs with Arturo and the increasingly animated ghost of Pierre Ménard. (*DS*: 1)

This preface is particularly complex. Bolaño claims that the story of Ramírez Hoffman, present in his previous novel, was told to him by his friend Arturo B., whom the reader is encouraged to recognize as Arturo Belano – the future protagonist of *The Savage Detectives* and Bolaño's alter ego. Belano was not satisfied with the result, so he and Bolaño write a better version of the story together. Apparently, though, Belano is the only author, despite Bolaño being the protagonist.

This is particularly relevant in explaining Bolaño's approach to post-modern poetics. Meta- and autofictional devices were developed by post-modern writers to blur the boundaries between fact and fiction, to challenge our perception of the real and, ultimately, to contest the existence of a univocal version of history, as indeed happens in Auster's work. Bolaño, however, uses them here to insert himself as the protagonist and a witness of events that never happened. These events, however, are set in a context that Bolaño *did experience* first-hand: Pinochet's coup and the subsequent mass exile of Chileans. The use of autofiction, then, is intended not to create confusion between fact and fiction, but to connect a personal experience with a symbolic figure, Wieder. The metafictional premise of the book, manifested in the claim that it was Belano and not Bolaño who authored *Distant Star*, simply aims to link the experience reported in the book with Bolaño's other works (which are crowded with vagabond poets such as Belano). In other words, Bolaño's meta- and autofictional devices are intended to give new and multiple voices to his personal experiences. For example, the reference to Pierre Ménard, a fictional character in a Borges's short story who rewrites the *Quixote* word for word, alludes to the postmodern tradition because the short story gives rise to questions surrounding authorship and interpretation that would later become pivotal for postmodern authors. Bolaño is never tempted to reduce the world to the purely textual; rather, he engages with it.

If we can say that Bolaño's use of postmodern strategies is atypical insofar as it generally tends towards serving or increasing realism, then his use of post-postmodern techniques confirms his commitment to material reality. Indeed, a typically post-postmodern feature of Bolaño's work is its realism. As we have seen in the introduction, post-postmodern realism is problematic. Although post-postmodern authors display a renewed attention to reality and its representation, their works continue to oscillate between mimetic and antimimetic features. This hybrid realism is very important in Bolaño's style. We have noted in the section about *2666* that Bolaño makes a serious effort both to recreate the circumstances in which the Holocaust took place and to replicate the bureaucratic language through which its perpetrators communicated. The same pattern can be observed across his novels. Bolaño deploys what Guido Mazzoni calls the 'environmental paradigm', which involves the accumulation of details that are unnecessary to the narration but enhance the description of the setting and the characters – making them, therefore, real (Mazzoni 2017: 268). Despite this mimetic effort (a constant that I will highlight in several other novels), Bolaño's fiction could hardly be considered realism in the traditional sense. The category of hybrid (or dirty) realism – which is to say, a realistic effort with unrealistic tendencies – seems to be more suitable. Bolaño's work is full of unrealistic (or rather surreal) elements, both stylistically (such as the use of metafiction and the genre plots we have noted or the elliptical development of the plot) and thematically. A sense of *unlikeliness* underlies Bolaño's novels. As Stefano Ercolino notes, it is not that the facts narrated are impossible, as we are never confronted with the openly supernatural in Bolaño, but rather that they are strange, grotesque and ridiculous (Ercolino 2015: 254). A mimetic effort in the recreation of certain circumstances is paired with the utter strangeness of the events narrated. For instance, the detachment and hyperrealism of the depiction of the femicides in Santa Teresa is intertwined, to use Ercolino's example, with the enquiry into a mysterious church desecrator with a supposedly giant bladder.

This oscillation between the real and surreal can be observed in the narrator. As Filippo Pennacchio convincingly notes, the narrator of *2666* has the traditional traits of omniscience and authorship, in opposition to the fragmented, feeble and unaware postmodern narrator. Bolaño's narrator is a rather classic third-person narrator, who is external to the events of the novel and uses the past tense (Pennacchio 2017: 203). This is particularly true in the first and fifth parts. In the second and third parts, the narration is almost entirely focalized through Amalfitano and Fate, whereas, in the fourth, the narrator employs the technique of impersonality. However, Bolaño often augments or deviates from certain characteristics of the omniscient narrator, for example, by using summaries in order to manipulate the temporality of the story (205). Moreover, despite the apparent precision of the omniscient narrator, Bolaño often gives the narrator implausible knowledge. The passage that Pennacchio mentions is significant in this sense. In 'The Part about the Critics', Pelletier is telling Norton about an episode in which he, Espinoza and Morini encounter a painter who mutilated himself and is now secluded in a Swiss asylum. During Pelletier's story, the focalization shifts from Pelletier to Morini to the painter, a transition that is evidently impossible as Pelletier cannot possibly be aware of Morini's and the painter's feelings.

Such oscillation between a classical model of omniscient narration and the violation of the model through playful imprecision and implausibility in Roberto Bolaño's oeuvre is once again typical of a post-postmodern poetics. Post-postmodernism is situated between a serious recovery of the tradition of the modern or modernist novel and the postmodern (although not ironic) freedom of this recovery. The same can be said of Bolaño's realism, his utilization of genre literature and his employment of auto- and metafictional devices. Similarly, Bolaño's representation of the Second World War as a symbol of absolute, yet contextualized, evil is suggestive of a thematic and stylistic 'return to the real', which gains greater importance as a result of the sustained critique of postmodern poetics in his work.

'It's Not Impossible': Narratorial Unreliability and Metafiction in Ian McEwan's *Atonement*

We have discussed the innovative use of metafictional poetics in Bolaño. My analysis of *Atonement* by Ian McEwan aims to deepen our understanding of the role of postmodern features in post-postmodern poetics. The metafictional structure of *Atonement* highlights the treacherous and deceptive nature of individual and public memory, reprising a distinctive trait of the postmodern approach to history without pushing it to its nihilistic extreme.

Ian McEwan's *Atonement* (*A*) was published in 2001, late in his career (McEwan was born in 1948), and immediately hailed as a major success. It is, in my view, the most remarkable novel about the unreliability of the memory of the Second World War, as well as the crucial relationship between memory and fiction. Its plot, which is divided into four parts or, better, three parts and a post scriptum, is well known. The first part is set in the luxurious country house of the Tallis family. Briony Tallis, a 13-year-old girl with literary ambitions, accuses her sister's lover Robbie Turner of raping her cousin Lola. Briony's accusation is based on a mixture of jealousy, her supposed dislike of Robbie (he is of a lower social class) and her misinterpretation of the romantic interest between Robbie and Cecilia. Specifically, Briony misunderstands a moment of sexual passion that the two lovers share as an instance of sexual violence. That same evening, while the whole family is outside searching for two missing children, Lola is raped by a man she claims she could not identify in the dark. Briony, who witnesses the culprit's escape, accuses Robbie of the crime, for which he is arrested and imprisoned. In the second part, Robbie has been freed on condition that he enrol in the army and is fighting in Dunkirk. Cecilia has become a nurse, in protest against her family who do not believe in Robbie's innocence. The two lovers have remained in contact during his imprisonment, without being able to meet, and have the chance to say goodbye before he leaves for France. In the third part, Briony, who now admits the falsity of her accusation, has also become a nurse and is willing to make amends. When she meets with her sister and Robbie, they both refuse to forgive her, but insist that she begin fixing her mistake by producing legal documents that exonerate Robbie from the crime and implicate a family friend (now married to Lola) as the real culprit. The third part terminates with the words 'BT / London, 1999' (*A*: 349). These epistolary formal devices – specifically, Briony's initials – suggest that what readers have read so far is a fictionalized account of events that has been provided by Briony herself. In the fourth part, a diary entry set in 1999, the now 77-year-old Briony is a celebrated writer. She explains that what we have read so far is her last novel, to be published after her death for legal reasons. In the final pages of the book, she informs her readers that Robbie and Cecilia did not survive the war, the former dying at Dunkirk and the latter during a bombardment, and thus did not have the chance to reunite. Briony's *atonement*, then, is not only the time she spends as a nurse, but also the novel itself, contained in the previous three parts.

The war plays a relatively small role in *Atonement*. Although central to the plot, it can be considered at first glance a marginal theme. And yet, *Atonement*'s complex metafictional frame, together with Briony's unreliability as a narrator, casts a shadowy light on the process of the memorialization of the Second World War. As Nick Bentley has summarized, 'this metafictional twist shifts the ontological status of the novel from objective account by an extradiegetic third-person narrator to a homodiegetic, historical (if somewhat fictionalized) memoir' (2004: 150). Briony, who is the fictional third-person narrator of the first three parts of the novel and first-person narrator of the last, is indeed an unreliable narrator – both because of her homodiegetic voice and because she claims to be suffering from vascular dementia (*A*: 354). She also claims that legal preoccupations have forbidden her to publish the book (*A*: 369–370), but preoccupations about the legal consequences of writing are a notorious topos of fictional writing, intended to suggest its truthfulness rather than to prove it. Moreover, we are made aware of Briony's unreliability through her lies; she hides the truth about the deaths of Robbie and Cecilia until the novel's end. Such a contradiction raises suspicions about everything that Briony as an implied or explicit narrator has said and her character is aware of that. As she has Robbie say in the third part, 'if you were lying then, why should a court believe you now? [...] You're an unreliable witness'

(*A*: 336; see also 358). Indeed, her contradictions invalidate the content of her confession and her attempt at atonement. It is certainly possible, as has been suggested, that the lovers did not die or that Robbie was truly the rapist (Jacobi 2011: 55–73; Marsh 2017: 1–19).

Moreover, Briony's unreliability is connected to the wider theme of the dangers of fiction (Möller 2001: 55). As a lonely child with a passion for literature, 'Briony's worldview has been shaped by aesthetic expectations' (O'Hara 2011: 76) and she is incapable of reading reality outside of the melodramatic romances she avidly consumes. This is symbolized by the play *The Trials of Arabella*, which she writes for the occasion of the family reunion. When she finds out what happens to her cousin, then, her reading of the misdeed is influenced by a novelistic preconception of Robbie as a brute – a view that refuses to take into account his different social class and the carnal aspects of romance. Sexual interest, in the literature Briony consumes, can only be interpreted as assault. Thus, paradoxically, literature ultimately leaves Briony unable to read literature itself: Robbie is considered guilty on the basis of a playful letter filled with obscenities directed at Cecilia (which Briony reads, although he did not intend to send it). Such a letter is evidently a product of imagination, comparable to D. H. Lawrence's *Lady Chatterley's Lover*, but Briony's literary background prevents her from reading it as such. She can only interpret it as further evidence of Robbie's criminal behaviour.

Significantly, the novel opens with a long epigraph from Jane Austen's *Northanger Abbey*.[15] Such an epigraph carries a double function: it alludes to the genre of the British country-house novel and signals the thematic importance of the dangers of fiction (Finney 2004: 70). In *Northanger Abbey*, Austen famously satirizes the reader's infatuation with the implausible plots of Gothic novels, constructing a story in which the heroine fails

15 The question of whether it is McEwan or Briony who places the epigraph there remains. If the *Northanger Abbey* quotation is considered Briony's choice, then we must interpret it as yet another part of *her* reflection on her own story in the first three parts. Otherwise, the quotation could be considered McEwan's comment on the entire novel, including the final post scriptum. I believe the quotation should be ascribed to the author and not to Briony, since it is placed before the beginning of the first part, right after the dedication of the book 'to Annalena'. Since this dedication is evidently McEwan's (we have no reason to suspect otherwise), it is fair to assume the same of the epigraph.

to accurately interpret the events unfolding around her because she forces them into the framework of the Gothic novels she so avidly reads. Briony evidently does the same thing, but her misreading has more dangerous consequences than those described in Austen's novel. Moreover, this reference to Austen signals that McEwan is adapting his style to fit the British modern (and modernist)[16] novel. Such a reprise, of course, also implies a critique of the ideological and classist aspects of the traditional country-house novel, in light of how class disparities are central and yet unproblematized in the genre (Quarrie 2015: 194–199). Moreover, considering that it is upper-class Briony who recreates the country-house novel and provides Robbie and Cecilia with a happy ending, it could be argued that her novel is an attempt not simply to achieve atonement, but also to return to 'a more innocent and intelligible time', which is, however, 'undercut by the guilt and horror that permeates the sections set during the war' (201–202).

Nevertheless, as Bentley argues, *Atonement* provides 'not only critical realism, but a critique of realism' (Bentley 2014: 142). Stylistically, McEwan deploys aspects of the modern novel (including plot, realistic characters, an omniscient narrator, mimetic realism, background characters) to reconstruct the Second World War and arouse sympathy for the fate of his protagonists. In her answer to Briony's story submission, the character of Cyril Connolly criticizes her experimental literary style as owing 'a little too much to the techniques of Mrs Woolf' (*A*: 312). She suggests that Briony's style should be less abstract and more plot-centred:

> Rather than dwell for quite so long on the perceptions of each of the three figures, would it not be possible to set them before us with greater economy, still keeping

16 Briony's aspiration to be a writer – which is part of the reason why she falsely accuses Robbie – persists into adulthood. We learn in the post scriptum that she becomes a professional writer. In the third part of the novel, she submits a story (a dramatization of the day her misdeed took place) to *Horizon*, a famous modernist literary magazine, and receives a response from Cyril Connolly. For further work on references to modernism and modernist literature in *Atonement*, see Robinson 2010: 473–495 and Mitric 2014: 715–740. As David K. O'Hara notes, Briony's evolution in aesthetic tastes is a form of atonement in itself, implying an understanding and condemnation of the melodramatic imagination that caused Robbie's imprisonment (2011: 82–83).

> some of the vivid writing about light and stone and water which you do so well – but then move on to create some tension, some light and shade within the narrative itself. Your most sophisticated readers might be well up on the latest Bergsonian theories of consciousness, but I'm sure they retain a childlike desire to be told a story, to be held in suspense, to know what happens. [...] Simply put, you need the backbone of a story. (*A*: 313–314)

Connolly's letter provides the first clue regarding the metafictional nature of *Atonement*, suggesting a correlation between the first part of the novel and Briony's short story and prefiguring the novel as a work of fiction. This is the case even though it is not explicitly stated that the first part *is* her story (Alden 2014: 168). Moreover, what Connolly suggests is precisely what present-day Briony does in the novel she writes (in which the letter is contained); indeed, it is what McEwan does. Through Connolly's critique, McEwan challenges the abstract quality of literature and at the same time upholds the necessity of engaging reality and evoking empathy in readers: 'How could [their death] constitute an ending? What sense or hope or satisfaction could a reader draw from such an account? Who would want to believe that they never met again, never fulfilled their love? Who would want to believe that, except in the service of the bleakest realism?' (*A*: 371). In other words, McEwan provides a recovery of the modern novel in *Atonement*, but with a metafictional twist – and the exorcism of the ingenuity that this recovery could imply. Such an oscillation between conventional novelistic commitment and postmodern meta-reflexivity is certainly a post-postmodern trait of *Atonement*. We are told: 'Robbie and Cecilia, still alive, still in love, sitting side by side in the library, smiling at *The Trials of Arabella*? It's not impossible' (*A*: 372). However, the very existence of the post scriptum undermines this hypothesis and Briony's unreliability only deepens readers' retrospective suspicion of what they have witnessed so far. Nevertheless, the emotions that the narrative has raised were real, despite their falsity. While McEwan warns against the dangers and sanitization that fiction, be it personal or national, can create, the sense of atonement implied in the novel's title can be obtained only through fiction (Cinquegrani and Re 2014: 209–214).

Finally, it is necessary to turn our attention to the representation of the Second World War. A central moment in *Atonement* is the description of the Dunkirk evacuation. The importance of this passage is accentuated by the ending of the novel, in which Briony tells the readers that Robbie did not survive, as they were previously told. Dunkirk was a primary subject of British propaganda during and after the war and still possesses a strongly evocative power, as the simple solemnity and the enthusiastic reviews of Christopher Nolan's recent film *Dunkirk* (2017) prove. The evacuation of the vast majority of the British Expeditionary Force (more than 300,000 men) from the shores of Dunkirk, besieged by land and air by German forces, represented a symbol of hope and resistance at a moment when the British Empire was suffering crushing defeats in Europe and Asia. The myth of the 'finest hour' of the British people and of the Commonwealth, which was, according to Paul Gilroy, 'produced with apparent spontaneity from below and sometimes engineered politically from above by crown and government' (Gilroy 2004: 97), largely depended on the capability of the army and the fleet to endure the military catastrophe and to prepare the counterattack that led to the final victory in the war.

Nevertheless, the part of the novel dedicated to the Dunkirk evacuation is far from propagandistic. McEwan carefully represents the conflict's chaos and the classism and internal struggles among British soldiers, debunking the official myth of the 'finest hour' (Bentley 2014: 151–152). In the novel, Robbie marches towards Dunkirk with two corporals who mock him for his manners and behaviour, which is highly symbolic of the class issues that pervaded Dunkirk and British society more broadly. Robbie was lower class, but had the chance to study at Cambridge thanks to a scholarship provided by the Tallis family. His manners and accent are contrasted with those of the corporals, who, as a result of their middle-class status, despise him. The three have dramatic encounters with officers who ask them to perform impossible military tasks and who therefore prove themselves unfit to command. One of these tasks is a last, desperate attempt to slow the German march, which Robbie and the corporals decline, thereby reaffirming their anti-heroic status. Moreover, on the shores of Dunkirk, the British troops almost lynch an aviator who is held personally responsible for the unsatisfactory effort of the Royal Air Force (RAF) and Robbie is tempted to participate. As Natasha Alden writes, McEwan's recreation of Dunkirk is far from the official myth of the retreat, showing instead how the evacuation happened in a chaotic 'moral vacuum' (2014: 149). The graphic, traumatic descriptions of the dead and wounded both in Dunkirk and in London testify to Alden's remarks. Most importantly, however, the profound reflection on the fragility of memory, the deceptiveness of fiction and the narcissism of self-representation that frame the account of the Dunkirk evacuation are intended to be a comment on the memory of the war itself. As Paul Gilroy writes:

> I think there is something neurotic about Britain's continued citation of the anti-Nazi war. Making it a privileged point of entry into national identity and self-understanding reveals a desire to find a way back to the point where the national culture – operating on a more manageable scale of community and social life – was, irrespective of the suffering involved in the conflict, both comprehensible and habitable. That memory of the country at war against foes who are simply, tidily, and uncomplicatedly evil has recently acquired the status of an ethnic myth. It explains not only how the nation remade itself through war and victory but also can be understood as a rejection or deferral of its present problems. That process is driven by the need to get back to the place or moment before the country lost its moral and cultural bearings. (Gilroy 2004: 97)

Gilroy labels Britain's problematic relationship with its past 'postimperial melancholia' (98). In *Atonement*, Briony's narcissistic personality, evidenced by her childhood mistake and her fictional recreation of it, is untouched by the consequences of history. By framing the memory of the Second World War within her account, McEwan warns readers of its status as a patriotic myth and recreates its contradictions. It is true that it is Briony who highlights these contradictions, but she does so in order to gain the atonement she seeks. Moreover, the reflection on the unreliability of the narrator invites us to problematize the whole reception of the memory of the war and its memorialization.

Bolaño's and McEwan's works contrast with one another. While Bolaño is concerned with the private experience and symbolic representations of fascism, McEwan is more interested in historical research. Nevertheless, the novels discussed in this chapter are situated at a liminal point between postmodernism and post-postmodernism, especially considering that both authors have produced nearly postmodern literary works in earlier phases of their career. The comparison between the two is useful in understanding the features of post-postmodern metafiction. As we see in Bolaño's work, post-postmodern metafiction – although concerned with the processes of memorialization and the transmission of history – does not question the boundaries between reality and fiction. While Bolaño is strongly influenced and fascinated by postmodern metafiction, as shown by his frequent deployment of inter- and intra-textual references and the constant presence of fictional writers and the act of writing in his work, his form of metafiction never challenges the knowability of history. On the contrary, Bolaño's only literary work structured around an auto/metafictional device, *Distant Star*, uses the author's persona to connect a historical event experienced first-hand to the symbolic character of Wieder. Although compromised by the unlikeliness that characterizes Bolaño's prose and narratorial style, in this sense auto/metafiction acquires an almost validatory function, rather than explicitly challenging the possibility of knowing history. In McEwan's novel, however, metafiction is employed to cast light on a specific historical event in order to challenge its official narrative. Narratorial unreliability in *Atonement* does not sanction the equivalence of facts and fiction, but rather undermines the credibility of a very specific version of the facts, which are represented as so factual and clear (although hidden by propaganda) through being supported by historical research and credible sources. In both Bolaño's and McEwan's fiction, then, we observe an innovative employment of metafictional devices, which go further than challenging historical knowledge. Paradoxically, *Distant Star* and *Atonement* seek to increase the participation of the reader in the creation of stories.

CHAPTER 2

A Collection of Parables: William T. Vollmann's *Europe Central*

Europe Central (*EC*) by William T. Vollmann is a complex, multi-layered, stylistically rich and carefully constructed book about the Second World War, its premises and its aftermath.[1] I begin my discussion of *Europe Central* by analysing its formal structure as it is part novel and part collection of short stories. This distinction is important since Vollmann defines the stories in the book as 'parables'. An enquiry into the narrative architecture of *Europe Central* is essential to understanding this concept and what it implies for our understanding of the work as a whole. I then provide a close reading of what I consider to be the text's most important short stories, focusing on the ethical distinction that shapes them – that is, the division between humanism and totalitarianism, which is to say between victims and perpetrators, and

1 William T. Vollmann is the author of twenty-six books, spanning fiction, non-fiction, memoir, philosophical speculation and cultural studies essays. Despite Vollmann's fecundity, very little has been written about him relative to the scale of his production. As Larry McCaffery argues, although Vollmann has been 'regularly (and mostly favourably) reviewed' and awarded and 'has achieved a kind of cult status among certain readers', there is so far 'no extended treatment at all, no book-length scholarly [study]' (McCaffery 2015: xiv; McCaffery here omits Hemmingson 2009, possibly because it is not, strictly speaking, a scholarly study). Although this remains generally true, things have changed slightly since McCaffery made this claim. McCaffery's contribution is part of a larger companion, edited by Christopher Coffman and Daniel Lukes, while other book-length discussions of aspects of Vollmann's work can be found in Qian 2012, Costa 2016, Palleau-Papin 2016, Özcan 2019, and in the monographic section of the journal *Enthymema*, edited by myself and Giuseppe Carrara (23, 2019). See also Coffman and Savvas 2020. Additionally, Lukes 2020 provides a collection of Vollmann's interviews.

the moral grey area between them. I consider these distinctions with the help of another of Vollmann's works, the essay *Rising Up and Rising Down* (*RURD*, 2005), which was written in the same years in which *Europe Central* was composed and provides an important insight into his theoretical premises. Finally, in the last part of this chapter, I draw a comparison between Vollmann's treatment of marginalized victims and the work of Rachel Seiffert and Sarah Waters.

A Collection of Parables

Europe Central is composed of thirty seven short stories, mainly featuring historical protagonists, arranged chronologically from 1914 to 1975 and set in Germany and the Soviet Union. These stories vary in length (from a couple of pages to 100 pages) and vary in tone from plain narration to lyrical sketch, dreamy divagation or metahistorical reflection, depending on the subject matter.

Critics are not unanimous in their definition of *Europe Central*'s form. This can be observed, for instance, in newspaper reviews accompanying the Penguin Books edition: *Europe Central* has been catalogued as 'part novel and part stories' by the *New York Times Book Review*, 'stories' by the *Los Angeles Times*, a 'novel' by the *Washington Post* and, generically, a 'work of fiction' by the *Boston Globe*. Meanwhile, the jury of the National Book Award calls it 'a half-continent of fictions – sketches, stories, novellas, a full-length novel'.[2] Ercolino, despite not discussing Vollmann's book directly, includes it in the canon of the maximalist *novels* (2015: 10). Finally, Michael Hemmingson argues that '*Europe Central* almost functions as a novel [...] an ambitiously big book of interlinked texts' (2009: 22). He compares it to *The Rainbow Stories* and *Thirteen Stories and Thirteen Epitaphs*, since all of them are not 'compilations of random short stories written over a certain

2 Judges' citation, available at: < https://www.nationalbook.org/books/europe-central/ > [last accessed 31 March 2020].

period of time, as many collections tend to be. Each is compounded on a high concept, a grand metaphor; the volumes are cycles of related texts with recurring topics and motifs' (22).

Half novel and half collection of short stories, Vollmann's text exemplifies the tendency of topic dispersion that seems to characterize the contemporary novel. Although certain elements lend cohesion to the separate stories, for example, recurring characters and uniform metaphorical imagery in relation to the musical and mythological aspects, the stories function autonomously. The characters, even the recurring ones, are always introduced as if they had not appeared before. For instance, we read in 'Opus 110' about 'Paulus, who if you don't keep up with such things was the Field-Marshal we'd capture at Stalingrad' (*EC*: 650), 'Lenin's widow Krupskaya' and 'that petty Nazi, K. Gerstein, who'd joined the SS in order to reveal its secrets' (*EC*: 694) – all of whom were protagonists in the previous stories. This is also the case for the recurring protagonists, such as Dimitri Shostakovich, Elena Konstantinovskaya and Roman Karmen. Although their love triangle occupies eight stories, as we will see, they are often introduced as if they have never been mentioned before (*EC*: 473 and 514). Similarly, the events they experience are narrated several times, as if they were happening, or at least being recounted, for the first time. This is the case for Shostakovich's indecision over whether he should be with Elena or his wife Nina, which is one of the subjects of 'Operation Barbarossa' and is also narrated in the previous story, 'Opus 40'.

These texts can be further defined as short stories because they meet the criteria according to which we define a short story: the brevity effect, the stories' unity as self-contained narrations of a single event and exemplarity (Zatti 2010: 15–18). The stories, as I have mentioned, are never longer than 100 pages (with longer stories qualifying as novellas) and have a sole protagonist and focalization. They are also strongly characterized by unity, be it thematic or chronological. Even the longest of them, 'The Last Field-Marshal' and 'Breakout', focus only on Paulus's life at Stalingrad and on Vlasov following the siege of Leningrad, respectively. When the entire life of an individual is narrated, this is done by insisting on a precise theme. 'Woman with Dead Child', for example, details the life of Käthe Kollwitz, focusing on the presence of grief and mourning. 'The Saviors' centres on the meeting between Krupskaya and Fanny Kaplan and the effects of this meeting on Lenin's widow's life. 'The Sleepwalker' enacts a parallel between Hitler's life and Nordic mythology. Even when the characters recur, the texts dedicated to them focus on a selected chronological period (the siege of Leningrad in 'The Palm Tree of Deborah', for example) or thematically concluded episodes (such as Shostakovich giving a book to Elena in 'Ecstasy' and Shostakovich at the stadium in 'Operation Barbarossa').

It is not superfluous, in the context of an analysis of the role of the Second World War in Vollmann's work, to focus on the form that his narrative takes. Like Roberto Bolaño, Vollmann tends to create narratives on the basis of a juxtaposition of implicitly connected episodes. For instance, the *Seven Dreams* books have an almost analogous structure to that of *Europe Central*, in that they consist of short narrative units, chronologically ordered. Vollmann, however, defines the *Seven Dreams* books as 'Symbolic History' (1990: 397), whereas, when he refers to *Europe Central*, he always calls the parts of which it is composed *stories* or *parables* (*EC*: 753). *Europe Central* could be referred to as a short-story cycle because the stories, however independent, are indeed 'so linked to one another that the reader's experience of each one is modified by his experience of the others' (Ingram 1971: 13).[3] Notwithstanding the author's own perspective, it has to be noted that in contrast to typical examples of this form, which is very popular in American literature, several stories in *Europe Central* are too long to qualify as short stories. They are, rather, novellas. Moreover, the chronological order in which the stories are collated is more reminiscent of the coherence of the novel than the relative freedom of the short-story collection – however

3 Specifically, Forrest L. Ingram suggests that the stories of a short-story cycle are so closely linked that 'the reader's successive experience on various levels of the pattern of the whole significantly modifies his experience of each of its component parts' (1971: 19). He argues that such cycles are regulated by 'the dynamic patterns of recurrence and development' (20). It is worth noting that these descriptions fit Vollmann's work perfectly, especially the many stories dedicated to Shostakovich. Nevertheless, it is the lengths of some of the stories that forbid us from defining all of them as short stories. In this sense, once again, *Europe Central* seems to place itself between a maximalist novel and a collection of stories, in a way that recalls (but does not coincide with) Ingram's categories. See also Nagel 2001: 1–17.

interrelated the latter's units may be. According to the author, 'the goal [...] was to write a series of parables about famous, infamous and anonymous European moral actors at moments of decision' (ibid.); therefore, parable, in this context, should not be understood as a 'rise-and-decline' story.[4] In *Europe Central*, we are presented with a series of related but autonomous short stories. Each one can be read independently, but all are held together by their moral meaning. Further, their moral meaning is highly influenced, as we will see, by the fact that these stories ask to be read as parables – although this term requires some clarification.

A parable is a short story that is used by an author to illustrate a truth or a religious teaching. If we imagine the parables contained in the Gospels or in certain Buddhist sutras, however, we will fail to recognize them in Vollmann's text. Without being too specific, a parable generally possesses two main qualities: brevity and clarity. A parable, it has been argued, is an extended simile, in contrast to an allegory, which is 'a series of extended metaphors' (Stein 2000: 31). Therefore, the meaning that can be attributed to a parable is singular, whereas allegory is open to a multitude of interpretations. Although Robert H. Stein warns against too strict an application of these categories, since Christ's own parables are in several instances indistinguishable from allegories, there is some truth in this distinction. Moreover, the differences between parable and allegory are strikingly significant when we consider Vollmann's 'parable'.

First of all, the stories that make up *Europe Central* are not entirely fictional because they tell the stories of real-life people and not stylized symbolical figures. Secondly, they are mostly excessively long, too long to be considered parables ('Breakout', 'The Last Field-Marshal' and 'Opus 110' are all more or less 100 pages long). Finally, and most importantly, they are profoundly ambiguous in their meanings. They take as their subjects, for instance, the life of a defeated German Field-Marshal, a Soviet traitor, a repentant SS officer and the blood-lusting East German Minister of Justice. In a critical article about Vollmann's text, Peter G. Christensen argues that

4 A common meaning of 'parable' is adopted from the name of the mathematic figure, 'parabola', which is a curve, hence the interpretation of a parable as a tale of a metaphorical curve, a 'rise-and-decline' story.

the model of the parable cannot be applied to *Europe Central*. Although his scathing critique is generally unbalanced because he mainly focuses on the historical imprecisions of Vollmann's depiction of Shostakovich and thereby fails to recognize that an artist can select his material and treat it as he wants, Christensen's position on the issue of the catachresis of 'parable' is useful. As Christensen writes of the parable, 'the reader should be able to see a cause and effect relationship in a clear narrative line' (2009: 98). In relation to Shostakovich's story, for example, Christensen argues that while Vollmann puts great effort into recreating thirty years of love suffering, the story of Shostakovich and Elena would need a proper resolution and a precise meaning in order to be classified as a parable (99).

Bryan M. Santin accuses Christensen of having a 'rigid, antiquated, didactic' view of the parable and of trying to impose on Vollmann a 'generically conservative definition of parables' (2015: 161, note 29).[5] However, I cannot discern the wider sense in which he seems to be suggesting we should interpret the concept of the parable in relation to Vollmann's work. Considering that the definition I provided earlier is the only one generally attributed to the parable, we can arrive at two different conclusions. Either the stories of *Europe Central* are actual parables in the sense that this definition suggests and present a clear meaning (which is unlikely, as Santin himself demonstrates in his essay on Gerstein's story) or Vollmann is using the word 'parable' in a very broad way, as a synonym for 'allegory' or 'metaphor' – thus, incorrectly.

My sense of Vollmann's misuse of the word 'parable' is also confirmed by the various references to the Kabbalah (*EC*: 215, 601, 671; and the story

5 It is also worth noting that Santin, in the title of his article 'The Tragic Parable of Kurt Gerstein', seems to use the word 'parable' in the sense of life progression, for how could a simile be tragic? In his article, Santin claims that 'in lieu of clear moral or spiritual edification, Vollmann's parables aim to mystify readers, instilling them not with self-assurance but self-doubt'. While this is certainly true, as ambiguity and paradox are key to understanding *Europe Central*, I do not understand how such an assumption can be logically consistent with the following: 'Vollmann adheres closely to the original etymological meaning of parable […] "to put side by side" or to "compare item 'a' with item 'b'"' (2015: 146). Indeed, given their ambiguity and their length, this is exactly what Vollmann's parables do *not* do. Santin does not explain in his article which 'item b' is supposed to match Gerstein's parable.

'The Saviors'), which is echoed, in different contexts, by the reflections on calligraphy (*EC*: 121–122, 209, 523, on the runes, *EC*: 224, and on Shostakovich's musical signature, *EC*: 94). Of course, the reprise of the Hebrew mystique can also be interpreted as a reference to Jewish culture, which is victimized in the text both by the Nazi and the Soviet regimes (*EC*: 628). However, in *Europe Central*, the Kabbalah lends the stories a mystical and allegorical undertone (unlike the parable, which is based on a simile) and, by implication, suggests that words and language contain an inexpressible, mystical meaning (Scholem 1970: 13).

I recognize that the Kabbalistic tradition's wide use of parables may appear to validate Vollmann's self-reading instead of undermining it. It seems, however, that Kabbalah is evoked in *Europe Central* not as a literary model, but, rather, for its mystical knowledge of the divine (*EC*: 628). In 'The Saviors (A Kabbalistic Tale)', we read about the Kabbalistic diagrams (*EC*: 15), which are symbols and not similes. A few paragraphs later, the exchanging of the rings between Lenin and Krupskaya is called 'a parable-within-a-parable' (*EC*: 16). It is not clear what this parable is supposed to signify, but Vollmann avoids attributing a precise meaning to it, suggesting instead that it has a supernatural symbolic value. The 'parable-within-a-parable' is said to possess an 'ironic symbolism' (*EC*: 16), but at the same time Vollmann claims that 'we need not detain ourselves here with mystic correlation and analogies, God being ineffable anyway' (*EC*: 17). Finally, Vollmann implies that the sense of the so-called parable lies in a hidden meaning, invisible to the non-initiated (*EC*: 18).

Although these references are indeed strongly connected to the teachings of Kabbalah, they are not connected to the concept of a 'parable' – not even the Kabbalistic parable. While Kabbalistic teachings are often complex and paradoxical, Kabbalistic parables rarely are (Scholem 1962: 59–60), especially in the most important of the Kabbalistic texts, the Zohar. It is important to highlight that despite the content of the Kabbalistic parables and their complex, paradoxical nature, they always present themselves as short stories, suggesting that they should be understood intellectually. Vollmann's, as I have explained, should not.

Vollmann's aim is to draw attention to people at the crucial moment of a decision, rather than evaluate the complexity or the context of that decision. As readers of *Europe Central* quickly come to appreciate, he is interested in depicting the psychological processes that come before and after a complex decision and not the relation of cause and effect behind it (thus, he refuses to elaborate specific economic and political circumstances). While Vollmann's stories do not suggest a precise meaning, they do present examples and even models of conduct, in a certain way. Therefore, I argue that, rather than parables, they are *exempla*, hagiographies, *passiones*. This change in terminology allows us to retain the religious and mystical meaning implied in the Kabbalistic parable, whilst also recognizing the structure and complexity of the texts.

Europe Central is rich in comparisons between characters and saints. For example, Gerstein's story is considered 'as rare, and hence as shocking, as full-figure reliefs of the saints on otherwise featureless walls' (*EC*: 425). Vollmann's characters act as exemplary figures, portrayed at a decisive moment of their life. They are victims, martyrs, witnesses and 'tragic heroes' (*EC*: 808). Shostakovich and Paulus exemplify this characterization:

> I see [Paulus] as the central figure of a parable, and therefore apathetic in spite of himself; in his long leather trenchcoat, his gloves and collar perfectly white even now, his loyalty gleaming, he was brought into the story of our Reich to illustrate a principle, to carry out a function, to think and suffer while things were done to him. (*EC*: 393)

If we consider the traditional meaning of the parable, these sentences seem contradictory. First of all, which 'principle' is Paulus supposed to be illustrating? Which 'function' is he supposed to be carrying out? The reader is never told and it is not made clear in the text. Moreover, the idea that Paulus's role is 'to think and suffer' does not accord with the parable's aim of bestowing a (moral) meaning as it constitutes a simile for something that is more difficult to comprehend. His tortured role suggests, rather, that Paulus is an example – a metaphor of the human condition – without explaining this analogy further.

In the first pages of the book, Vollmann suggests that his stories have some gnostic value, thereby implying a clear and immediately comprehensible meaning:

> Doesn't the parable possess greater integrity, greater righteousness we might almost say, than any other literary form? For its many conventions wave a holy covenant

> between the reader, who gets the mystification he craves in a bonbon-sized dose, and the writer, whose absence renders him divine. (*EC*: 13–14)

This passage, however, causes readers doubt whether there really is a 'bonbon-sized dose' of precise meaning in what they read. Having read the whole story 'The Saviors', we are forced to explore what its meaning might be. Given that integrity and righteousness are qualities that usually apply to human beings rather than to stories, I argue that Vollmann is using the word 'parable' to refer to something that is much closer to hagiography. While parables are used to explain a concept, providing a form and efficiency that a text would not otherwise have (Stein 2000: 35), they are not an object of contemplation like the life of the saints or a psychodrama to be reinterpreted by the reader. Parables require an intellectual understanding. As I have argued, Vollmann's stories are not intellectual theories; they require an emotional response. Participation and empathy are the means through which to comprehend a phenomenon in his fiction.

It is compelling and significant that the protagonists of these 'parables' are not only martyrs, as in Zoya's or Shostakovich's cases (and it has to be noted that, as Christensen points out, historical reality is modified in order to make Shostakovich look more like a martyr and less complicit with the regime; 2007: 100); they are morally ambiguous figures, as, for instance, in the case of Paulus, Vlasov or Gerstein. These characters are stuck in dynamics that partially dictate their fate and reduce their decisive action to the best decisions the context of the situation allows. Vollmann's short stories are psychodramas, in the same way that Christian *passiones* were (Brown 2015: 82). They invite readers to reflect and consider how these stories relate to their own experience and context, to find in them a metahistorical message and to change.

As in Christian hagiographies, Vollmann's protagonists are exceptional characters who distinguish themselves through their internal strength or the suffering they experience. Further, in much the same way as the lives of the saints are narrated only inasmuch as they show the presence of God and exhort the reader to imitate Christ – hence the variety in length and genre of the hagiographic patrimony – Vollmann reports his characters' lives minimally, only inasmuch as they testify to an opposition between humanism and totalitarianism. This opposition is central to his text, as we will see. Such allusive and metonymic use of character involves narrating almost the whole life of a character, but, crucially, focusing only on that character's losses and mourning (as in the cases of Käthe Kollwitz, Anna Akhmatova or Shostakovich). Alternatively, it focuses only on the climactic episode of a life (as for Zoya) or its aftermath (as for Paulus). In this sense, a comparison can be drawn between the oppositions of fable/fairy tale and parable/hagiography. Fables, due to their brevity, moral message and didactical purpose, are a kind of parable (Stein 2000: 31). Hagiographies, on the other hand, are similar to fairy tales in that they narrate longer episodes with a focus on a single hero and require emotional involvement rather than intellectual understanding. Parables (in the Gospels and Christian teachings) invite an understanding of the doctrine, while hagiographies aim to move the reader to the imitation of the saint and Christ.

In a passage of the story 'The Saviors', Vollmann characterizes the author as follows: 'the writer, whose absence renders him divine' (*EC*: 14). Interestingly, the author is never present in *Europe Central*. The narrators are different in each story (with one exception, to which we will pay further attention later). Generally, the narrators speak in the first person and tell stories about events they seem to have witnessed. They are both internal and external to these events. They are external or extradiegetic because the chronological gaps they mention and the evident unlikeliness of certain 'facts' make it impossible that they have actually witnessed the events. By way of example, in 'Mobilization', the narrator is implied to be at least 100 years old, without this remarkable age ever being discussed in the story (*EC*: 33). The narrators are also internal or intradiegetic because they are completely uniform with the cultural environment of the countries in which the stories are set. We will see this more clearly later, but for now let us just appreciate that there are no Russian narrators who are not communists and no German narrators who are not Nazis. This is made evident not only by their political proclamations, but also by the highly specific language they speak, influenced by Marxist materialism and Wagnerian mythology respectively. This contrast between Russian communists and German Nazis is made starker by the way in which, on several occasions, the narrators' (nationalist) perspectives change within the same short story, depending on the country in which the action is taking place. For instance, in 'Breakout', the protagonist is the traitor Soviet general Vlasov and the narrator is evidently Soviet while Vlasov is in the USSR ('Our Soviet Union', *EC*: 262), German as long as he is in Germany ('Our Führer', *EC*: 280) and Soviet again when he returns to the USSR (*EC*: 280). These narrators are not hypostasis of a single chameleonic narrator who writes in 2002 and switches roles according to the setting of the tale, since at least one of the narrators, Comrade Alexandrov, appears also as a character, and Manstein's veteran performs a monologue. On the contrary, the variety of narrators suggests the absence of a superior narrator, coinciding with the author, who judges his characters and provides a moral for their tales. In the author's own words, Vollmann remains divinely absent.

In the three-page story 'Denazification', there are three different narrators: one that might coincide with the writer ('the ageing of the blueprints as I study them in 2001', *EC*: 533), a Nazi ('Field-Marshal von Manstein had walked beside us smiling and alert', ibid.) and a Soviet ('And so we denazified them', *EC*: 535). This is not the only occasion when the author seems to coincide with the narrator. This also occurs (or at least seems chronologically likely) in 'The Saviors', 'The White Nights of Leningrad' and 'Far and Wide My Country Stretches'. For example, it is said that 'Roman Karmen has been called a great artist. And was he? In the year 2002, when I telephoned the University of Chicago film expert Yuri Tsivian, the following verdict came down' (*EC*: 229). The 'I' here could easily be Vollmann himself and it is worth highlighting that (as can be verified on the website of the University of Chicago) Yuri Tsivian is a professor of film studies and an expert of Soviet cinema.[6] However, this coincidence always seems casual, without much importance attributed to it. Therefore, the presence of the author is not fully exploited as a meta-fictional device (Santin 2015: 146). For instance, at the beginning of part 12 of 'Woman with Dead Child', the author intervenes as himself to point out the nature of his work and his inspirations: 'this story, like this book itself, is derivative. In his unsurpassable

6 <https://cms.uchicago.edu/profiles/yuri-tsivian>, accessed 19 November 2019.

A Tomb for Boris Davidovich …' (*EC*: 55).[7] However, just three paragraphs later, the narrator claims to have read the account of the fictional Comrade Alexandrov, to whom he claims to be very close (*EC*: 30). This oscillation simultaneously makes the author visible to the reader and refrains from drawing attention to him. Therefore, it cannot be interpreted as a metafictional, self-reflexive, postmodern device.

The author's distance from the polyphony of the protagonists and the narrators coincides with what Coffman calls Vollmann's 'moral non-intervention' (Coffman 2015: 15), meaning his consistent refusal to pass judgement. Literature, according to Vollmann, must be animated by the aim of pursuing the truth, which means a proper understanding of the circumstances in which characters act: 'other people's codes, until they tell us otherwise, must be presumed to be good enough for them' (Vollmann quoted in Coffman 2015: 14). In *Rising Up and Rising Down*, an analysis of the role of violence in human society and an attempt to understand whether it is ever justified, Vollmann explicitly states the importance of avoiding moral judgement in order to properly understand human actions:

> No credo will eliminate murder. But if we think about a sufficient number of cases we may be able to plant the seeds of a tentative ethics which others could consider, pick and choose from and hopefully benefit from even if they cannot improve. That is my hope for this book. I know that other people's advice has rarely made me better than I was. When it has, it was less often the advice itself than the spirit in which it was given which helped me, requiring me out of sheer respectful reciprocity to listen, search and consider […]. (*RURD*: 31)[8]

Due to Vollmann's refusal to pass judgement in the narration, it is no surprise that *Europe Central* so often contains unpleasant and disturbing

7 The work of Danilo Kiš explicitly influences *Europe Central*. For further information regarding Kiš's influence on Vollmann, see Cox 2015: 123–140. Vollmann also wrote the afterword for the Penguin edition of *A Tomb for Boris Davidovich*. This introduction is found in *Expelled From Eden. A William T. Vollmann Reader* (eds McCaffery and Hemmingson, 2004: 333–341).

8 Vollmann published two versions of this book, the first in seven volumes over 3,500 pages, the second in a single volume with significant cuts, which is only around 700 pages long. Here I am quoting the latter.

characters like Comrade Alexandrov, the Red Guillotine and Von Manstein's veteran. However, even in the case of those characters who behave in the most erratic and cruellest ways, Vollmann's guiding principle remains: 'no context, no judgment' (*RURD*: 36). Even when judgement is passed, it is accompanied by understanding and respect:

> My policy will always be to treat with empathy and respect anyone agreeing to be studied, interviewed, exposed. I would have been courteous to Eichmann. My obligation, however, is to the truth. But again, what is truth? [...] If, on the other hand, doubt has nowhere to hide, as in Eichmann's case, then one *must* condemn, but never without respecting the human being inside the evildoer. (*RURD*: 44)

This highlights the purpose of *Europe Central*, the reason behind the eclipse of its author and the narrators' uniformity with the cultural environments in which their stories are set. The text is a series of unique and exemplary 'parables' that help us to understand the moral circumstances and the meaning of the Second World War – not through intellectual statements, but through empathic reconstruction (Dushane and Vollmann 2007: 147).

Vollmann's ambition to enhance knowledge and understanding is expressed in the introductory story of *Europe Central*, 'Steel in Motion'. This *ouverture* enumerates almost all of the characters and actions that take place in the text, a function it shares, in a sense, with the map that opens the volume, which is chaotically filled with the names of the protagonists and military operations as well as portraits of the main characters and the most famous generals of the war. It mentions the vast majority of the main characters of the subsequent stories (Shostakovich, Akhmatova, Gerstein, Kollwitz, Krupskaya, Paulus, Zoya, the Sleepwalker, the Realist) and symbolically sums up the beginning and the end of the war. The cognitive value of *Europe Central* is expressed in the last sentence of the story, in which the narrator states his intention to 'invade the meaning of Europe' (*EC*: 10). However, again, the meaning with which the novel wants to supplant the meaning of Europe is shrouded with ambiguity and has a variety of possible interpretations pulsating within it. What the narrator (who, in this story, has all of the characteristics of the text's distinct narrators) seems to be suggesting is that no answer is definitive and absolute; rather, answers must be sought within each singular experience. As Vollmann states in *Rising*

Up and Rising Down, 'to describe universal forces, one must by definition take many excursions into alienness' (*RURD*: 31). Let us now prepare to explore the meaning of *Europe Central*.

Humanism and Totalitarianism

The meanings of the tales in *Europe Central* must be considered in the context of the opposition between humanism and totalitarianism. The terms of this opposition were, to my knowledge, first critically outlined by Christensen (2007: 6) as a trivialization of the complex (and, in his opinion, ambiguous) experience of Shostakovich under the Soviet regime. Although Christensen's illustration of these opposite poles was meant as a critique of Vollmann's novel, their structural function in the text is undeniable. According to Christensen, the presence of music in the stories about Shostakovich and the pervasiveness of references to Wagner's operas in the stories set in Nazi Germany create an opposition between Shostakovich's humanism and the nationalist völkisch ideology.

I would argue that this opposition should be extended to the structure of *Europe Central* and its cast of characters. It is not just an opposition between humanism and völkisch nationalism, but between humanism and totalitarianism. The sense of the word 'humanism' should now be explained. Not only is it never thematized in the text, but it seems to represent an absolute and entirely positive category, in contrast to the completely negative notion of totalitarianism. And while totalitarianism is considered negatively in the book (although not explicitly), it cannot be said that humanism is considered entirely positively as the situations and the characters that can be connected to humanism are mostly ambiguous. When I refer to this totalitarianism/humanism opposition, I mean the opposition between perpetrators and victims.

Totalitarianism, in *Europe Central*, is synonymous with Nazism and communism. I have already pointed out in the introduction the similarities and differences of these two political systems and their crimes. Vollmann is explicit on this point, suggesting that 'the moral equation of Stalinism with Hitlerism is nothing new. [...] Here it is merely a point of departure' (*EC*: 754). Even if Nazism and communism have different connotations, as I have mentioned in relation to the narrators, they both represent the side of the perpetrators, as opposed to the side of the victims. In several cases, moreover, they represent equally hostile environments for the same characters.

The opposition between totalitarianism(s) and humanism need not be interpreted as rigid. While it is true that *Europe Central* presents some extremes, including incarnations of evil, such as the Sleepwalker and sociopaths like Hilde Benjamin and Comrade Alexandrov, and, on the other hand, saint-like figures, such as Zoya and Kollwitz, it should also be noted that most of the characters are positioned in the context of ethical compromises and moral uncertainties (as in the cases of Paulus and Karmen). It is significant that Vollmann presents not only the victims, but also the persecutors. As he states in *Rising Up and Rising Down*, 'a major defining ethical constituent of violence is *the unique relationship between each victim and perpetrator at a given time*' (38). This division between victims and perpetrators, however schematic when we consider the book as a whole, is also useful when describing the situations faced by morally ambiguous characters. As we will see, characters like Vlasov and Gerstein hover between the roles of victim and perpetrator; in other words, between the human impulse to be merciful towards others and the compulsion to obey orders. Their tragedy lies in the difficulty of occupying this in-between position.

The Perpetrators

The perpetrators seem to be characterized by a lack, or a progressive loss, of compassion towards others. This is evident from the first story of *Europe Central*, after the introductory 'Steel in Motion'. 'The Saviors (A Kabbalistic Tale)' narrates the fictional (and unlikely) meeting between Nadezhda Konstantinovna Krupskaya, Lenin's widow, and Fanya Kaplan, Lenin's assassin, who reveals that she is a messenger of a godly revelation. Krupskaya, however, fails to understand this revelation and

Kaplan is sentenced to death (Christensen 2007: 99). The progression of Krupskaya's character is important in 'The Saviors'. Although she is described as a saint-like figure willing to sacrifice herself for others (*EC*: 14–15), by the end of the story her pity has been nullified and her compassionate love for others has turned into a fanatical devotion to the cause of the Revolution. Although the story is complicated by Vollmann's use of Kabbalistic references and by the obscure meaning of the message that Kaplan tries to communicate to the widow of the man she killed, it introduces, at the very beginning of the book, the theme of power as a source of moral corruption and the theme of devotion to a cause as an obstacle to acting mercifully. At the same time, the complex references to Kabbalah are suggestive of the complicated and self-referential mechanisms of the bureaucratic and political power that Krupskaya serves.

A similar attitude characterizes the two other Soviet examples of totalitarianism: Comrade Alexandrov and Hilde Benjamin. The fictional Comrade Alexandrov, alongside Comrade Alexeev, is the narrator of at least nine stories ('Woman with Dead Child', 'You Have Shut the Danube's Gates', 'Elena's Rockets', 'Opus 40', 'And I'd Dry My Salty Hair', 'Far and Wide My Country Stretches', 'The Second Front', 'The Red Guillotine' and 'Opus 110'). However, far more space is dedicated to Alexandrov than to Alexeev, who is only described as ignorant of music (*EC*: 94) and never expresses his own opinions, as Alexandrov does.

Alexandrov, a political commissar in Leningrad, is a constant presence since he is the person deputed to the surveillance of several of the protagonists, including Anna Akhmatova, Elena Konstantinovskaya and Shostakovich. As a commissar, Alexandrov exhibits detachment from and impassibility towards the faith of those under his control ('In 1933, when we arrested her son Lev for the very first time, just to tease him …', *EC*: 113) and anger against those he considers traitors of the revolution, to the extent that in one of Alexandrov's rants Shostakovich is called 'cocksucker' (*EC*: 107).

Alexandrov's idealism borders on sociopathy. As he says to Käthe Kollwitz in 'Woman with Dead Child', 'I used to believe that if I lived out my life without making anybody feel compassion for me, I would have done well. And I loved the masses because they didn't excite my compassion, even when they perished' (*EC*: 53). Although he reveals the relationship between his wife Elena and Shostakovich to Roman Karmen, and in the last part of the book interacts with Shostakovich himself, his emotional distance always seems unbridgeable. When referring to Elena, for instance, he claims that he 'never touched' her: 'I never introduced myself, not even when I arrested her' (*EC*: 74). He also insists on the superior position granted to him by his distance and observation: 'when she died in 1975, I respectfully refrained from attending her funeral' (*EC*: 74). Through Alexandrov's refusal to interfere on a personal level, even at the moment of Elena's death, Vollmann offers a portrait of a character so devoted to his cause that he behaves with formality and respect for protocol even when his task has ended.

Nevertheless, Alexandrov reveals ambiguities in his relationship with Anna Akhmatova that are not evident in his relationships with others (and are especially lacking in his relationship with Shostakovich). We are informed earlier, during his encounter with Kollwitz, that Alexandrov has a particular predilection for the arts (*EC*: 117) and is a great lover of classical music (*EC*: 65). This love of the arts does not make Alexandrov more pitiful and sympathetic in his persecution of Akhmatova, but it does result in a strange fixation with, and participation in, her poems. He expresses his knowledge and appreciation of her work through the story (*EC*: 112 and 117) and he is even moved by it (*EC*: 117).

Ultimately, Alexandrov (like Wieder in *Distant Star* or Maximilien Aue in *The Kindly Ones*) represents a variation of the archetype of the cultured, sensitive persecutor. Despite being far from insensitive, he is nevertheless untroubled in his duty by the emotions he feels. For example, he is disturbed by Akhmatova's poetry ('my head was filled with all kinds of ridiculous word-rubbish') to the extent that he cannot help thinking about it ('What was I to do?'). But he finds a solution to being emotionally stirred: *The Foundations of Leninism*. He tells us he 'read two pages at random. That cured me' (*EC*: 119–120). Nevertheless, Alexandrov admits that he 'still felt melancholic' (*EC*: 120).

On the contrary, the other communist persecutor of *Europe Central*, Hilde Benjamin, the East German Minister of Justice known as the Red Guillotine, is untouched by art and does not display any form of compassion.

Unlike Alexandrov (and despite being Walter Benjamin's sister-in-law), art does not become part of her life, nor is she ever moved to compassion, even in the worst scenarios. When asked by a delegation of doctors to allow German women to have abortions when raped by the soldiers of the Red Army and when confronted with the rape and consequent death of an 11-year-old German girl, her only response is, 'My feelings are of no relevance [...]. We brought it here ourselves. I refuse to discuss this case any further' (*EC*: 583). Indeed, Benjamin's formal and business-like language reflects her emotionless attitude.

Towards the end of her life, however, Hilde Benjamin is represented as a scared old woman deprived of her power by the younger generation (*EC*: 588–600). Just like Alexandrov's morbid interest in Akhmatova and her work, this final glimpse into Benjamin's life illustrates the humanity of this perpetrator. Vollmann is suggesting that power itself, and not necessarily individuals, is intrinsically evil because it corrupts everything it touches. Most importantly, we must highlight that, although they are negative characters in the balance of forces of the book, the perpetrators are never judged by the author for their evildoing; they are judged, rather, according to their intentions. Krupskaya, Alexandrov and Benjamin, for example, are convinced that they act for the good of humanity – or at least the benefit of their country.

Nevertheless, when we read *Rising Up and Rising Down*, it is clear that the author, although sympathetic towards the perpetrators as human beings, does not forget their deeds. They break what Vollmann defines as the 'Golden Rule', according to which violence is justified:

> 1. The Golden Rule: *Do as you would be done by*. But in the event that I would wish others to do unto me something which others would not wish for themselves, then the Golden Rule would not be justified. In fact, it would become the Zealot's Golden Rule. [Mostly justified]
>
> [...]
>
> 2. The Empath's Golden Rule: *Do unto others, not only as you would be done by, but also as they would be done by. In the case of any variance, do the more generous thing.* [Justified]. (*RURD*: 449)

Vollmann's Golden Rule is a reprise and expansion of Jesus's maxim intended to exclude too strict an interpretation of it. The Empath's Golden

Rule, moreover, suggests that one should always act not only in accordance with one's view of the world, but also with the intention of understanding the views of others. Nevertheless, as the comments in brackets show, Vollmann is open to the possibility of exceptions, even in the very moment in which he formulates his rules. Neither Alexandrov nor Benjamin (or Hitler, to move to the other ideological extreme) would accept the violence they inflict upon others or think that others would accept it. According to Vollmann's system, violence is also justified 'in legitimate self-defense or the defense of other human beings against imminent physical harm' and 'in defense of individual right' (*RURD*: 461). In this context, 'legitimate self-defense means that the provocation and thus the initial threat lie largely on the other side'. While Vollmann does not explicitly judge characters such as Alexandrov or Benjamin, one should not take this silence for sympathy or support. In Vollmann's text, his silence and refrainment from commenting are the basis of narration, but the evidence of the moral failure of the characters is evident in the way in which they are represented and the style in which their stories are written, for example, the harsh yet ambiguous judgements of Alexandrov or the severe and bureaucratic sentences of Hilde Benjamin.

Völkisch Ideology: The Sleepwalker and Colonel Hagen

Völkisch ideology in *Europe Central* is characterized by a continuous evocation of myth. The mythological references originate from aspects of German mythology, mainly the *Poetic Edda* and the *Nibelungenlied*, often filtered through Wagner's operas. Mythological elements are appropriated without any particular coherence in the spelling of proper names, in order to be faithful to the incongruence and variety of the fonts (*EC*: 754).

Mythology is central to the language of the German narrators, in contrast to the Soviet narrators who openly repudiate it ('in our Soviet literature of today [...] there is scant room for epics and suchlike old trash', *EC*: 64). This language gives form to an idea often implicit in, and yet central to, fascism. Vollmann describes fascism not only as an ideology, but also as a *magical* attempt to transform the present into a mythical time, to cancel history and therefore 'to push death aside for ever and ever' (*EC*: 12), creating a 'time without time' (Esposito 2015: 287; Galli 1989: 5–7; Mazower 1999: 26–31). As Colonel Hagen underlines, there is no difference between the Norse epics and the military effort of the Nazis: 'He said to me: "How well do you remember our national epic?" / "The one that's seven hundred years old, or the one we're writing now?" / "They're the same"' (*EC*: 103). In order to convey this feature of fascism, Vollmann's narrators speak a language full of mythological references that is constructed as a mythological discourse. Norse mythology is not used as a contrast to events contemporary to the narrator. It is used as a parallel, as if it were unfolding in the very same moment. In *Europe Central*, historical events are narrated as if they were mythological tales and mythological tales are presented as real events:

> What else was happening when Parzival killed the Red Knight? On the far side of Myrkvith Forest, where ogresses ride wolves and use snakes for reins, past Sun Fell and Snow Fell, in Sowjet-Russland, another Red Knight (I mean Kirov) fell to Russia's Parzival, who attended the funeral, called for vengeance, and launched his Great Terror. It was a year after Erich von Manstein had been promoted to Colonel and a year before Friedrich Paulus would be promoted to Colonel. (*EC*: 84)

The nickname that Adolf Hitler is given throughout the book, the Sleepwalker, suggests that his actions are either taking place in a mythical, dream-like landscape rather than in history – and, as we have seen, in 'The Sleepwalker', Wagnerian references serve as parallels to Hitler's story – or that history itself is shaped as myth. Although Vollmann is the only author I study who explicitly uses this nickname to refer to Hitler, sleepwalking is also employed in relation to Nazism by Bolaño (in *Distant Star*, Wieder is said to commit his first crime 'like a sleepwalker, without hesitation', *ED*: 22) and Littell (Max's matricide is carried out in a non-conscious state). The recurrence of this theme signals that it is modelled on a certain magical and mediumistic interpretation of Hitlerism.

Sleepwalking connotes a dream-like condition that is situated outside of history and logic. In this sense, like the proliferation of mythical metaphors and images in the book, sleepwalking reflects the irrational (meaning non-logocentric) ideas that underlie fascism and its ambition to create a time outside of history and outside of time itself (a 1,000-Year Reich). Moreover, this reference to sleepwalking is surely intended to refer to the almost medium-like and spiritual qualities that Hitler, as an orator, was said to display by his contemporaries (Galli 1989: 100–102); he excited the masses as if he were possessed. On the contrary, when Stalin is given a nickname, he is suggestively called 'the Realist'.

The elimination of historical time in favour of a mythical, circular time is a key feature of fascist ideology that is highlighted by Vollmann, who places it at the centre of his representation of fascism. It is a philosophical vision that structures the thought of two of the main right-wing, anti-modern thinkers of the twentieth century: Julius Evola and René Guénon. From the time of Evola's seminal work, *Rivolta contro il mondo moderno* [*Revolt against the Modern World*] (1931), his thought – inseparable from magical and esoteric elements and full of references to Tantrism, Indian philosophy, Gnosticism and Neoplatonism – centred around the concept of Tradition (always capitalized). Tradition is not tied to cultural heritage; it is, rather, a set of absolute and eternal principles – authority, hierarchy and discipline – in a perennial struggle against chaos and dissolution (Cassata 2003: 77–90; Furlong 2011a: 33–34 and 2011b: 37–52; Cassini Wolf 2016: 481–482). Evola explicitly underlines the coincidence between historical time and the time of modernity, suggesting instead that his esoteric research focuses on a time outside history. Guénon's Traditionalism (also known as Perennialism), like Evola's ideas, is founded on an eclectic and syncretic reading of Christian, Hindu, Taoist and Sufi mysticism; further, it focuses on the existence of an absolute and ahistorical truth.[9] It is important to notice, therefore, in relation to the image of the Sleepwalker, the existence, in the self-representation of fascism, of a gnostic path that can lead to the knowledge of an absolute, metaphysical truth, which fascism as an ideology attempts to restore on Earth. Sleepwalking in the text, then, not only represents a mythical action (the performance of a certain rite, for instance), but also a mythical vision of human history.

9 See Sedgwick 2004: 21–54 on Guénon, and 95–118 for further details regarding the relationship between Traditionalism and fascism.

The Sleepwalker's story is often critically read in relation to (and enriched by) references to the great German epics of *Nibelungenlied* and *Parzival*, both of which were also appropriated by Wagner in his operas. I will refer to the *Nibelungenlied* and its meaning in Hitler's parable later in this section; however, I shall first consider Hitler's comparison with Parsifal. This comparison is less emphasized and more obscure than Hagen's story, even if only because it is a comparison and not a symbolic figuration and therefore there are two terms to explain rather than one. Vollmann refers to the hero, Parzival (using the old spelling and not the Wagnerian diction, Parsifal), in the story 'When Parzival Killed the Red Knight'. He evokes two episodes detailed in Wolfram von Eschenbach's *Parzival*, specifically in books III and IV: the killing of the Red Knight and the liberation of the city of Queen Condwiramus through the killing of Galogandres, standard bearer of the besieging King Clamidê. It is not particularly clear what these episodes are supposed to signify. Whilst the killing of the Red Knight is rather arbitrarily paralleled with the elimination of Röhm's SA[10] (*EC*: 81; is it possible that Röhm is called a 'red' knight because of the socialist sympathies of his Brownshirts?), the references to Galogandres and Condwiramus seem rather obscure. The aim of the inclusion of such legends in the text is to obfuscate historical events and reflections, situating them in a haze of Germanic references that serve as totems.

However, if we consider the version of the myth in Wagner's *Parsifal*, we can more coherently deduce the meaning of Vollmann's comparison. In Wagner's opera, Parsifal was raised by his mother, whose husband and other sons were killed in war. Parsifal is unaware both of his name and of the ideals of knighthood. However, having met a group of Knights of the Round Table, he expresses his desire to become a knight himself. Therefore, he represents an image of a *tumbe klâre* – a pure idiot, a primitive saint – and is thus the only one capable of accomplishing the task of healing King Amfortas. To an extent, then, this comparison reflects the certainty felt by Hitler (whose obsession for Wagner is notorious and often recalled in the book) that he was some kind of reincarnation of that principle of holy

10 Moreover, it is worth noting that at the end of the story Stalin is defined as 'Russia's Parzival', his Red Knight being Kirov (84).

naïveté represented by Parsifal. This feeling was shared, to a certain extent, by his contemporaries and was part of the political mythology of the Führer, such that Ezra Pound famously wrote that Hitler was a modern Joan of Arc.[11] Moreover, two of the main personal biographical details of Wagner's Parsifal are also shared by Hitler. One is Parsifal's chastity (Wagner's main innovation in his reprise of the myth; McGlathery 2005: 56), since, although Hitler had sexual relations in his lifetime, these were not known to the general public and he famously disapproved of promiscuity. The other is the saviour-knight's vegetarianism (Manacorda 1997: xv–xvi), as we know that Hitler was a vegetarian (at least for propaganda purposes).[12] In other words, the attribution of Parsifal's pure madness to Hitler (however preposterous and the result of Hitler's own self-representation and indirect discourse) serves to reinforce the very same meaning implicit in the image of the Sleepwalker. That being said, I believe that, although it may be possible to explain the general meaning of the parallel with Parsifal, the specific references are not all supposed to have a precise meaning. They aim, on the contrary, to create a sense of uniformity and mythological dreaminess in the language of the German narrators.

In strict correlation with the linguistic pattern of the narrators and Hitler's figuration as the Sleepwalker is Hagen, who is the protagonist of the stories 'Operation Magic Fire' and 'Operation Hagen' and who makes appearances in several others. Hagen (who also appears under the name Hogni and plays a significantly less important role in the *Poetic Edda*) is one of the main characters of the *Nibelungenlied*, the thirteenth-century epic poem that merges the stories[13] of Siegfried and Kriemhild's love and the destruction of the people of the Burgundies at the hand of the Huns. In this poem, Hagen constitutes an ambiguous figure. On the one hand, especially in the first part, he seems to incarnate the reason of state and serves

11 Hans Rudolf Vaget has written extensively on this topic (2007: 95–114).

12 According to Galli (1989: 105), Hitler derived his vegetarianism from Wagner's example and the moral of *Parsifal*.

13 The stories that compose the *Nibelungenlied* are so different, and sometimes contradictory, that critics have questioned its structural and thematic unity (DeVane Brown 2015: 356). This contradiction is clearly reflected in interpretations of the figure of Hagen, who 'is typically seen either as a loyal and capable vassal or as the central villain of the poem' (365).

as a symbol of loyalty and devotion to his king (Mancinelli 1972: LIV). It is, in fact, for King Gunther's sake that he uses deceit to kill Siegfried and for the glory and safety of the Burgundies that he deprives Kriemhild of the treasure. On the other hand, Hagen seems also to represent a desire for death and the voluptuous and heroic acceptance of it in the name of honour. It is significant that Hagen's first appearance coincides with a mention of Wagner's *Ring Cycle* (*EC*: 100), which seems to suggest that Hagen is both a symbol of the German national spirit and a product of the self-representation of German identity.

This is especially evident in the second part of the poem. At the end of the first part, Hagen, with the consent of King Gunther, kills Siegfried after having deceived his wife Kriemhild into telling him where the only vulnerable part of Siegfried's body is. After killing him, he throws Siegfried's hoard into the Rhine in order to prevent Kriemhild from using it to secure revenge against the Burgundies. Years later, King of the Huns Etzel (Attila) asks Kriemhild to marry him and she accepts in order to gain the means to exact revenge. Despite Hagen's reluctance, the Burgundies accept Kriemhild's invitation to Hungary, where they are all killed after a gruesome battle. In *Europe Central*, the acceptance of Etzel's invitation is represented by the Second World War. During the crossing of the Danube (a situation that takes the form of a katabasis into the realm of the dead), the nymphs of the river inform Hagen of the woeful death that awaits the whole expedition: 'it is fated that no one of you shall survive there apart from the King's chaplain [...] as is well known to us. Only he will get back to Burgundy alive' (*Nibelungenlied* 1969: 194). After he attempts to annul this prophecy by killing the chaplain, Hagen, upon seeing the chaplain reaching the opposite shore alive, accepts the fate of death that they are inevitably going to meet. He does not accept it with melancholic resignation, but with a furious effort, almost transforming the nymphs' words into a self-fulfilling prophecy. He is the one who destroys the boats, thereby preventing all of the Burgundies from returning, and he starts the hostilities with the Huns, first provoking Kriemhild by wearing Siegfried's sword and then decapitating Attila's infant son. As Laura Mancinelli writes, Hagen gains heroic status because of the obstinacy with which he consciously provokes and hastens the fall of the Burgundies (Mancinelli 1972: XLIX; Lionarons 1998: 170). This attitude is exemplified by the purposeless assassination of Etzel's son.

In *Europe Central*, Hagen (who now appears to be an SS colonel) plays a far less prominent role. He is one of several characters that crowd the stories and could easily be overlooked by a reader unfamiliar with Norse literature. However, the significance of his presence in the book should not be underestimated. Hagen represents both the incarnation of the sense of duty and loyalty towards the state and the fascination with death that infects Nazi ideology. In the *Nibelungenlied*, Hagen is proud to take the blame for the evil deeds that he suggests and that his king commits ('let me take the blame', he says when he convinces Gunther to steal the hoard from Kriemhild; *Nibelungenlied* 1969: 148). Similarly, in *Europe Central*, his only function seems to be to take the blame for the crimes of Germany ('so we retreated, laying down land mines like metal suitcases, and next to me a shellshocked colonel with sunken eyes kept saying over and over again: my name is Hagen. My job is to take the blame', *EC*: 511).

Curiously enough, Hagen seems to be acting as a Christ-like figure, offering himself as a sacrifice in order to save and purify his people. And yet, the meaning of this purification is ambiguous insofar as Germany made an attempt to 'resurrect' so-called 'purity' through ethnic cleansing during the war. Whilst, on the one hand, Hagen serves as scapegoat for Germany's crimes (just as Germany has been turned into a scapegoat for crimes that involved other countries in Europe), he is also the incarnation of Germany's will to self-destruction. As the narrator of 'Woman with Dead Child' says, 'this war [the Great War] was Siegfried's war. The next war would be Hagen's' (*EC*: 40). The narrator is referring to the total destruction that the Second World War visited on Germany, in parallel to the fall of the Burgundies. Despite his reluctance to go to war (*EC*: 525), Hagen is a symbol of the Hitlerian *cupio dissolvi* that led to a war on multiple fronts: 'now [Hitler] comprehends in his soul why Gunnar and Hogni could not resist the Hunnish invitation: although it meant doom and sister-woe, at least they'd win that brilliant if sinister moment of light when they drew near their foemen's forecourts' (*EC*: 136). This will to self-destruction is both explicit, as in Hitler's case, and implicit, when it manifests itself in fanatical devotion to the principles of law, honour and duty (as, for instance, in the case of Paulus). In *Europe Central*, as in the *Nibelungenlied* (Gentry 1998: 77), an excess of zeal in obedience leads to catastrophe. As the anonymous soldier narrator of 'Operation Citadel' states, 'it wasn't our task to win [...]. It was only our job to take the blame' (*EC*: 486).[14]

Martyrs and Tragic Heroes

Europe Central is a book that is filled with depictions of victims. With the exception of the perpetrators, specifically when they enact forms of persecution – whether that be corporeal violence or the inappropriate use of bureaucratic language in cases of human rights abuses – all of the characters of the book are victims to some degree, be it through pure and simple violence or the obligation to collaborate with the perpetrators. Of course, Vollmann's victims are not only threatened with or subjected to violence; they become victims because of the way their shared inclination to act pitifully, to help, understand and take care of others and to sacrifice

14 We should also recognize that it is not only Hagen's meaning and acts of purification that are ambiguous, but also his name. Together with the onomastic oscillation between the *Nibelungenlied* and the *Poetic Edda*, it is unclear which historical figure might have served as a model for Colonel Hagen. The only two people named Hagen that could be compared with the Colonel Hagen of *Europe Central* are Albrecht von Hagen and Herbert Hagen. The first was a German jurist known for participating in the plot to assassinate Hitler in 1944 and hanged thereafter. The latter was an SS-Sturmbannführer, a collaborator of Adolf Eichmann's – involved, therefore, in the extermination of Jews. Herbert Hagen seems to be the most likely candidate as Colonel Hagen's historical double; however, he was only a commandant, never a colonel. Moreover, the book's Hagen is presented as already powerful and influential in 1936, at the beginning of 'Operation Magic Fire', whereas, in 1936, Herbert Hagen is only 23 years old. Whilst I understand that Vollmann may not have intended to refer to anyone other than the mythological character, I also believe that this ambiguity enriches the character's complexity. Finally, there is a coincidence that, however random, Vollmann must have been aware of, having read Friedlander's biography of Gerstein: Hagen is also the name of the town where Gerstein spent his early years. Vollmann seems to be deliberately using these coincidences in order to add layers of interpretation to the text. Most importantly, by pluralizing the possible identifications for Hagen, Vollmann renders him a German *everyman* that can function as a symbol for Germany.

themselves (all qualities, as noted, that Krupskaya loses when she gains power). In other words, whilst the perpetrators – although not deprived of human impulses and moral shades – are presented as sociopaths incapable of perceiving the suffering of others, the victims are depicted as those who constantly suffer, mainly because they are incapable of helping others or preventing the damage being done to them.

The prototype of all the victims of totalitarianism in *Europe Central* is Zoya Kosmodemyanskaya, known in the book simply as Zoya. A Russian partisan famously hanged by the Nazi occupants, Zoya functions as a prototype because of her lack of characterization. Throughout the novel, she is referred to only by her first name and her identity is alluded to by the famous photograph of her hanging and her equally famous last words ('you can't hang all hundred and ninety millions of us', *EC*: 268). Her function, in other words, is that of an icon – thus reinforcing the idea that the characters of *Europe Central* are meant to be examples, rather than similes.

If 'The Saviors', at the beginning of the book, evokes a reflection on the loss of compassion in the life of Krupskaya, 'Woman with Dead Child', the story of the life of Käthe Kollwitz between the two wars, introduces the theme of victimhood. In this story, the constant references to Kollwitz's artistic career and to her grief-ridden paintings and sculptures (in parallel with her own personal story and her difficulties) introduce the mass of obscure, yet real, people who suffered and died during and between the wars. Since the First World War, the focus of Kollwitz's work has been the miserable conditions of the lower classes, portrayed in a style that merges realistic details and allegorical figures, not unlike Vollmann's prose.

Kollwitz can be considered an antithesis to the lack of empathy of the perpetrators because of her personal life (she lost her son during the First World War and her grandson during the Second World War) and especially because of her artistic work, which merges social themes, such as the suffering of the working classes, with universal, isolated figures of grief, as in her famous *Woman with Dead Child* (1903). Of course, this perpetual witnessing of suffering cannot but lead to pain for the witness and a reduction, in Vollmann's universe, to a destiny of martyrdom. As Lucy R. Rippard writes, 'the real burden Kollwitz was trying to express was the burden of caring too much, the almost tragic concern of a person who cannot ignore what happens around her, to whom social justice is necessary as food and shelter' (Rippard 1981: x).

A figure that lends herself to comparison with Kollwitz is, of course, Anna Akhmatova, the delegate of the literary world in *Europe Central* (since Vollmann notably only depicts one character for each form of art: Shostakovich the musician, Akhmatova the poet, Kollwitz the painter, Karmen the film director). I have already discussed Akhmatova's life in opposition to her persecutor, Comrade Alexandrov; it is worth noting the fear of Alexandrov manifested by Kollwitz during her journey in the Soviet Union (*EC*: 56) and the morbid abuse she is subjected by an officer who is clearly obsessed with her personal life and her work. What Kollwitz and Akhmatova have in common are their reactions to the losses they suffer and the pain inflicted on them – reactions that do not, like Shostakovich's, constitute compromises and do not provoke nervous breakdown, but rather take the form of grief. Both women undergo a kind of private suffering that does not allow their persecutors to take anything more from their lives.

The story of Käthe Kollwitz also functions as a means of depicting Nazi Germany and Soviet Russia at the beginning of the book, since she, as a communist sympathizer, is invited to exhibit her works in the USSR. This geographical duplication (which, as we will see, can be compared to that of Vlasov) transforms her, paradoxically, into a victim of both the regimes. The conclusion of the story is suggestive in this sense, since it underlines the equivalent distance of both these political systems from that quality of human compassion incarnated by Kollwitz:

> In the end, her art got supplanted in both zones. A grief-stricken mother holding her dead child is all very well, but perhaps a trifle too universal – or, as Comrade Stalin would say, incorrect. For how could our ends be served by implying that everybody, even the enemy herself, grieves over dead children? Better by far that famous poster of the Red Army woman with one hand on her hip, another on her bemedaled breast, standing sentry-straight before a bullet-pocked German wall, her red-starred cap at an angle to show off her hair (short, yet feminine) as she smiles into the sideways future! Thus runs the Russian view. On the other side we merely need to quote our Führer's dictum that *the Germans – this is essential – will have to constitute amongst themselves a closed society, like a fortress.* (original emphasis; *EC*: 62–63)

The most present, although not the most important of these victims, is Dimitri Dimitriyevich Shostakovich. The life of the composer and his romantic relationship with Elena Konstantinovskaya are at the centre of several of the book's stories. However suggestive and sensuously written, their love story (by Vollmann's own admission, widely exaggerated and fictive in several of its parts, *EC*: 807–808) does not contribute very much to our understanding of the meaning of *Europe Central*, despite Vollmann's claim that 'above all Europa [*sic*] is Elena' (*EC*: 808). This refers to her attractiveness, her mysteriousness and her capacity to love and be loved. Indeed, the name 'Elena' encourages us to see her as a metaphor for a continent destroyed by the conflict of two factions, an allusion to the *Iliad*. In *Europe Central*, Shostakovich represents the prototype of the victim-hero, an ambiguous martyr like Gerstein: 'when I think of Shostakovich, and when I listen to his music, I imagine a person consumed by fear and regret, a person who [...] did what little he could to uphold the good – in this case, freedom of artistic creation, and the mitigation of other people's emergencies' (*EC*: 808).

Shostakovich is persecuted by the Soviet regime for his formalism – in other words, a deviation from the canon of socialist realism that the minister, Andrej Ždanov, preached. Like Akhmatova, Shostakovich is profoundly sympathetic in all his fears and tics (such as the way he continuously mutters 'you know') and even in 'his selfishness, his ugly spitefulness, his narcissism' (*EC*: 214). He represents passion and artistic freedom in the face of totalitarianism's attempt to enslave such creativity. In this sense, his burning love for Elena seems to function as a simile for the effort and passion he puts into his music, which Vollmann describes in powerful, emotional passages (*EC*: 180).

Shostakovich's life is not depicted as a progressive rise-and-decline parable; instead, it seems to be a sort of fearful stillness. From one of the first stories, Shostakovich is described as threatened by the Communist Party, as in 'The Palm Tree of Deborah', in which the disastrous performance of *Ledi Mekbet* in Moscow in the presence of Stalin himself leaves Shostakovich feeling terrified because the dictator leaves the theatre before the end of the production. The accusations of formalism, and therefore of reactionism, are a leitmotiv throughout the whole book (*EC*: 175, 190, 623, 629, 634, 638) and Shostakovich undergoes every form of humiliation, from accepting that his son is forced to denounce him (*EC*: 638) to receiving lessons about Stalin's political thoughts (*EC*: 656). However, it is worth noting that Shostakovich refuses, for the majority of his life and notably during Stalin's dictatorship, to become a member of the Communist Party. This is a sign of his unwillingness to participate in the suffering of others by joining the perpetrators in exchange for a better life, since when he finally does join the party, the conditions of artists in Soviet Russia have improved significantly.

Despite Shostakovich's fame in the present day, of which readers (or at least those interested in classical music) are likely to be aware, the end of his story, much like the end of Kollwitz's, resembles the outcome of the lives of so many of the protagonists in *Europe Central*: after lives full of suffering, they are forgotten. Notwithstanding his critical success and the public position he attains in his later life, Shostakovich is a loser, since the persecutions he faced prevented him from reaching the success and fame he deserved:

> One might think that his reputation was embalmed as safely as was Lenin in the mausoleum (Stalin, I'm afraid, had been secretly taken out once his fame decayed). And yet the regime might have felt some bitterness about his formalist infidelities. I may be imagining things. However, *The Soviet Way of Life*, published the year before his demise, mentions the interesting results obtained from a poll conducted in industrial enterprises in the Urals. The workers were asked to name their favourite artists. Of the composers, Tchaikovsky gets mentioned first, and Mussorgsky last, with a couple of foreigners in between. Dmitri Dmitriyevich Shostakovich does not appear. After all, no one individual can be indispensable in our Union of Soviet Socialist Republics, the greatest and most perfect country in the world, whose borders touch a dozen seas. (*EC*: 727)

It is not important that these words are, in reality, false. What matters is that the narrator of the story has pronounced them, therefore emphasizing the victory of the Soviet state over their citizenry.

Although he cannot be listed among the perpetrators, Roman Karmen's obedience to the Soviet regime and his enthusiasm as a propaganda artist make him the ideal opposition to Shostakovich. While their relationship with Elena is described as a triangle, it more closely resembles two oppositional poles, with Shostakovich's freedom in musical composition (his 'formalism') leading to persecution and with Karmen representing the artist immanent to the regime due to his enthusiastic, yet cold and shallow work. In a kind of retaliation, Karmen is to be forgotten and the quality of his work underestimated, in contrast to Shostakovich's posthumous triumph, of which the reader is aware (*EC*: 229). However, the narrator does not judge him for the apparent modesty of his artistic efforts: 'poor Karmen! And yet, what if Professor Tsivian was wrong? For that matter, even if he were right, how was Karmen supposed to act? All we can do in our life is our best' (*EC*: 229). The oblivion into which Karmen fades after his death, in other words, is real, as stated by an impartial narrator similar to Vollmann himself and a scholar of Soviet cinema in the material world. Shostakovich's destiny recalls Comrade Alexandrov's empty proclamation.

Despite their differences, the two specular characters Andrei Vlasov and Friedrich Paulus represent the opposition between politics and military ethos and the attempt to find a space in between in which the good can operate.[15] These two characters are interesting in that they both commit errors and crimes because of the faith they have in their countries and their leaders. However, at the same time, the suffering that their obedience causes for their soldiers is no less than the suffering they bring on themselves, which transforms them into victims.

Andrei Vlasov is a Soviet general captured by the Nazis during the Leningrad siege who guides the Russian Liberation Army (a military organization promoted by the Germans) in an attempt to garner support for their occupation. However, the creation of Vlasov's army encounters great resistance in the high ranks of the Nazi party and it is forbidden to operate until the very last days of the war. In this sense, Vlasov, like Kollwitz, is crushed between the two opposing totalitarianisms. During his service in the Russian forces, he proves himself to be a brave and competent general, but he is forced to sacrifice the lives of his men during unsuccessful attempts to defend the front. In response to his objections that a retreat is necessary and would save the lives of his soldiers without causing any damage to the war effort, the political commissar of his unit says, 'everything you say may be correct from the military viewpoint, but politically speaking it's quite incorrect', and reminds him that his 'eldest brother was shot for anti-Bolshevik activity during the Civil War' (*EC*: 266).

15 On Vlasov and Paulus, see Schwieger 2010.

Vlasov meets similar political opposition to the rational conduct of war affairs in Germany, when Hitler repeatedly forbids his army to operate (*EC*: 311). Vlasov is aware of the brutalities of the Soviet Communist Party and the Nazi party, since he is informed of the massacre of Babi Yar (*EC*: 277) and the existence of death camps (*EC*: 290–291). However, in the interstice between these two totalitarianisms, Vlasov desperately attempts to make the choice that would be best not for him, but for the people he is asked to guide.

Paulus, the Field-Marshal in command of the Sixth Army during the disaster of Stalingrad and later a prisoner of and collaborator with the Soviets, serves a similar function to Vlasov. In a passage I have previously quoted above, Paulus is explicitly said to be part of the story of Germany in order 'to illustrate a principle, to carry out a function, to think and suffer while things were done to him' (*EC*: 393–394). Paulus is one of several figures in Vollmann's books that find meaning in an almost gnostic path of suffering and degradation (Coffman 2015: 15). In his case, the end of this gnostic path through suffering is reaching the grade of Field-Marshal, a role he yearns for, with patience, obedience and devotion to his Führer.

Of course, Paulus's devotion is not to Hitler or his ideology, as exemplified by how, 'immediately upon succeeding to command of Sixth Army, he'd canceled our late Field-Marshal von Reichenau's order 10.10.41 to proceed with extreme measures against subhumans' (*EC*: 347–348). His devotion is, rather, to Hitler as an incarnation of Germany. Like Vlasov, he accepts the sacrifices he has to make – 'against all your objections I speak two words: Adolf Hitler' (*EC*: 372) – and, like Vlasov, he does not commit any crime out of cruelty (*EC*: 347–349).[16] The suffering and the humiliation he endures are mitigated by the trust that Hitler seems to have in him: 'then he was happy again. Our Führer still believed in him. Our Führer's confidence was as vital to him as is gasoline to our troops at Stalingrad' (*EC*: 376).

Despite his faith, which is not dissimilar to Vlasov's faith in Russia during the defence of the country, Paulus ultimately faces the very same destiny as the Russian general. He is captured and forced to join a group of collaborationist officers and, after the war, he is held captive in East

16 Vollmann, commenting on the aforementioned quotation about order 10.10.41, contrasts Paulus with the more criminally implicated figure of von Manstein (*EC*: 808).

Germany, where he is used for propaganda purposes (whereas Vlasov is executed in 1945). In this sense, their tales can be compared. In Vollmann's representation of them, despite their involvement with criminals, their intentions always seem pure and they are never ignorant of the suffering of others, nor are they spared pain. In contrast, another general, von Manstein, is often presented as pretentious and hypocritical and Vollmann explicitly expresses a negative judgement of him (*EC*: 805).

Kurt Gerstein is, in many ways, the main hero of *Europe Central*, or at least the hero whose tragedy is most striking and significant for Vollmann's purpose. Gerstein is a devoted Christian who joins the SS in order to gain information regarding their crimes, denounce them and sabotage them – as he does throughout the war by damaging the loads of toxic gas he is supposed to look after and trying to inform several foreign dignitaries about the Holocaust. Gerstein's tragedy is that the only way in which he can influence the course of the narrative (and, by extension, history) without consequences for his innocent family is by participating in deplorable actions. Paradoxically, he must contribute to the extermination of the Jewish people in order to denounce their extermination. As Santin writes, 'Gerstein's moral dilemma is not characterized by an obvious choice between "right" and "wrong", which is a recipe for melodrama, but by an exigently tragic collision between "right" and "right"; he must make a crushing moral choice between saving the life of innocent Jews while also keeping his family safe' (Santin 2015: 141–142).

In this sense, Gerstein's dilemma differs from the dilemmas of Vlasov and Paulus, who find themselves in a moral struggle between obedience to orders and the wellbeing of their soldiers, and those of victims Shostakovich or Kollwitz, who are simply persecuted. Like the generals, Gerstein attempts to fulfil two opposite demands. But unlike them, he only collaborates with the perpetrators in order to further his purposes and does not personally benefit from this collaboration. Vollmann unambiguously asserts Gerstein's righteousness and his 'clean hands' – something he does not do for any other character. In reference to the expression 'ambiguity of good' used by Saul Friedlander, Vollmann comments: 'I firmly believe that there was nothing ambiguous about Gerstein's good, unavailing though it proved to be. He is one of my heroes' (*EC*: 784).

The expression 'ambiguity of good' is derived from the first serious study on the figure of Gerstein, Friedlander's *Kurt Gerstein ou L'Ambiguïté du Bien* [*Kurt Gerstein: The Ambiguity of Good*] (1967). The meaning of this expression, which draws on Hannah Arendt's banality of evil, is explained by Friedlander in the introduction. He comments on Gerstein's suicide in the prison where he was held as he awaited judgement. Despite his being 'a convinced Christian', according to his friends, and 'a man of absolute purity', Friedlander quotes Otto Wehr:

> A figure such as Gerstein, judged in half-light, or better still, in the glaring light of bourgeois criteria, cannot fail to seem improbable. His uncanny skill in hiding his deep, inner, Christian life under a mask, for the sole purpose of helping others, defies judgment. It is impossible to do justice to this man [...] if one applies normal moral standards or if one attempts to explain him in political or psychological terms. (Quoted in Friedlander 1967: x)

What emerges from Friedlander's (and Vollmann's) portraits of Gerstein is a tormented man who desperately tries to help others using all the means he has. Notwithstanding Gerstein's apparently exemplary moral character, after his death he is not recognized as a hero, nor is he condemned as a criminal. He is perceived simply as a sort of accomplice. His name, says Vollmann, is not written in the list of the just nor the list of persecutors: 'what then is Gerstein? Wherein should he be inscribed? GEHEIM' (*EC*: 425; *geheim* means 'secret'). Gerstein's destiny is, like the destinies of other characters, characterized by silence and inattention. After the war, he reveals his actions during the conflict to the Allies and kills himself. He is posthumously condemned as a 'petty Nazi' by the Denazification Council of Tubingen. Finally, as Vollmann notes, his pardon in 1965 goes unnoticed because it is too late for him to function as a popular example (*EC*: 471).

Those that would judge him refute his apparent ambiguity, claiming that his hands are not clean at all. Gerstein himself is painfully aware of this contradiction: 'Herr Gerstein, forgive me for asking this, but have you ever personally taken part in the actions against the Jews? / I have clean hands, he replied through clenched teeth' (*EC*: 464). However, as Santin notes, 'Kurt Gerstein's moral conscience remains "clean" precisely because he gets his hands "dirty" – that is, because he makes difficult, messy moral decisions without "washing his hands" of Nazi atrocities' (2015: 158).

Gerstein is not a typical hero and he is certainly not the typical hero of a tale of resistance against totalitarianism. The nature of his task and efforts is hidden (*geheim*) to everyone else, and, in addition to the posthumous disdain of his judges, he experiences resistance from his family and friends. Gerstein's family opposes his intent not only through the pressure they put on him, but also in the way they actively obstruct him. His wife opposes his efforts (*EC*: 439) and his father, a judge, repeatedly denies the pre-eminence of Christian compassion over the laws of the state (*EC*: 430 and 464). A friend of his accuses him of exaggerating the extermination campaign and the plight of those held in concentration camps and also accuses him of secretly enjoying his own martyrdom (*EC*: 467). Apparently, no one is able to accept a hero who stands between two evils and does not fit into precise, rigid categories of heroism or martyrdom. However, 'his story is as rare, and hence as shocking, as full-figure reliefs of the saints on otherwise featureless walls' (*EC*: 425; the alliteration of the 'f' is suggestive of the nobility of the alliterative poetry of the ancient epic poems of the German and Anglo-Saxon tradition). By placing such emphasis on the profound ambiguity of a main character, Vollmann performs two functions. He exonerates Gerstein's reputation, showing that, to an extent, his good actions were not so ambiguous and could only be performed through compromise. At the same time, he illustrates through Gerstein's perpetual sense of guilt that even morally right and heroic behaviour can lead to self-destruction.

To conclude, now that we have considered the intrinsic ambiguity of Vollmann's heroes in relation to Gerstein, who, more than any other, exhibits and is immune to heroism, and observed the continuous moral non-intervention of the author, we should return once again to the concept of the parable evoked at the beginning of this chapter. As we have established, despite Vollmann's semantic shift, what he calls a parable is a key concept that allows us to understand *Europe Central*. As Santin writes, 'in Vollmann's fiction, imaginative empathy precedes moral logic because his fiction does not demand that readers *assent* to a philosophico-ethical belief; instead, it asks readers to *imagine* a particular moral actor's historico-ideological matrix and then draw their own conclusions' (2015: 144). I have already stated that Vollmann's use of the word 'parable' is a catachresis and that he might instead have called the stories *exempla*. Santin, despite sometimes misusing the word, actually emphasizes this point. Vollmann offers his readers no answer to the question he asks and no solutions for the problems he evokes. Instead, the aim of his narrative is to raise such questions and problems by recreating the moral circumstances in which they take place and seeking a personal, empathic understanding from his readers, rather than an intellectual understanding.

Literature as Experience

According to Theophilus Savvas, Vollmann, like David Foster Wallace and Jonathan Franzen, belongs to a 'lost generation' of 'reluctant heirs to the first generation of postmodernists', who 'retain some of the impulses of postmodernism, but want to say something more directly than they believe postmodernism has the capacity to' (2011: 160). Indeed, among the authors considered in this book, Vollmann is the one most influenced by American postmodernism. This is evident in the anti-mimetic, strange lyricism of his prose, which has been identified in the oscillation of narrators and in his extensive employment of mythological references in the depiction of hostilities. Nevertheless, as Savvas states, Vollmann's work is distinguished from postmodernism by the profound attention Vollmann pays to reality and its complications. While it is true that he does not indulge in mimetic realism, as Bolaño or Littell do, and that he does not care to recreate the material conditions in which the actions of his heroes take place, preferring instead intrusions of the fantastic and the supernatural, the psychological realism of his work is striking. As we have seen, Vollmann's characters are represented when making important moral decisions and recreated with precision as they experience their internal struggle. Moreover, even the continuous deployment of supernatural and mythical elements that characterizes the German narrators must be understood as a form of ventriloquism. That is, the confusion of myth and history and the presence of Kabbalistic tales are used to characterize the narrators and the protagonists, but are not a feature of the novel as a whole.

Except for few symbolic characters, such as Zoya, Vollmann's characters are not the uncertain characters of postmodernism, but well-rounded figures with strong motivations who engage in deep introspection. The continuous shifts in narrator and focalization are not intended to suggest the characters' lack of identity. This is evident, for instance, in the case of the Sleepwalker. The use of supernatural evidence and mythical references aims to frame a reading of Hitler's story, but it does not reduce it to mere allegory. Instead, by imitating the words of Nazi propaganda, it transforms Hitler into a character coherent with the ideological world in which he lives.

Similarly, the alternation of narrators does not suggest the 'death of the author' or a confusion of personalities and viewpoints. All the narrators are strong characters and share the ideological framework of their countries. Their alternation, therefore, aims to produce a chorus of voices rather than a narrative of schizophrenia. Similarly, the narrators' oscillation between omniscience and the first person (as in Bolaño's fiction) simultaneously makes the author visible to the reader and obscures him. Therefore, the narrative voice cannot be interpreted as a meta-fictional, self-reflexive, postmodern device.

The notes in *Europe Central* do not create a metafictional space or a hypertext or continue the narration of the main text – as in David Foster Wallace's *Infinite Jest* (1996) and Mark Danielewski's *House of Leaves* (2000), in which the notes contain so many digressions from and developments of the main story that, in Danielewski's case, they cannibalize and dissolve it. Rather, *Europe Central*'s notes aim to provide actual sources for the story, although these are sometimes deformed or superficially interpreted (Christensen 2007: 100–102). Except for a few remarks, some of which I have already quoted, the notes are not intended to be read as part of the narration or as supplementary comments. The story does not evolve into them and only occasionally do they contain more than bibliographical references. Vollmann's use of notes has evolved over the course of his literary career; in his earlier works, he made more metafictional and polemical use of notes, paratexts and bibliography (see, for instance, Bucher 2016 on *The Rifles*). In contrast to the *Seven Dreams* series, in which there are multiple autofictional figures, competing chronologies, shifting temporalities and various representations of geographies, the main aim of *Europe Central* is not to challenge the authority of the primary texts, but rather to support and explain the narration. It is significant that an author such as Vollmann, so versed in historiographic metafiction (of which *The Rifles* is a primary example), can also display such an apparent faith in historical documentation, thereby indicating that history can indeed be factually understood. While Vollmann is not so ingenuous as to believe that historians are always to be completely trusted, as he proves in the *Seven Dreams*, he can nonetheless write historical fiction without polemical intents. This illustrates that, for post-postmodern authors, historiographic metafiction can be a useful tool, but it is but a tool amongst many others.

Together, these post-postmodern features – the eclipse, but not the death, of the author; psychological realism; truthfulness as a purpose – create a literary form in which the experience of the protagonists is shown in all its complexity and depth, such that their narrative lives may be experienced by readers themselves.[17] The variety of experiences and stories contained in the book suggests that *Europe Central* seeks not to pass moral judgement on its characters, but, rather, to present them as examples of the difficulties of moral behaviour in troubling times. In *Rising Up and Rising Down*, Vollmann reports that 'the translator of two old collections of Zen koans has noted that there is no "correct" answer to a koan, and, indeed, one student's right answer may be wrong if uttered by another' (*RURD*: 445). Indeed, the idea that truth is, to a certain extent, performative shapes the parables of *Europe Central*. The characters are never judged according to an abstract or universal system of values, but are rather judged based on their capacity and their will to act in the situations they are forced to be in. By way of example, Gerstein is not defined as a villain for participating in the Holocaust, nor is he defined as hypocritical because he tries to sabotage the organization he joined. He is presented as a hero because he does everything in his power to help others, unlike Alexandrov, for instance.

In other words, Vollmann chooses the Second World War as an archetypal case study for what he described theoretically in *Rising Up and Rising*

17 An analysis of this characteristic of Vollmann's literary production is provided in Palleau-Papin 2016, with reference to *The Rifles* (1994).

Down and takes the opportunity to fictionalize the conflict. The Second World War, as a historical, memorialized event, has an exemplary status that cannot be meaningfully conveyed by everyday violence or the late twentieth-century wars and genocides described in Vollmann's theoretical essays. Insofar as *Europe Central* appears to represent the literary practice of the theoretical framework described in *Rising Up and Rising Down*, we might conclude that, for Vollmann, literature presents itself as the only form in which he can successfully communicate a message and convey the violence of human society. Vollmann himself reflects on the importance of literature as a tool to promote participatory interpretive and moral reflection:

> The colors of the Burmese jungle at twilight, or the scorched smell of a shelled city, do not themselves further analytical understanding. [...] [However] descriptions of personalities, appearances and the settings in which people act and react will hopefully provide further means for the reader to make that re-creation himself, and thereby to evaluate my judgment. (*RURD*: 48–49)

Europe Central, which is eminently more readable and enthralling than *Rising Up and Rising Down* because of the quality of its prose and the importance of the Second World War, can answer the theoretical questions Vollmann raised in his essays in a practical manner. Vollmann, as a theorist, is very much aware of the power of fiction. Consequently, he chooses to set aside his theoretical reflections in *Europe Central*, rather that inserting them and commenting on the novel from a meta-narrative position of superiority. On the contrary, the stories of *Europe Central* perform the function of questioning the readers' certainties. They serve as an invitation to readers to experience the very same dilemmas that led Vollmann to write *Rising Up and Rising Down*.

Marginalization and Ambiguity in Sarah Waters and Rachel Seiffert

By way of concluding this chapter, I want to analyse two novels that, although very different from one another and Vollmann's work, share with

Europe Central a nuanced and complex analysis of two themes. The attention Vollmann devotes to the sufferance of non-combatant marginalized characters during the war, such as Kollwitz or Shostakovich, can be compared to Sarah Waters's careful recreation of the lives of several queer characters in wartime London and their struggle to survive during the war and retain their new lifestyle after it. In Rachel Seiffert's collection of short stories, two themes emerge that allow a comparison with Gerstein's story: the ambiguity of a character's moral behaviour and the collective dimension of the atrocities of the Holocaust. A closer look at Waters's work can offer further insights into the differences between postmodern historiographic metafiction and post-postmodernism, while Seiffert's book allows us to further explore the postmemorial transmission of the Second World War, a theme that has often been evoked in this book.

Blank Spaces, Queer Spaces: The War as a Renegotiation of Roles in The Night Watch

It is a common topos of war writing that the war represents a blank space that allows for the redefinition of individual and collective identities. This topos of war as the opportunity to rearticulate identity can be found in a series of contemporary texts, such as *White Teeth* by Zadie Smith (2000), *Small Island* by Andrea Levy (2004), *The Night Watch* by Sarah Waters and *Burma Boy* by Biyi Bandele (2007).[18] That the Second World War can facilitate the rearticulation of identity is a direct consequence of its *total* nature. The war was a conflict between imperial, transnational forces. It represented a moment when the balances of power across empires (often linked to ethnicity, as well as caste, religion and occupation) began to be renegotiated. For the British Empire, specifically, the Second World War engendered a progressive loosening of the bonds of domination between the 'mother country' and the colonies. Yet citizens of the British Empire were mobilized to fight in the war. Smith, Levy and Bandele are

18 In *White Teeth* by Zadie Smith, the friendship between the English Archibald Jones and the Bengali Muslim Samad Iqbal is pivotal. Their friendship is made possible by the temporary redefinition of social and class roles during the Second

all concerned with the role of the colonies in the Second World War and represent Pakistani, Jamaican and Nigerian subjects of the British Empire dispatched to fight for interests other than their own in distant and foreign countries. At the same time, this transnational dimension of the war, with the patterns of migration and the destruction and reconstruction that it implies, generates the possibility of new identities: both individual and collective.

Similarly, by eliminating the distinction between home and front (as the air bombardments created a *physical* home front, not just a metaphorical one), the *total* nature of the Second World War elevates women to the position of direct subjects. Whereas previously women could only be involved in the war in the case of direct invasion or as relatives of the fallen soldiers, the new air technologies employed in the Second World War dissolved the differences between the army and civilians. The front line was at Coventry no less than at Dunkirk. Moreover, to a greater extent than the Great War, the Second World War represents the moment when women began to be employed en masse. As Penny Summerfield has argued, the war was a moment when female labour was employed not only in the traditional patriarchal context, but also in the framework of a capitalistic economy, and in these contradictory economic systems different needs

World War. Smith's novel explicitly criticizes the post-imperial memorialization of the war and the erasure of the contribution of colonial subjects to the war effort. Significantly, the representation of the 'official' historicized version of the conflict that falsely claimed that there was little to no participation of non-British subjects is continued, in the novel, by a senile character suffering from dementia. Similarly, Andrea Levy's *Small Island*, set in Jamaica and England during the Second World War and its immediate aftermath, is concerned with the possibilities of emancipation that the war opens up for colonial subjects and women and the denial of their effort in the official representation of the war. Racism is a problem in Britain and the Jamaican characters struggle to navigate it. One of the strengths of *Small Island* is that it contests the presumption that, since the Allied forces fought against a racist ideology, their own countries did not enact racist policies. Finally, *Burma Boy* by the Nigerian writer Biyi Bandele again depicts the transnational dimension of the war by representing the battles between the Japanese and a Nigerian regiment of the British forces in Burma. As a colonial soldier, the protagonist fights a war that he does not understand for a country other than his own, against enemies he has nothing against.

and demands coexist and clash (Summerfield 1984: 29–31). The effects of the war did not last long after its end, as the number of female workers on the job market quickly diminished (187). Moreover, a significant portion of the jobs women secured during the war were still, in many ways, gendered, to the extent that this process resulted in the reinforcement of gender inequality after the war, rather than diminishing such inequality (185). Nevertheless, the Second World War was a moment when women had access to positions that had previously been reserved for men, with some of the freedom granted by these positions. Waters's novel is dedicated to this subject and to the sexual liberty (both hetero- and homosexual) that the resulting economic freedom engendered. Waters treats this alternative vision of the war as a blank space in which minorities and excluded subjectivities can claim their identities.

Sarah Waters's *The Night Watch* (*NW*) thematizes the Second World War as a space for the emergence of non-conforming sexualities. The novel follows several intertwined characters, all of whom exhibit sexual and behavioural deviations from the monogamous, heterosexual norm. Viv, a heterosexual woman, is the lover of Reggie, a married man. She is the colleague of Helen and the former lover of Kay – a masculine, lesbian ambulance driver who saves Viv's life during the war after she experiences complications from an illegal abortion that Reggie forces her to have. Helen cheats on Kay with Julia, Kay's former lover, who then cheats on Helen. Finally, Viv has a brother, Duncan, imprisoned during the war because of his involvement in an attempted double suicide in which only his friend (and implied lover?) is killed. For clarity, we can deduce that he attempted suicide in a bid to escape being drafted by the military.

The Night Watch overturns conventional gender roles. Whereas the female characters are heroic in the face of the bombardments, the men appear cowardly (Reggie) or apathetic (Duncan). In the novel's climactic scene, Viv finds out that she is pregnant with Reggie's child. First, he suggests that she take poison to get rid of the baby and, later, he organizes an appointment with an illegal abortion doctor. After the abortion, however, she falls ill and starts bleeding heavily, at which point Reggie deserts her out of fear of damaging his reputation. Her life is saved by Kay and Mickey, two masculine-presenting lesbians who work as ambulance drivers who arrive on the scene. Duncan's imprisonment can be interpreted as a punishment for evading his duties as a man and citizen.

Furthermore, in Waters's novel, it is the war that allows the development of otherwise illicit relationships: 'London is imagined as a blank space open to potential re-inscriptions' (Wood 2013: 313; O'Callaghan 2016: 314).[19] The time when social norms were effectively suspended as a result of the German blitz can be regarded as a 'queer time' (O'Callaghan 2017: epub). In 1944, Helen and Julia begin seeing each other in abandoned, ruined houses. Their first romantic meeting takes place during a blackout in the ruins of a church, which is similar to the way Kay and Helen meet for the first time during a bombardment in 1941. Likewise, Viv and Reggie's relationship is made possible by the suspension of norms brought about by the war, since Reggie, a soldier, is forced to leave his family; thus, their relationship is queer in its rejection of the social (and spatial) norm (O'Callaghan 2017: epub) of the heterosexual family unit. Moreover, the space of the prison in which Duncan spends the duration of the war 'encourages homosexuality' because of the 'forced proximity' it creates between inmates (O'Callaghan 2017: epub).

The end of the war, however, terminates this realm of possibilities and, once the benefits the war brought have been lost, all of the characters are, in one way or another, haunted by negative memories of it. Viv's affection for Reggie is compromised by the memory of her abortion; Kay is tormented by the memory of Helen's betrayal; Helen faces up to Julia's betrayal and Duncan is forced into the very same prison rhythms despite being a free man, since he lives with a guard of his former prison. More specifically, it is Kay who benefits most during wartime and who experiences the greatest loss after its end. As a very masculine-presenting woman who often wears male clothing and is mistaken for a man (*NW*: 94; in contrast her friend Mickey, who looks like 'a male impersonator on the stage': 331), Kay is granted a professional position as an ambulance driver during the war. As we have seen, the lack of male labour during wartime offered women access to professions that had previously reserved for men.

19 The openness of the bombed city contrasts with the suffocating stiffness of British homes (Jones 2014: 36).

Similarly, wartime fostered relative tolerance towards homosexual affairs, even public ones. Nevertheless, Kay's freedom to express her identity is only permitted during the war and ends with it: '[wartime] tolerance is not the same as acceptance' (O'Callaghan 2017: epub). After the war (and at the beginning of the novel, which follows a reverse chronology), without a job or a social position, Kay lacks identity and purpose. She becomes 'a person whose clocks and wrist-watches have stopped, and who tells the time, instead, by the particular kind of cripple arriving at her landlord's door' (*NW*: 3). Moreover, Kay has lost her lover, since Helen leaves her for Julia. Tired of her lack of identity, Kay invests in her romantic relationship with Helen, fearing the lonely outcome of a life of meaningless relationships (*NW*: 241). Significantly, Waters ties Kay losing her job to Helen's betrayal. When she learns that a bomb has fallen near their home, she takes the ambulance without permission and goes there – only to find that Helen is safe, since she was with Julia. According to O'Callaghan, 'Helen and Julia's affair functions (troublingly) as a form of punishment to Kay for her apparent investment in heterosexual idealism', that is, Kay's desire for a monogamous relationship with Helen (O'Callaghan 2016: 208). Like Vollmann's victims, Waters's characters are stuck between the danger represented by the enemy and the oppression of their nation and consequently no safe space is available to them, except temporarily.

The Night Watch is a carefully researched historical novel and Waters exhibits her sources in a conclusive note to the book (*NW*: 471–473).[20] Natasha Alden argues that *The Night Watch* should be regarded as historiographic metafiction due to its polemic attitude towards official historiography and its focus on minorities and the excluded (Alden 2016: 65; see also Boehm 2011). Well-made though her argument may be, I would argue that the text does not cohere with the ideological values of this category. While it is true that the novel contests the official vision of history by giving new relevance to those excluded by the public memory of the war, such as homosexuals and women outside of heteronormative married relationships (Stewart 2015: 420), Waters does not contest the possibility of knowing history. Note again that she provides sources to demonstrate the fidelity of her account. Further, the novel does not make use of metafictional devices.

20 See also Alden 2013: 70–83 for a closer examination of Waters's sources.

Nevertheless, Waters does criticize the traditional values of Britishness, revealing their ambivalence and their role as obstacles to the characters' abilities to be themselves, such as the topos of the pastoral idyll, which, for Viv, turns into unpleasant and unwilling intercourse with Reggie (Cavalié 2014: 84–100).

In other words, if we understand historiographic metafiction more broadly as a narrative contesting assumptions about national histories and official propaganda, Waters's novel could be categorized as such. However, I argue that such an understanding would have significant limitations because it is too general and fails to recognize the differences between postmodern historiographic metafiction and post-postmodern historical writing. As in the work of Vollmann (an author who has practised both forms of writing), contesting a given narrative is an important element of continuity between the two modes, but does not represent a form of metafiction per se. In Waters's novel, the difference between the two modes is evident. Far from undermining our understanding of historical mechanisms or historical sources as Vollmann does in his *Seven Dreams* series (in which Western historiographical positivism and native American mythology and traditional thought are merged), Waters simply provides, like McEwan, a different understanding of the events based on alternative sources.

Another element of *The Night Watch* that has led to it being read as historiographic metafiction is its reverse chronology. It starts in 1947 and proceeds to 1944 and 1941. This peculiar organization of the narrative material is certainly influenced by postmodern writing, but is not, strictly speaking, a quality of historiographic metafiction. As Mitchell notes, the reverse chronology of the novel challenges the notion of historical progress and underlines the role of past trauma in defining the characters (Mitchell 2013: 87; Stewart 2015: 230). This kind of chronological framework differs, for example, from that of Levy's *Small Island*, in which the narration constantly shifts from the war period to its aftermath, and Martin Amis's *Time's Arrow*, in which the same non-linear style playfully undermines the possibility of knowing history and the idea of personal responsibility.

These novels exemplify, as Seymour Chatman puts it, the difference between an episodic and a semantic reversal (2009: 31–55). These are, respectively, the reverse ordering of narrative units, which follow an internal chronological order, as in Waters, and a more consistent reversed progression of the story, consisting, for instance, of answers before questions in the dialogue, effects presented before their causes and actions represented backwards, as in Amis. The first approach, 'which offers a mirror-image of the linear novel, arranging material in a consistently retrograde C-B-A pattern, at a macrosequential level over the course of a complete text' (Ireland 2010: 31), is still 'relatively conservative' (30). Waters's novel, which uses reverse chronology in order to illustrate the extent to which the past can influence and haunt the protagonists' present, is not nearly as radical as Amis's postmodern novel. Moreover, by presenting the miserable conditions of the protagonists at the very beginning of the novel, Waters undermines the idea that the Second World War was a seminal moment of liberation for women, suggesting instead that it should be read as a parenthesis between equally problematic times. Once again, post-postmodern authors reprise specific postmodern techniques – in this case, historiographic metafiction and reverse narration – but they do so not to challenge realism or historiographical knowledge, but, rather, to strengthen their claims and re-readings of official historiography and to enhance the readers' involvement in the story.

'Anything to Make Them Unclear': Complicity and Memory in The Dark Room

Rachel Seiffert's highly praised novel *The Dark Room* (*DR*) is a remarkable reflection on the problematic nature of memory, which questions the reliability of personal memory as a source of historical knowledge and historical knowledge as a source for understanding of human events. The book is composed of three unrelated stories set in Germany,[21] all of which focus on perpetrators and their heirs at different points in time. Each takes its title from the name of its protagonist. In 'Helmut', set during the rise to power of the Nazi party and the first years of the war, the protagonist is

21 Born in England to a German mother and an Australian father, Rachel Seiffert 'was raised bilingually and visited Germany regularly. She has kept a close relationship with her German relatives, and even lived in Berlin for some time' (Martínez Alfaro 2013: 268).

a boy employed in a photography shop, and a photographer himself, who witnesses – without necessarily understanding – events related to the war on the Eastern Front and the extermination of Jews. In the second story, Lore is a young girl who leads her brothers and sisters through Germany in the immediate aftermath of the war. She is the daughter of an SS officer, her mother has been arrested and her father is missing. In the last story, set between 1998 and 1999, Micha is a German schoolteacher who finds out that his grandfather was a member of the Waffen SS. He starts to investigate the activity of his grandfather's unit only to discover that it was involved in the extermination of Jews.

Seiffert's style is influenced by the technology of photography itself, as photography is a 'dispassionate, objective, even quasi-documentary style that, for the most part, precludes editorial comment or prescriptive judgments' (Zeitlin 2006: 223). It is worth noting that the use of the points of view of two children in the first two stories has a distancing effect that allows the narrator to present the events in an innocent light that lacks, at a first glance, comprehension of the meaning of what happens (ibid.). Indeed, Seiffert's decision to narrate the second story from the point of view of a child results in a certain degree of ambiguity towards the paternal figure, whom the readers know to be an SS officer, despite Lore having no real idea of his job and tasks. In this sense, Seiffert 'challenges the very possibility of an innocent subject position' (Baackmann 2017: 166).

As the title of the book suggests, all of these stories highlight the problematic nature of photography as a historical source. In the first story, far from serving as a denunciation of the Nazi regime, Helmut's portfolio coincides with the official propaganda of the regime as it mainly contains pictures of architectural and technological innovations and mass assemblies (Rau 2006: 300). However, Helmut does not fit into this triumphalist view of the world since he was born with an arm defect that prevents him from joining the other boys during gymnastics at school and, later, from joining the army. In the climactic scene of the story, he witnesses a round-up of Romanis but fails to understand what is happening and is simply frightened by the Romani people, rather than horrified by their arrest. In his eyes, his disability does not reinforce the similarities between him and the excluded and persecuted. It only strengthens his will to be part of the 'normal' group. At the end of the story, during the useless defence of Berlin against the Red Army, Helmut is enrolled in a reserve force 'with the fat boys and the boys with the bad teeth, the old men and the amputees' (*DR*: 62). Glad to be part of the army despite the desperation of the defence, Helmut is depicted in the last sentence of the story 'standing high on his rubble mountain, over which Soviet tanks will roll with ease [...] smiling' (*DR*: 63).

In 'Helmut', photography fails to become a means of comprehension, while in 'Lore', it becomes a means of deception. Lore's mother destroys the family portraits, and therefore the evidence that her husband was an SS officer, which allows Lore to travel unrecognized through Germany. During their journey, Lore and her siblings meet Thomas, a man who says he has been in prison for a long time and offers to help them. Later in the story, however, Lore finds out that the man is not who he pretends to be, but a German war criminal. Thomas has stolen the documents of a Jewish man who resembles him and is using them to travel safely in the country. As Hirsch notes, Thomas's deception utterly undermines 'the evidentiary authority of photography' (2012: 65). Even images of the concentration camps do not offer a representation that is free of doubt. When she first sees a picture of the prisoners of a concentration camp, Lore does not immediately understand what she is looking at:

> In front of Lore is a picture of a rubbish heap, or it might be ashes. She leans in closer, thinks it could be shoes. Below each of the photos is a place name. One of them sounds German, but the other two don't. [...] The pictures are of skeletons. Lore can see that now, pulling her hands back, tugging her sleeves down over her glue-damp palms. Hundreds of skeletons; hips and arms and skulls in tangles. Some lying in an open railway carriage, others in a shallow hollow in the ground. Lore holds her breath, looks away, sees the next picture; hair and skins and breasts. [...] People. Lying naked in rows. Skin thin as paper over bone. Dead people in piles with no clothes on. (*DR*: 103)

The tragic photographs of the dead are difficult to comprehend. The people suggest that 'it's all a set-up. The pictures are always out of focus, aren't they? Or dark, or grainy. Anything to make them unclear. All the people in the photos are actors' (*DR*: 175; see also 202–203). Paradoxically, photographic evidence does not provide clarity, but can instead lead to more confusion and deception (Pividori 2008: 89). As in the case of Kurt Gerstein, no matter how many proofs are presented, the existence of the death camps is countered by hypocritical incredulity and reticence, when not met with open hostility – as in the case of Gerstein's father.

Similar events take place in 'Micha', the last story of the book. Micha, a progressive German schoolteacher, finds out that his dead grandfather was a Waffen SS and was held prisoner by the Russians for more than a decade. Disturbed by this discovery, Micha starts investigating the tasks and misdeeds of his grandfather's unit in Belarus. He travels there to meet a survivor, Jozef, who witnessed the actions of the Germans and later confesses to having been a collaborationist. After long talks, during which the ghastly activities of the SS in the region are revealed, including the deportations and mass shootings of Jews and partisans, Micha shows the collaborationist a photograph of his grandfather, whom the man recognizes and remembers. Nevertheless, the photograph may not prove beyond doubt that Micha's grandfather is guilty of war crimes. Although the collaborationist remembers him, he never witnessed him participating in the shootings; however, he does remember those who did not participate: '– Did you see my Opa [grandad] do anything? [...] – He killed people. I am sorry, Michael. He killed Jews and Belarussian people. [...] – You saw that? [...] – I know that he did' (*DR*: 362). When Micha enquires further, Jozef answers: 'there were so few who didn't do it. I could tell you all the names and faces who didn't do it because they were so few' (*DR*: 363). As Berberich notes, Micha's search for the truth about his grandfather's past soon alienates him not only from his parents, the generation born just before the war, but also from his own generation: his older sister Luise and her partner Mina (Berberich 2011: 273). In this sense, his character is similar to Gerstein in that both of them fail to reconcile their dedication to the truth not only with their national history, but with their family, too. Gerstein experiences conflict with his father, his wife and his friends during the war; Micha has the same experience fifty years after its end. Although Seiffert's book is not explicitly postmemorial, as it does not involve the author's personal recollection of or dealings with family memories, 'Micha' represents a clear instance of postmemorial involvement and national history mediated not through the protagonist's personal recollection, but through a familial story and a related imaginative effort.

As Petra Rau argues, 'Seiffert does not equate photography with historical proof. On the contrary, she repeatedly contests that photographs are effective mnemonic devices or unequivocal pieces of evidence. At best, they are a version of "reality" or merely a synecdochal representation' (2006: 297). Photography is one of the most trusted technologies where public and individual memory is concerned, yet it proves to be deceptive both in the comprehension of the present (as in 'Helmut') and in the reconstruction of the past (as in 'Lore' and 'Micha'). Of course, Seiffert does not intend to deny the possibility of knowing the past. Despite the apparent uncertainty in which he is left, Micha knows that his grandfather *did* participate in the shootings. However, the ambiguity of photography, which is consistently not portrayed as a means of achieving clarity, suggests that readers should exercise caution when relying on photographs to understand the past. Indeed, Seiffert's problematization of photography implicates the wider problematization of memory, which is distinct from history as it is not completely reliable (as Micha's indecision proves), but which nevertheless provides access to an otherwise unattainable experience.

It is worth comparing Vollmann's and Seiffert's approaches to photography. As we have seen, Seiffert undermines the validatory function of photography: in her stories, photographs do not serve to aid in the understanding of history and do not even represent a definitive clue for the protagonists regarding whether an event took place. The ambiguity of photography in Seiffert's stories contests the traditional mechanisms regulating historical knowledge and the transmitted versions of historical facts and is the reason for the centrality of photographs in the plots. It is this very ambiguity that leads Micha to doubt his grandfather's past. Without suggesting that historical facts cannot be accessed, Seiffert, by highlighting the ambiguity of photography as a medium and acknowledging its mediating function, offers a problematic understanding of historiographical knowledge. Vollmann's interest in photography, on the contrary, tends to have quite a positive value. Although *Europe Central* does not contain photographs, Vollmann has often employed pictures in his reportages (as in *Poor People*, 2007, or *Carbon Ideologies*, 2018; on these books and their iconotext, see, respectively, Carrara 2018 and Malvestio 2019). In these works, Vollmann uses photographs to stand in for what he himself has witnessed in order to illustrate his point and persuade the reader. In the case of *Carbon Ideologies*, for instance, photographs are used to testify to Vollmann's presence at the sites described in the reportage and to give a face to those interviewed. In this sense, his use of pictures signals at least a partial faith in their capacity to provide precise information about the world, in the proper context.

Europe Central, however, contains a drawing by Vollmann himself – the map at the beginning of the book. Chaotically filled with portraits of generals and names of characters and military operations, the map is not intended to be a useful tool for interpreting the text or to guide the reader through the narrative, nor does it help the reader to follow the peregrinations of the characters. It features the names of military operations that have no particular relevance in the text (Operation Blau, for instance) and the name 'Roman Karmen' is written on the Spanish part of the map, despite Karmen being in Russia for most of the novel. The map should be interpreted, just like the *ouverture*, as a way of evoking and summing up the themes and the places involved in the war without providing an explanation or an accurate historical and geographical context. The allegorical value of the map is also evoked in the text (*EC*: 7). The partial purposelessness of the map and its arbitrary depiction of names and people is, nevertheless, balanced by the abundance of notes at the end of the book, which confirm that Vollmann's understanding of history differs from the doubtful understanding of history that characterizes postmodernism. Whilst Vollmann's decision to employ a useless map rather than photographs could lead us to believe that he undervalues photographs as a source of knowledge, this perspective is undermined by the fact that photographs are used to confirm and validate the material of the reportages. At the same time, the presence of the map, together with the liberties Vollmann takes in his narration, signals a more creative approach to historical writing than that of the classic historical novel and is certainly influenced by his experience of historiographic metafiction.

In sum, despite their differences in terms of style and narratorial choices, a comparison between the works of Vollmann, Waters and Seiffert allows us to observe the emergence of different traits of post-postmodern writing. Among these texts, Seiffert's lies closest to postmodern doubtfulness regarding historical transmission. Nevertheless, by adopting a postmemorial perspective and therefore a closer focus on the reactions of the characters, rather than historiography itself, she incorporates postmodern concerns about the transmission of history. However, they are not central to her enquiry; they are present and generate consequences, but it is their effect on the characters that is pivotal. Similarly, Vollmann and Waters, like McEwan, contest established versions of history, but they do so using the very same means of traditional historical enquiry, involving bibliographical research and the rediscovery of contradicting sources. Thus, Vollmann and Waters adopt a non-monolithic and plastic postmodern vision of historiography, but strongly refuse the outcomes of the linguistic turn. Some postmodern traits survive in post-postmodernism, but, as I have demonstrated, the most problematic aspects of postmodernism are discarded in favour of a style that shares more similarities with classic works.

CHAPTER 3

'A Real Morality Play': Jonathan Littell's *The Kindly Ones*

The Kindly Ones by Jonathan Littell (*KO*) abandons postmodern irony and avant-garde experimentalism, instead recovering formal aspects of the traditional (eighteenth- and early-nineteenth-century), modern (late nineteenth-century) and modernist (early twentieth-century) novel. Mimetic realism, which I believe to be amongst the most important stylistic features of the novel, together with the length of the book and its chronological and thematic variety, contributes to making *The Kindly Ones* one of the most significant examples of the post-postmodern epic. In this chapter, I highlight Littell's stylistic reprises of the traditional novel, especially in terms of mimetic realism, and analyse the employment of these stylistic reprises in the representation of the Second World War and the Holocaust. Littell's realism, I argue, problematizes the protagonist's reliability and forces readers to confront him and deal with their feelings of sympathy towards him. I go on to discuss Littell's use of Greek mythology as a hermeneutical tool in order to understand the Holocaust as a historical phenomenon. Finally, in the last section of this chapter, I draw a comparison between *The Kindly Ones* and two other novels: *HHhH* by Laurent Binet and *The H Twin* by Giorgio Falco. Both of these novels demonstrate a critical approach to the historical novel as a traditional form and exhibit metafictional and essayistic traits. My comparison aims to prove the innovative value of Littell's realistic approach.

The protagonist and narrator of *The Kindly Ones* is Maximilien Aue, SS-Obersturmbannfürher, an incestuous homosexual who kills his mother. When it was published, the novel was met with hostility and polemics, inciting opposing reactions amongst French critics (Thierry 2010: 11–18)[1] and generally negative reviews in the United States (Goslan 2010: 174–183) and Germany (Theweleit and Nunan 2009: 21–34; Asholt 2012). Critics focus mainly on two issues. First of all, they consider Littell's decision to make an SS officer the narrator scandalous, in addition to which this character's reasons and excuses for his actions make *The Kindly Ones* shocking to some. Secondly, and more importantly, its style has been critiqued. Some critics have wondered how it is possible in the twenty-first century to write as if William Faulkner, James Joyce, Marcel Proust or the Structuralists never existed, not to mention Michel Houellebecq, Toni Morrison or Salman Rushdie. Littell's novel, in other words, is anachronistic as it seems to uncritically recover a literary tradition that has been surpassed (Mazzoni 2008: 233).[2] I only partially accept this critique because Littell does not write exactly as if he was part of the nineteenth-century literary tradition and, as we will see, is well aware of the existence of Joyce (and Houellebecq). However, this accusation points to something that has been overlooked by several critics who focus primarily on the *ethics* of the novel: that Littell, narrating Aue's history, recovers the style of the traditional novel by abandoning the experimentalism of the twentieth-century avant-gardes and the parodying dimension of postmodern literature.

Lermonier highlights that despite winning the prize of the French Academy and the Goncourt Prize in 2006, Littell is, surprisingly, American (2007: 11). Littell's cultural and linguistic identity is significant. Littell was born in New York on 10 October 1967, finished high school in Paris in 1985 and continued his studies at Yale University. His father Robert is a Sovietologist and the author of several bestselling novels. During the 1990s, Littell worked with NGOs and witnessed some of the worst massacres of the late twentieth century in Bosnia, Rwanda, Chechnya and Afghanistan. Even after the publication of *The Kindly Ones*, Littell returned to work in Chechnya (*Tchétchénie, An III* [*Chechnya, Year III*], 2009) and

1 Paul-Éric Blanrue reports that 500,000 copies were sold in 2006 alone (2006: 9–15).

2 These names have been listed by Sylvain Bourmeau in a review of the novel on *Les Inrockuptibles* (2006; quoted in Mazzoni 2017: 340).

Syria (*Carnet de Homs. 16 janvier – 2 février 2012* [*Syrian Notebooks: Inside the Homs Uprising January 16 – February 2*], 2012).

It is worth bearing in mind Littell's cosmopolitanism since it influences his stylistic choices. Refusing formal and linguistic experimentalism, he also rejects the idea that the novel is bound to a specific national tradition. Littell is primarily inspired by Russian (Tolstoy, Dostoevsky, Grossman), Anglo-Saxon (Joyce), German (Hofmannsthal, Mann) and classical (Aeschylus) authors – and only marginally by French authors (Maurice Blanchot and Georges Bataille). In a passage previously mentioned in the introduction, Littell emphasizes his refusal to consider literature a national product:

> Tout ce que vous [Richard Millet] dites est vrai si l'on se place d'un point de vue qui n'est pas le mien, qui est qu'il existe des littératures nationales. Pour moi, le découpage littéraire national a eu certainement une réalité à l'époque où les transmissions étaient beaucoup plus longes. Du fait de l'isolement, là il y avait de grandes distinctions entre les littératures nationales [...]. Aujourd'hui, à l'ère de la communication et de la connexion de masse, c'est beaucoup moins vrai. Les interpollinisations d'un pays à un autre se font à une échelle de temps tellement rapide que tout écrivain digne de ce nom est nourri par toute la littérature – dans mon cas la russe presque autant que la française ou la littérature en langue allemande, ça peut tout aussi bien être les littératures asiatiques, africaines, etc. C'est pourquoi l'idée de littératures nationales me semble un mythe, aujourd'hui. (Littell and Millet 2007: 16–17)
>
> [Everything you [Richard Millet] say is true, from a perspective that is not mine, according to which national literatures exists. In my opinion, the division into national literatures certainly occurred in the past, when the circulation of texts took much more time. Because of their isolation, there were great differences between national literatures. [...] Today, in our age of mass communication and connection, this is significantly less true. The cross-fertilization between different countries takes place so fast that a writer worthy of the name must be nourished in all literatures – in my case, Russian literature almost as much as French literature or literature in German, but it could also be African or Asian literatures, and so on. That's why the idea of national literatures seems to me to be a myth, today.]

It is clear that Littell as an author aligns with the global dimension of contemporary literature (or at least of a Francophone, rather than French, literature; Moura 2012: 253–265) and the post-postmodern tendency to non-ironically repurpose the traditional features of the novel. In particular, in Littell's work, three typical elements of the nineteenth-century novel are non-problematically and non-ironically recovered: plot, characters, time (Tirinanzi De Medici 2012: 167).

Littell recovers from the traditional novel of the eighteenth and early nineteenth centuries the focus on a specific individual, immersed in everyday life in a precise and carefully recreated environment, and is interested in the individual's relationship with the surrounding ambient. The nineteenth-century novel, known as the novel of modernity, provides Littell with the figure of the intellectual hero, while the mythical method is inspired by modernism, although this use of myth, as we will see, differs from the modernist tradition in significant ways.

Plot, Characters, Time

Two elements signal the influence of the traditional novel in *The Kindly Ones*: a recognizable plot and mimetic realism. According to Stefano Calabrese, the modernist novel endorses the decline of plot (2005: 22). This depreciation of plot survives in postmodernism. Prior to the advent of modernism, the novelist carefully tried to achieve a balance between the centre of the story (the close-ups) and its satellites (the spatial and temporal settings); by contrast, in the third decade of the twentieth century, the satellites started to gain priority whilst the centres dispersed, scattered in a 'galaxy of epiphanies' (22). Littell, however, unironically chooses a clear plot. *The Kindly Ones* tells the story of Maximilien Aue from 27 June 1941, the beginning of Operation Barbarossa, to 28 April 1945, two days before Hitler's suicide. The narrator is writing during the 1960s and 1970s and several flashbacks cover the period from 1919 to 1941. Aue's history proceeds with precision, starting in Ukraine, where Max, who is part of the Einsatzgruppe C, witnesses the Babi Yar massacre, and continuing on to the Caucasus, following the march of the German army. Aue is then moved to Stalingrad because of a fight he has with another officer who insinuates that he is homosexual and because he is less than convincing whilst pursuing the case against the Bergjuden. Later, after the fall of the Kessel, he is urgently sent back to Berlin. He is commended by Heinrich Himmler for his courage in battle and hired to collaborate with Eichmann in the supervision of the Polish death camps and the deportation of the Hungarian Jews. During the siege of Berlin, Max finally succeeds in escaping, joins the civilian refugees and reconstructs himself in France.

Aue significantly changes his behaviour and perception of the world after the head wound he receives in Stalingrad (what he calls his 'pineal eye', the location of the human soul according to Descartes, *KO*: 443) and gradually loses control of himself. Until that moment, the model that regulates the development of the plot is the classical novel. It is no coincidence that Stendhal is a recurring presence in the first half of the novel; Aue reads his works between Ukraine and the Caucasus. Moreover, Aue's proud, rebellious character – he is more cultured and sensitive than his colleagues – could be modelled on the impulsive behaviour of Julien Sorel in *Le rouge et le noir* [*The Red and the Black*] (1830) since, ultimately, his conduct leads to his punishment and transfer to Stalingrad. Whether or not this is the case, Max is moved by a vague but irrefutable ambition in the first half of the novel, as is typical in the nineteenth-century Bildungsroman (Luperini 2007: 16).

As I have intimated, after the battle of Stalingrad, the plot runs aground, mirroring Aue's psychological decline. I will return to this topic in more detail later in this chapter as the disintegration of the plot is typical not of the traditional novel, but of the modern novel. For now, it is worth noting that the first part of the novel has an adventurous plot, whilst the second part prioritizes introspection over action. The first half of the novel is geographically located on the Russian front, from chapters 'Toccata' to 'Sarabande'. Not only is it geared towards the representation of Nazi atrocities and the war, but it is also a way to pay homage to the Russian writers Littell admires, such as Fyodor Dostoevsky (Nivat 2007: 56) and Vasily Grossman (and therefore, indirectly, Tolstoy; Nivat 2007: 58–60). Specifically, a reference to Grossman is made in the reappropriation of the famous interrogation scene from *Žisn'i sud'ba* [*Life and Destiny*] (1980), in which a Nazi officer and a Soviet prisoner discuss politics (Panichi 2014: 129), while Mikhail Lermontov is mentioned in several episodes in the Caucasus (*KO*: 243 ff.).

Referring to epic novels like Tolstoy's and Grossmann's and mimicking their serious tone and aspiration to totality (*The Kindly Ones* is1,000 pages long) is Littell's way of telling the story of the *absolute* war. The explicit presence of references to these authors in the novel, therefore, allows Littell, by extension, to enhance the epic proportions of the work, which, according to Watts, represents one of the greatest epics of contemporary literature (2012: 155).

Another notable element of Littell's recovery of the nineteenth-century model in *The Kindly Ones* is his mimetic effort to recreate, plausibly and in detail, a world that he did not experience first-hand (Mazzoni 2008: 233). This mimetic effort represents one of Littell's most significant novelties in the narration of the Second World War. Maximilien Aue is not a metaphysical incarnation of evil, like many Nazis in low and high cultural products, but a specific man, inhabiting a precise and carefully recreated ambient. Aue meets and interacts with other particular beings, is identified by a personal story and a set of personal data, aims to satisfy his ambitions and moves with realistic rhythms in a recognizable physical and cultural landscape, of which he is a product. As we have seen in the introduction, postmodernism is characterized by a disregard for realism. If we compare *The Kindly Ones* to postmodern attempts to portray Nazi perpetrators, such as Martin Amis's *Time's Arrow*, the novelty of Littell's effort becomes clear. Amis's book refutes realism by way of its very narrative structure. *Time's Arrow* narrates the life of a Nazi doctor involved in the Holocaust, but in reverse chronological order. The narrator is a sort of second consciousness of the protagonist. These narratorial and chronological choices evidently forbid mechanisms of causality and responsibility from emerging. On the other hand, as Michael Mack writes, 'the hyperreality of Littell's novel is of course not that of the nineteenth-century realism, but it is certainly removed from the playful accounts of fantasy and bricolage' (2014: 206).

How is this mimetic effect achieved in *The Kindly Ones*? We can identify four different strategies employed by Littell to achieve such realism: a first-person narrator who often assumes the qualities of an omniscient narrator; the exhibition of historical characters; the reproduction of the cultural ambient and its language; and the exhibition of precise details.

The Kindly Ones is staged as the memoir that Aue writes some decades after the war. This device allows Littell to give Max both the partial point of view of the protagonist and the totalizing point of view of the narrator of the historical novel. Littell makes him, in other words, both a witness and an omniscient narrator (Pennacchio 2018: 55–88). Aue writes of events that could be reconstructed by consulting history books (something his character admits he has done to aid his memory), which makes his testimony acceptable and credible. That being said, on several occasions, Aue proves to be an unreliable narrator as, for the duration of the novel, he denies killing his mother. Aue speaks in the first person to move readers to identification and encourage them to forget that they are reading a novel, despite the evident falsity of some of the details contained in the text. This oscillation between omniscient and first-person narration is not uncommon in post-postmodern novels, as we have seen in *2666*.

Another validatory mechanism that Littell exploits is the presence of historical characters. The majority of the characters represent real-life people. With the exceptions of his family, his protectors (Mandelbrod and Leland), his prosecutors (Clemens and Weser), his friend and double, Thomas, his semi-fiancée Hélène, three colleagues Voss, Hohenegg and Osnabrugge and a few other minor characters, Aue interacts only with non-fictional characters. This is more significant if we consider, as I explain later in this chapter, that the fictional characters mainly have a symbolic role. Aue has the chance to meet Reinhard Heydrich and Hitler, works for Himmler, is close to Albert Speer and is a colleague and a friend of Adolf Eichmann. But beyond these famous names, the nebula of minor hierarchs, officials and functionaries creates a safety net of validation that allows the narration to proceed without incredulities. These characters include Waldemar von Radetzky, Paul Blobel, Walter von Reichenau, Otto Ohlendorf, Lucien Lippert, Ernst Jünger, Helmut Knochen, Werner Best, Louis-Ferdinand Céline, Robert Brasillach, Lucien Rebatet, Richard Korherr, Ernst Kaltenbrunner, Odilo Globočnik', Hermann Höfle, Ilse Koch, Rudolf Höss, Josef Mengele, Hans Frank and Otto Hermann Fegelein.

Furthermore, like Aue, these characters are not merely empty symbols of absolute evil. For instance, although Littell generally subscribes to Hannah Arendt's thesis, Max portrays Eichmann as a photographic negative of the profile of him in *Eichmann in Jerusalem*. In Arendt's text, Eichmann insistently complains that he did not have a brilliant career (1963: 49); according to Aue, these missed promotions are the result of the structural problems of the organization for which he works (*KO*: 511–512). Whereas in *Eichmann in Jerusalem*, Eichmann is systematically depicted as forgetful and unable to recall basic facts about his private and public life (53), Aue praises Eichmann's excellent memory (*KO*: 519). Arendt depicts Eichmann's well-known interest in the Kantian imperative as deceptive, while Littell emphasizes the Obersturmfürher's sincere fascination with the work of Kant (*KO*: 521–524). Aue carefully underlines that Eichmann was not 'the incarnation of *banal evil*, a soulless, faceless robot, as some sought to present him after his trial' (*KO*: 569). Although the author's conclusions differ to those of his narrator, Littell attempts to provide a fair and complete depiction of Eichmann as a complex human being who inhabited a specific cultural landscape: a man with passions, interests and defects who was talented and brilliant in the execution of certain tasks. Littell is trying, in other words, to paint Eichmann as 'a very talented bureaucrat, extremely competent at his functions, with a certain stature and a considerable sense of personal initiative, but solely within the framework of clearly circumscribed tasks' (*KO*: 569–570) and not simply as someone who never understood the consequences of his actions. This attitude towards Eichmann is also suggestive of Littell's fundamental disagreement with Arendt's work, which is not with Arendt's understanding of Eichmann's personality, but rather with her unsympathetic representations of him. In Littell's opinion, it is more useful to present readers with a character they can relate to and may even admire, rather than someone they despise (Palumbo Mosca 2014: 108–109). I will return to this point later in this chapter.

The historical characters that Littell presents are credible not only because they have real-life counterparts, but also because of the realism of the language they speak and the ambient they move in. This environmental paradigm, again, is inherited from the nineteenth-century novel tradition (Mazzoni 2017: 269 ff.). Littell's characters speak in an accurate and non-stereotypical way that is in accordance with Nazi ideology. Even Aue, who is an atypical Nazi, thinks in line with the official doctrine of the party and therefore believes in pseudo-scientific racism and is scandalized when the linguist Voss exposes its lack of scientific credibility (*KO*: 298–304). Even when he is depicting the worst absurdities and vileness, Littell tries to be historically faithful. Examples of this include the discussion of the *Führerprinzip* between Aue and Eichmann or, during the siege of Stalingrad, the soldiers' debate regarding the racial inconvenience of eating the corpse of a Russian and the moral inconvenience of eating the corpse of a German, which ends with them agreeing on the compromise of eating a Ukrainian Hiwi (*KO*: 376). Or we might consider the grotesque results of Nazi racial theory, such as Governor Hans Frank's intentions to build a zoo for the extinct human races in postwar Kraków (*KO*: 683–686). Or we could note Himmler's enthusiasm for a brief essay, written by Aue in a feverish delirium, suggesting the relationship between red and green Martians in Edgar Rice Burroughs's books as a model for the racial politics in the occupied territories (*KO*: 822–833). These absurdities are not explicitly mocked at the moment of their appearance in the book, since Aue considers them to be coherent with the framework of Nazi ideology. This ideology was, notoriously, a synthesis of magic and advanced technology; Hitler was a man pursuing irrational aims with rational means (Severino in Galli 1989: 11). Similarly, the at least partly esoteric roots of anti-Semitism (Galli 1989: 55) and Hitler's foreign politics are well known (145). It is historically credible that Himmler, who was convinced that he was the reincarnation of Henry the Fowler (155) and consented to being involved in an expedition to find the entrance to the Hollow Earth in the Baltic Sea (159), was persuaded by the theories contained in a book for children.

Not only are names and cultural issues portrayed accurately; Littell's topographical precision is impressive. While it is true that Aue's omnipresence in important situations and at crucial moments is unlikely and almost magical, the abundance of precise place names, whether readers know them or not, serves to validate the words of the narrator.[3] Moreover, in the depiction of the bureaucratic processes regulating life in the Third Reich, the use of a specific lexicon is important. Littell always uses the German word for the institutions of the Reich, the divisions on the Russian front

3 Denis Briand (2010: 99) provides a list of all the places on the Eastern Front that Max visits in the novel.

and the military grades of the Wehrmacht, the SS and the Waffen-SS. He even provides a glossary at the end of the book. Aue reflects on the hypnotic and intimidating power of these specific words for the survival of the regime and the extermination process, implying that readers are subjected to the same effect:

> Then, little by little, the signification [of *Endlösung*, the final solution] had slid toward the abyss, but without the signifier changing, and it seemed almost as if this final meaning had always lived in the heart of the word, and that the thing had been attracted, drawn by it, by its weight, its fabulous gravity, into a black hole of the mind, toward the point of singularity: and then we had passed the event horizon, beyond which there is no return. We still believe in ideas, in concepts, we believe that words designate ideas, maybe there's really nothing but words, and the weight peculiar to words. And maybe thus we had let ourselves be led along by a word and its inevitability. (*KO*: 630–631)[4]

The reality of the war and the extermination of Jews is not depicted as a metahistorical epic or a sacred memory, but as a series of human events that necessarily depends on a myriad of material circumstances and practical details. Describing the genocide in Ukraine, for instance, Littell exposes their logistical difficulties and portrays the Nazis as men trying to find the most acceptable solution to a practical problem. For them, it does not matter that this practical problem is how to kill the highest number of people in the easiest and quickest way (*KO*: 97–101). A similar argument can be made for the parts of the novel dedicated to Auschwitz and Hungary, including the chapter 'Menuet (en rondeaux)'.

One of the moments that exemplifies Littell's interest in the practicalities, rather than the metaphysical or moral dimensions of Nazism, is the discussion regarding the Bergjuden. During the occupation of the Caucasus, the SS and the Wehrmacht must decide whether to proceed with the deportation of these people of ancient Hebrew heritage. The SS want to deport them, whereas the Wehrmacht does not. What is shocking in this passage is the way in which the destiny of an entire people is bound to the

4 Élise Lamy-Rested (2014: 40–41) argues that in passages such as this Littell implicitly quotes Victor Klemperer's *Lingua Tertii Imperii. The Language of the Third Reich* (1947), which reflects on the Nazi use of language as a means of propaganda.

misleading, dull and completely irrational discussions of the Nazi officers ('their Jewish character is as plain as day. Their manners are insinuating, and they even tried to corrupt us', *KO*: 320). The casual, unexpected and off-stage, so to speak, death of the linguist Voss – one of the few positive characters in the book and an opponent of the deportation – almost results in the SS triumphing. They are unsuccessful only because of a stratagem employed by a Wehrmacht general, who proposes to delay the debate until the occupation of the original land belonging to the people, Daghestan. It is clear, by that point in the conflict, that Daghestan will not be conquered, but it would be unpatriotic of the SS to admit to this and so they are forced to accept the delay.

The large quantity of historical details, which Aue himself ironically admits are excessive, creates the base upon which Littell's novel functions and causes the reader to identify with the protagonist. I will clarify the way in which the novel encourages an empathic response in more detail later in this chapter. For now, it is important to observe that Littell models his mimetic effort on a non-ironic appropriation of the traditional novel form, naturally ('con sprezzatura') using details that are unnecessary to the development of the plot, but that create, for the reader, the impression of reality (Mazzoni 2008: 233).

On this matter, we must remember that the novel does not tell the story of an ordinary man, but that of an SS officer involved in the most important events of the Second World War. Therefore, the importance of the allusions to Russian literature becomes even clearer. By describing in detail the environment in which the protagonist moves, Littell portrays the relationship between the cultural milieu and his protagonist and therefore the influence of circumstances and chance on human life. Littell's mimetic effort aims to demonstrate that the evil committed by people is never absolute, unencumbered by context, but generated and cultivated at a specific time in certain circumstances (Tirinanzi De Medici 2012: 176). This pivotal concept, partially discussed earlier in reference to Bolaño's character Leo Sammer, is of the utmost importance in the context of a war that has become a symbol of absolute evil in public memory. Littell's realism serves to restore an everyday dimension to the war, suggesting that it does not belong to a parallel metaphysical dimension, but to a realm of concrete possibilities.

Objections

Two objections have often been levelled against the realism of *The Kindly Ones*. The first concerns Littell's abuse of kitsch and pulp expedients in the representation of the protagonist and other characters. The second concerns the scant credibility of Maximilien Aue as an SS officer.

It is true that the choice to narrate the story, which contains many scatological and sadistic scenes, from the perspective of a homosexual and incestuous SS officer makes the novel vulnerable to accusations that it belongs to the Nazi-porn genre (Levéel 2010: 141–154). Aue could simply be perceived as the last in a long series of stereotypically sexually perverted Nazi officers. The sexualization of the Nazi legacy is a typical trait of several films from the late 1960s and 1970s. This first began in high-culture movies such as Luchino Visconti's *La caduta degli dei* [*The Damned*] (1969), Liliana Cavani's *Il portiere di notte* [*The Night Porter*] (1974), Lina Wertmüller's *Pasqualino Settebellezze* [*Seven Beauties*] (1975) and Pier Paolo Pasolini's *Salò o le 120 giornate di Sodoma* [*Salò, or the 120 Days of Sodom*] (1975) and can be traced back to Roberto Rossellini's representation of the Nazi officer in *Roma, città aperta* [*Rome, Open City*] (1945; Hake 2012: 131–134). Although these films were attempting to create a connection between sexual deviation and the perversity of power, their imagery was soon adopted by several low-budget, semi-pornographic films. These movies, which establish the so-called *Nazisploitation* canon, include Don Edmonds's *Ilsa, She Wolf of the SS* (1975), Cesare Canevari's *L'ultima orgia del III Reich* [*Gestapo's Last Orgy*] (1976), Luigi Batzella's *La bestia in calore* [*The Beast in Heat*] (1977), Sergio Garrone's *Lager SSadis Kastrat Kommandantur* (1976) and Bruno Mattei's *Casa privata per le SS* [*SS Girls*] (1977) and *KZ9 – Lager di sterminio* [*Women's Camp 119*] (1977), together with the more artistically ambitious *Salon Kitty* by Tinto Brass (1975) (Hake 2012: 150).

This relatively exhaustive list aims to underline how prevalent and pervasive the stereotype of the sexually perverted Nazi is in contemporary culture. Such imagery, as Carlo Tirinanzi De Medici notes, is still evident, for example, in Quentin Tarantino's *Inglourious Basterds* (2009) (Tirinanzi De Medici 2012: 188). Although Littell explicitly claims to despise the so-called *Nazisploitation* genre (Littell and Nora 2007: 40), it is hard to deny that several details in the novel belong to the same kitsch paradigm. I am thinking, for instance, of Max's seduction of his comrade Partenau in Crimea ('I showed him the cover: "*The Symposium*. Have you read it?" – "I must confess I haven't". I closed it and held it out to him: "Take it. I know it by heart"', *KO*: 194); the description of the excesses of the SS in Poland, which are imbued with a hint of sexual morbidity (*KO*: 574–578); the introduction of the mysterious doctor Mandelbrod, complete with a cat on his knee, like a James Bond villain (*KO*: 450), and his 'amazons' Hilde, Helga and Hedwig, who offer their bodies to Max and recall *Ilsa, She Wolf of the SS* (Lermonier 2007: 40). Furthermore, the very notion of a detective subplot in the Third Reich (when Clemens and Weser investigate the deaths of Aue's parents) recalls B-movies, pulp detective stories and kitsch bestsellers like Robert Harris's *Fatherland* (1992), rather than Philip K. Dick's alternate-history classic *The Man in the High Castle* (1962).

While it is true that these superfluous, overtly sexual or popular culture details, which caused critics to define Littell as a fanatic of Nazi kitsch, stand out against the normality of the background and the dull bureaucratic processes depicted, it must also be underlined that they are infrequent in this over 1,000-page novel. In my view, since they are relatively scarce, they do not spoil the credibility of the historical reconstruction (Sandberg 2014: 250). This merging of high and popular culture may lead us to associate *The Kindly Ones* with postmodernism as pastiche, as we have seen, is an important element of postmodernist poetics. However, Littell's intent is never ironic. The reprise of pulp and kitsch details is intentional and contributes to, rather than undermines, the narrative impact that the novel has on the reader. Pierre Nora has spoken of 'quelque chose de parfois juvénile dans [le] livre' [something even juvenile in the book] (Littell and Nora 2007: 29). Littell expresses his admiration for cinematographic works such as *Apocalypse Now* and *The Shining* (6 and 14), suggesting that so many midcult elements are included in his novel because of the incisiveness of many of their scenes. The author asks his readers to assume a kind of naïveté typical of post-postmodernist fiction. He encourages them to ignore the falsity of the *mise-en-scène*, which is openly admitted, in order to completely enjoy and therefore understand the novel. Thus, Littell's intention is typically post-postmodern because he looks seriously to cultural products of mainstream and pop culture as models for his work.

The second critique levelled against *The Kindly Ones* – the scant credibility of Max as an SS officer – is more significant. If the traditional novel interests us because it narrates the lives of ordinary individuals in a recreation of their society, why should readers be interested in as eccentric, problematic and unlikely a character as Maximilien Aue? First of all, it must be said that the objection that Aue is an unlikely Nazi because he is too smart and cultivated (the readers face exchanges such as: '"Have you read Plato?". He looked at me, taken aback: "What?" – "No, it's nothing"', *KO*: 34) does not cohere with what we know historically and biographically. This objection is the consequence of a naïve and simplistic prejudice against the Nazis, who included among their number not just bloodthirsty animals, but also educated people, as in every social and political group. The aim of the novel is precisely to insist that crimes of monstrous proportions, such as the Holocaust, were carried out not only by normal people like Eichmann, but also by highly formally educated people – opera lovers and readers of Plato, Stendhal and Gustave Flaubert. In other words, the Holocaust was not the result of a lack of intelligence and culture; it was coherent with European culture itself. We must remember that among the Nazis there were men like Carl Schmitt, Martin Heidegger, Ernst Jünger, Albert Speer and, working for the SS, Otto Ohlendorf, in whom critics recognize the most likely model for the character of Maximilien Aue (Compagnon 2012: 117 ff.).

Aue's eccentricity, moreover, is always confined *in interiore homine*. Therefore it is false, as Husson says (2006), that it would not have been tolerated among the SS. Heydrich and Himmler never have the chance to witness Aue's psychological problems and his homosexuality is largely gossiped about, but never witnessed, by the people around him (*KO*: 253–254). It is true, therefore, that Aue is a peculiar kind of Nazi, but it cannot be argued that these characteristics would have been an obstacle in his career – not least because there were several openly homosexual Nazis, such as Robert Brasillach and Lucien Rebatet. The fact that Aue is an atypical Nazi does not make him an impossible Nazi, as some critics have suggested. I will focus later in this chapter on the reasons that led Littell to choose certain peculiar psychological features for Aue. Nevertheless, it is true that Aue's peculiarity distances him from the stereotypes of his time and places him cognitively and culturally closer to his readers. This is achieved through literary references, relativization and sexual morbidity. Such closeness is necessary for readers to fully empathize with the protagonist.

However, Aue's unlikeliness raises another doubt about *The Kindly Ones*. Aue is an extremely self-aware narrator who displays extensive knowledge of rhetorical mechanisms and a high degree of erudition. Moreover, he admits to readers that he has been consulting historical sources in order to write his memoir. At the same time, Aue is an unreliable narrator who refuses to admit the obvious truth that he killed his mother (or at least he convinces himself he is not guilty). His potential implausibility as a Nazi officer is encapsulated by the unlikeliness of certain passages of the plot, such as the final pages, in which Aue bites Hitler's nose, and the kitsch morbidity that characterizes several characters and situations. These features suggest that *The Kindly Ones* belongs to the genre of historiographic metafiction, rather than the genre of the historical novel.

It has been argued that Littell's work can be considered metafictional (Grethlein 2012: 92). Philippe Carrard suggests that

> [i]t is this use of actual rather than fictional characters as middlemen that makes *The Kindly Ones* into a piece of historiographic metafiction. [...] By challenging the conventions of the historical novel, at least those identified by Lukács [according to whom historical characters traditionally have the role of middlemen], Littell's text becomes self-reflexive. (2014: 184)

A similar effect is produced by the presence of a glossary of terms at the end of the novel, which 'constitutes a reflection on the relations between text and paratexts in a novel that aims at factual accuracy' (185). Despite significant narratorial and authorial self-awareness (suggesting a degree of metafictionality), *The Kindly Ones* cannot be considered historiographic metafiction in the sense outlined by Linda Hutcheon. Littell's focus is not on the way in which we know and understand the past, nor is it on the fact that we can only know the past through its representations. Although Aue uses books and historical sources to structure his narration, his main source of knowledge and validation is his own direct testimony. Although Aue acts as an unreliable narrator in some parts of his story, this never undermines the reader's faith in the truth of what is being narrated. Aue's unreliability does not cast doubt on the historicity of the Holocaust or the way it has been transmitted to us. On the contrary, the narrator's testimony endorses the truthfulness of direct witnesses and survivals, while his admission that he uses historical sources endorses the work of historians. Littell's exploitation of metafiction is not a playful and dubitative way of discussing the hermeneutic value of literature, but rather, as we will see, an attempt to convey further meaning that does not contradict the mimetic effort.

Max Aue, an Intellectual Hero

Another book is often evoked during the second half of Littell's novel, after the battle of Stalingrad. Gustave Flaubert's *L'Éducation sentimentale* [*Sentimental Education*] (1869), a Bildungsroman and historical novel (Imbaud 2010: 186), accompanies Aue until the very last moments of the history of the Reich (*KO*: 867) and is recalled by the name of his stepfather, Moreau, which is the surname of Flaubert's protagonist. The meaning of this choice seems clear, as the second part of the novel narrates, mainly through flashbacks, the love story of Max and his sister Una. The promise that Max made to her when he was a teenager never to love anyone else recalls the promise made by Frédéric to Madame Arnoux in *Sentimental Education*. Moreover, for Flaubert's Frédéric, this promise serves as an excuse for his irresoluteness and allows him to avoid making a serious commitment to Madame Dambreuse. Similarly, Aue abides by the promise he made to Una (who subsequently married) to stay anchored to an infantile incestuous fantasy that prevents him from having a mature relationship with Hélène.

Another meaning can be attributed to Littell's inclusion of Flaubert, in connection with the new literary tradition instantiated by *Sentimental Education*, which is also partially evident in *The Kindly Ones*. According to Romano Luperini, Flaubert's novel can be interpreted as the milestone between the traditional and the modern novels, a turning point in that characters are not moved by defined purposes and desires, as had previously been the case, but rather by confusing, undetermined and impractical aspirations (Luperini 2007: 19).

It is significant, therefore, that Littell introduces Flaubert at the juncture of Aue's psychological impasse, after the more eventful and active first part of the novel, which was written with Stendhal in mind. The battle of Stalingrad signals the end of the Axis initiative in the war and the beginning of their defeat. In this second part Aue, as a result of his head wound, loses his sense of will and moves from *acting* to *being acted on* by the circumstances in which he finds himself. He seems capable of continuing to perform his duties with the usual efficiency, but he is unable to perform all larger-scale actions, with the exception of his frustrated desire to be transferred to France.

In the first part of the novel, Aue acted on his own initiative, as in the Caucasus, where he pays for his actions with the transfer to Stalingrad. Now, his activities are regulated by the mysterious figures of Leland and Mandelbrod, who recommend him to Himmler and Speer. Aue's passivity becomes almost total at the end of the novel, specifically in the long, delirious chapter 'Air', in which Flaubert's novel is explicitly mentioned. Aue's will, like Frédéric's, manifests itself in sudden, arbitrary and fleeting acts of pride, evident when he kills a Prussian Junker (*KO*: 929–930) and his former lover, Mihai, out of rage (*KO*: 949).

Aue's condition is, of course, metaphorical. His intellectual and psychological disarray is a symbol for the state of decay in which Germany finds itself at the end of the war. If it is true, to quote Giuseppe Di Giacomo, that the importance of *Sentimental Education* lies in the dramatization of inaction and erosion (1999: 68), then it seems clear that Flaubert represents an important intertext through which to read the second half of Aue's story. From the modern (late nineteenth-century) novel, Littell borrows distinct features, which he bestows on his protagonist. Aue is a flâneur and an intellectual hero.

Aue's flânerie is evident on a structural level. Given the reference to Baudelaire in the first lines of the novel (Dambre 2012: 173), it could be said that it is evident from the very beginning of the book. Max travels throughout Europe during the war, following a path that precisely traces the stages of German military expansion and retreat (Ukraine, the Caucasus,

Stalingrad, Poland, Hungary), as well as the symbolic progression of the Holocaust (from the France of the Enlightenment to the concentration camps; Briand 2010: 87–102). Aue visits Paris, the capital of flânerie (Davies 2010: 176), and registers the actions and impressions of the people he meets. As a flâneur, Aue is mainly an observer. Except for during his time in Hungary, he is never asked to work actively. In Paris, before the war, his job is to analyse the inclination of the French political right towards the Nazis. In the Caucasus, he is tasked with studying the Bergjuden in order to determine whether they are real Jews. In Stalingrad, he is charged with investigating the morale of the troops, while in Poland he controls and supervises the camps.

Aue's flânerie is intimately connected to another important characteristic. He is represented as an eccentric hero, both intellectually (Bougnoux 2007: 67) and psychologically. I have already mentioned that this eccentricity has led many to consider Aue an unlikely character and that I disagree with this critique. What I now want to underline is the role that this intellectual and psychological diversity plays in the novel. According to Littell, 'une grande partie de la fonction de Max Aue est de servir de regard sur les autres. Etant effectivement un personnage décalé par rapport à son environnement, il peut apporter ce regard lucide, qui balaie presque comme un scanner' [a great part of Max Aue's function is to provide a gaze on others. Being actually a character out of context in his environment, he can provide a lucid gaze, that sees through things like a scanner] (Littell and Millet 2007). In other words, Aue's eccentric personality is the result of his liminal shape-shifter persona, which adopts characteristics appropriate to the different material circumstances he inhabits. Aue's mutable identity is also signalled by his native land Alsace, a borderland with a contested and mixed cultural identity (Tame 2010: 218), and by his name, which not only sounds French, but is also a sonorously *liquid* name, in stark contrast to the asperity of all the German names that crowd the novel (Bougnoux 2009: 69).

Aue is a problematic hero. According to György Lukács's definition, he is a character fighting against himself and the external world (Tame 2010: 218; Ferdjani 2010: 265). Consequently, in various parts of the novel, he exhibits irony (one of the typical traits of characters in the modern novel; Di Giacomo 1999: 32–36). For instance, when looking closely at Heydrich and Himmler, he realizes how unpleasant they look. This irony is the result of the confrontation between him and the world, of which he perceives the absurdity.[5] It is an implicit perception, however, not an explicit one. Aue never openly ridicules what he believes in.

Aue's eccentricity manifests itself psychologically in his sexual perversions. In order to fully understand the meaning of Aue's behaviour, we must consider the author's essay *Le sec et l'humide* [lit. *The Dry and the Wet*] (2008), which represents a kind of preparatory sketch for *The Kindly Ones* in the form of a commentary on Leon Degrelle's autobiography and which is heavily influenced by Klaus Theweleit's *Männerphantasien* [*Male Fantasies*] (1977; Littell 2008: 25). According to Theweleit,

> Le modèle freudien du Ça, du Moi et du Surmoi, et donc de l'Œdipe, ne peut pas lui être appliqué, car le fasciste, en fait, n'a jamais achevé sa séparation d'avec la mère, et ne s'est jamais constitué un Moi au sens freudien du terme. Le fasciste est le "pas-encore-complètement-né". Or ce n'est pas un psychopathe; il a effectué une séparation partielle, il est socialisé, il parle, il écrit, il agit dans le monde, de manière hélas souvent efficace, il prend même parfois le pouvoir. Pour y parvenir, il s'est construit ou fait construire – par le truchement de la discipline, du dressage, d'exercices physiques – un Moi extériorisé qui prend la forme d'une "carapace", d'une "armure musculaire". Celle-ci maintient à l'intérieur, là où le fasciste n'a pas accès, toutes ses pulsions, ses fonctions désirantes absolument informes car incapables d'objectivation. Mais ce Moi-carapace n'est jamais tout à fait hermétique, il est même fragile ; il ne tient réellement que grâce à des soutiens extérieurs : l'école, l'armée, voire la prison. En période de crise, il se morcelle, et le fasciste risque alors d'être débordé par ses productions désirantes incontrôlables, la "dissolution des limites personnelles". Pour survivre, il extériorise ce qui le menace de l'intérieur, et tous les dangers prennent alors pour lui deux formes, intimement liées entre elles : celle du féminin et celle du liquide [...]. (Littell 2008: 26)
>
> [The Freudian model of Id, Ego and Super-Ego, and thus of the Oedipus, cannot be applied, because the fascist, in fact, has never achieved the separation from the mother, and has never constructed an Ego in the Freudian sense of the term. The fascist is the 'not-yet-completely-born'. He is not a psychopath; he has achieved a

5 On Aue's and, more interestingly, Littell's irony, see Boisseleau 2010: 277–298.

> partial separation, he is a social being, he talks, he writes, he acts in the world (unfortunately often in an effective way), he even attains power. In order to succeed, he has built or has had something else build – through discipline, training, physical exercise – an exteriorized Ego that takes the form of a 'carapace', a 'muscular armory'. This remains inside, where the fascist has no access to it, all the urges, his desiring functions, completely shapeless because he is incapable of objectivation. But the Ego-carapace is never completely sealed, it is very fragile; it only holds together thanks to its external supports: school, the army, even prison. In periods of crisis, it becomes fragmented, and the fascist risks being overwhelmed by his uncontrollable desiring productions, the 'dissolution of personal boundaries'. In order to survive, he externalizes what threatens him from the inside, and all the dangers thus take for him two forms, intimately connected with one another: the feminine and the liquid [...].]

Based on this portrait of the fascist as someone in desperate need of 'an exteriorized ego', Aue is both a typical and an atypical fascist. Like Theweleit's fascist, Aue is tormented by nightmares involving liquid and scatological fantasies and his discomfort with the tasks he has to carry out manifests itself in violent diarrhoea that turns into constipation after the war. The social and political contradictions of his character start to emerge after Stalingrad and reach their climax in the 'Air' chapter. The condition of siege (from the Latin *obsidere*) makes Stalingrad 'an obsessed city' (*KO*: 386), the inevitable place for Aue's insanity to start manifesting itself violently. On the other hand, Aue openly embraces this obsession for the humid and the feminine, as evidenced by his desire to be a woman like his sister, Una, who, however, accuses him of still being a child (*KO*: 486).

Max Aue's calm acceptance of his sexual peculiarity contradicts the intimidating masculinity of Theweleit's fascist. For this reason, it is inappropriate to consider Aue's depravation as a metaphor for the moral depravation of Nazism, as Samuel Moyn does (2012: 132). Aue does not indulge in acts of sadism. His sexuality does not compensate for an internal weakness, he does not try to create master–slave relationships with his lovers and he is not sexually aroused by the idea of killing his victims (Levéel 2010: 143). This contradiction, like Aue's intellectualism and bilingualism, allows him to critically examine the reality around him and makes him seem more sensitive than we would expect based on our usual perception of common fascists.

A German Orestes

Littell models the structure of *The Kindly Ones* on the early nineteenth-century novel and the modern novel. However, the book is littered with references to literary modernism. As well as meeting Céline and Jünger, Aue reads Blanchot's *Faux Pas* [lit. *False Steps*] (1943) and the use of the expression 'pineal eye' is a clear homage to Bataille's theories. Littell, listing his sources, mentions the classics of literary modernism – Samuel Beckett, Blanchot, Bataille, Robert Musil (Littell and Millet 2008: 24). Moreover, the main feature of literary modernism that can be observed in the text is the structural importance of myth.

Myth is important for modernist poetics as it represents an attempt to close the 'ontological gap between event and meaning'. Myth gathers, conserves and condenses a series of sometimes incompatible but yet coexisting meanings (Gould 1981: 6). In the works of some of the most important modernist authors, including Ezra Pound, Saint-John Perse, H. D., Virginia Woolf, T. S. Eliot, James Joyce and Thomas Mann, myth gives deeper meaning to narrative and symbolism and serves to trigger latent meanings. In other words, myth highlights the lack of authenticity in the contemporary world and the persistence of an archetypical pattern (Dei 2015: 78). In *Ulysses, Order and Myth*, T. S. Eliot defines the *mythical method*, arguing that the reuse of myth by Joyce succeeds 'in manipulating a continuous parallel between contemporaneity and antiquity' and that the mythical method 'is simply a way of controlling, of ordering, of giving a shape and a significance to the immense panorama of futility and anarchy which is contemporary history' (Eliot 1923: 201). As Eric Gould notes, to say that myth is a structure does not simply mean that novelists are free to steal, rewrite or juxtapose classic stories because they are worthy of being told again; rather, they find themselves stuck with the logic of mythical thinking every time they try to make sense of their material (Gould 1981: 137). The modernist myth is therefore a source of discipline, illumination and order (Donoghue 1997: 211).

White outlines two characteristics of what he calls the 'mythological novel': first, 'that the mythological parallel is suggested as an analogy or contrast to the contemporary world in which the main events of the novel occur' and, second, 'that the parallel is an extended one and could be described as a motif' (White 1971: 7). There is no doubt that these two formal characteristics can be identified in both *Ulysses* and *The Kindly Ones*. In this sense, there is an undeniable analogy between the way in which myth is adopted by Littell and the way in which it is adopted by Joyce. What differs, however, is Littell's relationship with myth, which alters the meaning of this reprise. As with Vollmann's deployment of myth, there is an unbridgeable distance between the modernist appropriation of myth and Littell's. In *The Kindly Ones*, the use of myth does not recall some absolute, metahistorical meaning, in which the author can no longer believe, but which has an eminently argumentative function, as if part of a metaphor. Whilst the modernist mobilization of myth looks to anthropological works like James Frazer's *The Golden Bough* or psychoanalytical works, like those of Carl Gustav Jung and Károly Kerényi – who connect mythical structures to the basic behavioural and psychic structure of man – Littell approaches myth through its secular form: tragedy.

At the same time, Littell's utilization of myth is not driven by the parodying motivations of postmodernism. The postmodernist use of myth is characterized by an ironic approach that signals a writer's disenchantment with epistemology. In the work of authors like Julio Cortázar, Thomas Pynchon, Paul Auster and David Foster Wallace,[6] mythical content is part of a broader parody of our capacity to know the world and myth's hermeneutic value is explicitly ridiculed. This is not the case in *The Kindly Ones*. In Littell's novel, myth is employed in a serious manner to draw parallels between Aue's personal life and the Holocaust, and is never the object of parody or irony. What I am trying to suggest is that Littell's reprise of myth is essentially post-postmodern. It does not replicate the modernist faith in a metaphysical order that is opposed to the chaos of contemporary society, but yet it represents an integral part of the novel's structure.

6 For critiques of the use of myth in the first two authors' works, see Hocevar (2012: 107–118) and Monballieu (2012: 131–144). Auster does not use an actual myth, but rather the 'myth' of Don Quixote, which is used to structure the first novella of the *New York Trilogy*, 'City of Glass', in a way that replicates the way Joyce uses the Odyssey. On this topic, see Ciccarello di Blasi (1995). For critiques of Wallace, see Ercolino 2015: 150–153.

The title of *The Kindly Ones* reminds us of the myth of Orestes, which appears in the *Oresteia* by Aeschylus. Aue mirrors Orestes because he kills his mother and her lover (whose name, Aristide, is an anagram of Atrides) in order to vindicate his father, whom they had declared dead and who was, like Agamemnon, a famously ferocious soldier. Descriptions of Aue's mother parallel the descriptions of Clytemnestra in Aeschylus' tragedy. She is more determined and resolute than her lover, even showing her breast to her son while he is killing her (967–968). Aue's incestuous relationship with his sister also replicates the ambiguous relationship between Orestes and Electra, although it is said to be explicitly modelled on *Una and Monos* by Edgar Allan Poe (Raciti 2013: 18) and not, as Georges Nivat suggests, on Nabokov's *Ada* (Nivat 2007: 56), which Littell detests (Littell and Millet 2007: 20). Other possible inspirations could be Albert Camus's *Caligula* (Levéel 2010: 151) or Musil's *Der Mann ohne Eigenschaften* [*The Man Without Qualities*] (Nivat 2012: 19–31). Moreover, Littell sets part of the novel in Crimea, a region famously connected to the saga of the Atrides by the sacrifice of Iphigenia and classically known as Tauris.

The other figure who mirrors the myth of Orestes is Thomas, Aue's close friend, whom Brasillach refers to as his Pylades (*KO*: 57). Thomas stands by Aue throughout all the difficulties he faces and incites him to act. In the same way, Pylades pronounces his only line to convince Orestes of the necessity of the matricide.[7] Thomas's aid unfortunately causes Aue to enrol in the SS. He remains present throughout the novel, helping Aue and making suggestions. Thomas's instinct for career reveals his most diabolical traits: 'my friend had a strange and infallible genius for finding himself in the right place not at the right time, but just before; so that he seemed every time as if he had always been there, and that the ups and downs of bureaucratic precedence did nothing but catch up with him' (*KO*: 59). He is an almost supernatural figure because his capacity to recover from a wound seems unnatural to Aue (*KO*: 411–412), just as it seems unnatural to him

7 'Orestes: "Pylades, what am I to do? Shall I respect my mother, and not kill her?". Pylades: "Where henceforth shall be the oracles of Loxias declared at Pytho, and the covenant you pledged on oath? Count all man your enemies rather than the gods!"' (Aeschylus 2014: 155, vv. 899–903).

that Thomas has parents. Thomas's surname, of course, is Hauser: it would not have seemed strange if, like Kaspar Hauser, his origins were unknown.

The novel concludes with Max Aue killing Thomas and stealing his false documents, which will allow him to escape to France. Thomas, like Una, is Aue's double (Fusillo 1998: 25), but he is a demonic one: 'thus does the devil expand his kingdom', Max comments when Thomas convinces him to join the Einsatzgruppe in Ukraine (*KO*: 60). Una and Thomas represent two opposite aspects of Aue's personality: respectively, discomfort with the world in which he lives and the tasks he has to carry out and his cynical obedience and adherence to völkisch societal norms. The presence of two doubles of the protagonist, the feminine Una and the demonic Thomas, is important not only in relation to the mythological parallel, but also (as we will see) in relation to the novel's reflection on the very nature of Nazi anti-Semitism.

Most significantly, Aue is tormented by the Erinyes, the 'kindly ones' of the title, personified by Clemens and Weser, the detective duo investigating Aue on suspicion of matricide. Clemens is a suggestive name ('benevolent' in Latin) and the two are described, in a reappropriation of the traditional iconography of the Erinyes, as a couple of bulldogs (*KO*: 800). Their persistence in persecuting Aue is somewhat irrational, insofar as they continue even after the official end of the investigation and during the catastrophic fall of Berlin. Ironically, as noted by Dominick LaCapra, the two detectives have the same names as two infamous Nazi criminals (LaCapra 2013: 102).

Littell mobilizes myths from both Aeschylus' *Oresteia* and Sophocles' *Electra*, rather than just one of them, as Mercier-Leca suggests (2007: 47). Although the novel does not include the actual moment of Aue's judgement (Aeschylus's *Oresteia* concludes with Orestes' judgement), the Erinyes are physically present in the novel, whereas in *Electra* they are not. Other important sources are Seneca's *Thyestes* and *Agamemnon*, relevant due to the political meaning of the myth of the Atrides and its abundance of gory details. The ubiquity of this myth in German theatre is also significant, since it takes place at the dawn of the recovery of the classics (Turato 2014: 153) and in Hofmannsthal (340), and also because, among the ruins of Berlin, in Hauptmann's work (497). I would not take into consideration the myth of Oedipus, which Wladimir Troubetzkoy (2010: 19–30) and Pauline de

Tholozany (2010: 197–212) believe should be substituted with the myth of Orestes. They argue that, like Aue, the figure of Oedipus merges the political novel, the family novel and themes of incest and parricide (Troubetzkoy 2010: 25); however, there are too many references to the *Oresteia* to substitute it with another entirely different myth.

There is a text that, more than any other, isolates the conceptual centre of the myth of Orestes: *Faux Pas* by Maurice Blanchot, which is even mentioned in the novel. Blanchot highlights the core of Orestes' dilemma:

> Orestes makes himself guilty by obeying. He is not master of his crime. He is only the indispensable link in the chain of infamies. [...] The young righter of wrongs, before this insoluble situation that, whatever he does, whether he abstains or whether he kills, transforms him into a guilty man, does not lament over his undeserved fate. He submits to it but he accepts it. The entire drama of *The Libation Bearers*, the preparation for crime, the son's cry to his father, signifies only the ever-deepening acquiescence in the bloody act of vengeance, Orestes' effort to change himself on his own in this night of evil and horror that Agamemnon's death represents – in short Orestes' will to enter into his own death. (Blanchot 2011: 59)

Blanchot describes how a crime may be committed simply by obeying the superior and inescapable will of the god of reason. If we apply this rationale to *The Kindly Ones*, we can observe that Max Aue's crime of matricide is depicted as an inevitable crime, committed on the basis of a warped perception of duty to his father. That being said, only on a very elementary level is the inevitable crime that of matricide. Matricide here is allegorical for the Holocaust: 'necessity, as the Greeks knew already, is not only a blind goddess, but a cruel one too' (*KO*: 589). When I referred to an indissoluble relation between the two parts of the novel (thematically, the narration of historical facts and Aue's psychic life; structurally, the traditional and the modernist novels), this is precisely what I meant. Just as Littell's mimetic effort reveals an infinite chain of events in which apparently no one is guilty, the reference to the myth of Orestes represents the evil committed as necessary and inevitable.

As Giuseppe Raciti points out, the real assassin in the *Oresteia* is Apollo (2010: 72), who orders Orestes to commit matricide and promises him forgiveness. As Pylades says: 'count all man your enemies rather than the gods!' (Aeschylus 2014: 155, v. 903). Apollo is also the assassin in *The Kindly Ones*. I am not simply referring to the demonic and supernatural figures who push Aue towards increasingly wicked and criminal acts, like Thomas and Mandelbrod (Lermonier 2010: 38). Littell's effort is far more elegant and profound. Aue's characterization suggests that the root of Nazi evil is the rational spirit of the Enlightenment. The Holocaust, as I insisted in the introduction, is the most extreme product of European modernity and Littell's protagonist is extremely aware of that, as he repeatedly states:

> The destruction by our deeds of the people of Moses did not stem solely from an irrational hatred of Jews [...] but above all from a firm, well-reasoned acceptance of the recourse to violence to resolve the most varied social problems, in which, moreover, we differed from the Bolsheviks only by our respective evaluations of the categories of problems to be resolved [...]. In Europe at least, from the eighteenth century onward, all the distinct solutions to the various problems – public torture for criminals, exile for the contagiously ill (leprosarium), Christian charity for the imbeciles – converged, under the influence of the Enlightenment, toward a single type of solution, applicable to all cases and infinitely variable: institutionalized imprisonment, financed by the State, a form of inner exile, if you like, sometimes with pedagogical pretentions, but above all with a practical finality [...]. But then why, you might ask today, the Jews? What do the Jews have in common with your lunatics, your criminals, your contagious? Yet it's not hard to see that, historically, the Jews constituted themselves as a 'problem', by wanting to remain apart at all costs. (*KO*: 669–671)

This passage echoes Foucault's theories (see also Littell and Nora 2007: 38 and Savattieri 2008: 242), as well as the sense of fury that, long before Foucault, characterized Faust as one of the most iconic symbols of the ambiguity of modern science and development. Indeed, this passage illustrates how a 'desire for *development*' (Berman 1982: 39) and 'the drive to create a homogeneous environment, a totally modernized space' (68) move Faust to kill Baucis and Philemon.

Littell's thesis is historically founded and coherent with several interpretations of the Holocaust as a historical phenomenon. If we consider European history between the two wars, it is clear that conservative and anti-democratic doctrines were more popular than democratic policies (Mazower 1999: 3–4) and that the myth of a 'pure nation' (41) was the theoretical basis for territorial distribution after the Great War, even for liberal democracies. This anxious quest for purity coincided with the extensive diffusion of genetics policies on the home front. The Third Reich was but one of the countries that adopted forced sterilizations and other coercive methods of population control (77–105) and even the most extreme of these policies were widely supported (xii–xiii).

In his important study *Modernity and the Holocaust*, Zygmunt Bauman warns against considering the Holocaust as significant only for Jews and simply counting it among the many massacres pervading European and world history (Bauman 1989: 1–3). For Bauman, the Holocaust represents a paradigmatic case of modernity's capacity for destruction and dehumanization; European anti-Semitism itself does not constitute a satisfactory explanation for the Holocaust, which would be inconceivable without Enlightenment thought and industrial modernity. Bauman argues that the Holocaust does not represent the emergence of the dark tendencies of human nature, nor does it contradict the motivations and outcomes of human civilization thus far. Rather uncomfortably, the Holocaust is historically coherent with human civilization and represents a consequence of modernity: 'The Hobbesian world of the Holocaust did not surface from its too-shallow grave, resurrected by the tumult of irrational emotions', he argues, but rather 'arrived [...] in a factory-produced vehicle, wielding weapons only the most advanced science could supply, and following an itinerary designed by scientifically managed organization' (Bauman 1989: 13).[8]

Whilst capitalist modernity builds a world in which the old ethnic and caste identities dissolve and change, nationalism functions as a separate space in which these differences are still clear, insofar as nations derive their identities from distinguishing themselves from other nations. According to Bauman, as a nation without a state, Jews were never able to fight using the means of the nation-state and therefore represented in the minds of their enemies physical corruption in the healthy body of the nation (Bauman

8 Universality, extra-temporality and extra-territoriality were defined as characteristic of 'the Jew', which made him or her an easy target for propaganda. Jews were codified as empty vessels able to incarnate – depending on the occasion – the essence of capitalist or Bolshevik cosmopolitanism, the refractoriness of adherence to the nation-state or the cowardice of not having a nation to defend (Bauman 1989: 41; see also Fritz 2011: 4–5).

1989: 35).[9] In the context of the equalization of citizens in terms of the law and the neutralization of religious differences, anti-modern thought reacts by re-codifying the Jew as no longer physically separate (inhabitants of the ghetto), but biologically different: 'the distinctiveness of the Jews had to be rearticulated and laid on new foundations, stronger than human powers of culture and self-determination' (Bauman 1989: 59). This is the foundation of the pseudo-scientific notion of race.

Paradoxically, despite progressing from pre- and anti-modern ideas, the extermination of Jews cannot be conceived outside of the context of modernity. The nation-state and the notion of scientific racism are modern, like the means used to practically eliminate Jews. As recognizably modern as the discourses and technologies that facilitated the Holocaust may be, its unprecedented meaning lies in the notion that extermination was no longer a method of conquering a land or to impose someone's will, but a purpose (Bauman 1989: 91; see also Traverso 1998: 304 and Diner 2000: 196–199). The Holocaust is inconceivable without the biopolitics of the nation-state. As Bauman sardonically remarks, 'modern genocide, like modern culture in general, is a gardener's job' (1989: 92).

The Holocaust required the synchronization of 'some ordinary factors of modernity which are normally kept apart' (Bauman 1989: 94). Some of these factors are incidental to modernity, but not in contradiction with it, such as racialized anti-Semitism and the exceptional state of war. Others are fundamentally modern: the presence of a strong centralized state, the ability to control an efficient bureaucracy and the moral neutrality of the majority of the population (94–95). The concentration

9 It would be an error to think that the statelessness of the Jews was only perceived as a problem by the Nazis: the same situation arose, for instance, in the Soviet Union. In 1934, 'the Soviet government established the Jewish Autonomous Region [that] was designated as the national homeland of the Soviet Jewry' (Weinberg 1998: 13). More generally, anti-Semitism has been (and indeed still is, even if it is sometimes disguised as anti-Israelism or anti-Zionism) a typical feature of anti-capitalistic literature. According to Michele Battini, the existence of an 'anti-Jewish anticapitalist paradigm' (2010: 3) can be backdated to the Catholic reaction to the French revolution and characterized European culture for more than a century. This paradigm identified the new market economy with finance and finance with the Jews.

of violence caused the hierarchization of work and therefore the replacement of *ethical* responsibility with *technical* responsibility (98), the dehumanization of bureaucratic objects and the fall of moral safeguards that these forms of dehumanization would ordinarily imply (98–116; see also Diner 2000: 165) – all of which are modern factors typical of the capitalist factory. The extermination of Jews, in sum, was enacted according to the logic of industrial modernity with the means, instruments and symbols that typically belong to it. As Traverso argues, the 'industrial methods of execution' used in Auschwitz closely resembled factory production and so did the architecture of the death camp and 'its position at the centre of an industrial zone and an important railway junction. Production and extermination were indistinguishable, as if massacre [...] was simply a particular form of production' (2003: 37).

The positivistic mechanisms that structured the process of extermination also shaped the language of the killing bureaucracy. As I underlined in the first part of this section, Littell's Greek tragedy portrays a world in which personal initiative is accorded little or no space. Just as the victims cannot avoid death, the perpetrators cannot avoid killing. In this sense, Littell's vision is profoundly deterministic, as reflected by the use of a specific lexicon comprised of formal yet vague terms. The monstrous dimensions of the bureaucratic machine, evident in the very language they speak, leads the men to their crimes:

> And perhaps that, at bottom, was the reason for our *Sprachregelungen*, quite transparent finally in terms of camouflage (*Tarnjargon*), but useful for keeping those who used these words and expressions – *Sonderbehandlung* (special treatment), *Abtransportiert* (transported onward), *Entsprechend Behandelt* (treated appropriately), *Wohnsitzverlegung* (change of domicile) or *Executivmassnahemen* (executive measures) – between the sharp points of their abstraction. This tendency spread to all our bureaucratic language, our *Burokratische Amtsdeutch*, as my colleague Eichmann would say: in correspondence, in speeches too, passive constructions dominated: 'it has been decided that ...', 'the Jews have been conveyed to the special treatment', 'this difficult task has been carried out', and so things were done all by themselves, no one ever did anything, no one acted, they were actions without actors, which is always reassuring, and in a way they weren't even actions, since by the special usage that our National Socialist language made of certain nouns, one managed, if not completely to eliminate verbs, at least to reduce them to the state of useless (but nonetheless decorative) appendages, and that way, you did without even action, there were only

> facts, brute realities, either already present or waiting for their inevitable accomplishment, like the *Einsatz*, or the *Einbruch* (the breakthrough), the *Verwertung* (the utilization), the *Entpolonisierung* (the de-Polonization), the *Ausrottung* (the extermination). (*KO*: 631)

The Nazi imperatives of order and purity are inevitably frustrated by reality and by their own inconsistency. In *The Kindly Ones*, this frustration is represented by the long digressions detailing dull bureaucratic processes, the practical and physical difficulties of carrying out extermination and Aue's nervous breakdown.

The task dictated by Apollo, behind whose 'cold, calm, inhuman beauty' (*KO*: 500) Max Aue hides, turns into a terrible nightmare. With regard to the matricide, it is significant that Littell's protagonist commits the crime in state of unconsciousness and never admits to being the assassin. The crime is committed when he is not able to control himself and is therefore guided by his most obscure passions. How can we not recall, in this context, Hitler's famous sleepwalking metaphor? Like Bolaño and Vollmann, Littell invokes a sleepwalker to suggest the mediumistic nature of fascism and its capacity to rouse the enthusiasm of the masses as if by hypnotism. At the same time, the portrait of the Holocaust as an apparently inevitable event, culturally and linguistically, creates a parallel between Aue's individual crime and the collective crime that was committed in that period.

In light of all that we have discussed, it would be difficult to classify Littell's use of the myth as experimental. While the twentieth century novel could be defined as an anti-novel because the reader does not follow a clear and consequential plot with a beginning and an end, instead wandering aimlessly in a fictional universe (Di Giacomo 1999: 121), *The Kindly Ones* contains frequent moments of oneiric delirium. The chapter 'Air', for example, is structured in a chronologically and topographically precise manner. Even in those moments when Littell's prose abandons itself to something similar to a stream of consciousness, as in the pages on Himmler's discourse of 6 October 1943 (*KO*: 663–672), it is still clear, controlled and lucid. In the commentary on Himmler's discourse, the lack of punctuation across several pages does not make Aue's reasoning more difficult to follow.

'A Real Morality Play'

It is necessary now to summarize the different arguments I have made thus far and attempt to give them a coherent meaning. In order to understand why Littell wrote a despairing and provocative novel like *The Kindly Ones*, we must consider why he chose to thematize the Second World War and why he chose a perpetrator as his protagonist.

The narration of the Holocaust has, for decades, been dominated by witnesses and their heirs (and rightly so). However, *The Kindly Ones* does not belong to 'the era of the witness', as Annette Wieviorka has called it (1998). It is a historical novel in which the protagonist is a fictional witness. The reader is well aware of the protagonist's fictionality and cannot mistake Aue for a real person. New York-born Littell is not a Holocaust survivor, nor is he the son or grandson of one (Luzzato 2008: 222; Tirinanzi De Medici 2012: 190). Although he did not personally experience the tragedies he narrates, Littell chooses to exploit the emotive weight that develops around these tragedies. As I have argued, the Holocaust was not a massacre amongst many others, but the defining massacre of the twentieth century. Just as the Second World War is *the* absolute war, the Holocaust is *the* absolute tragedy – the one with the greatest symbolic value.

In the context of this symbolic density, it might seem strange that the aim of Aue's discourse is to seduce us (Razinsky 2012b: 147). Everything in the book attempts to make us sympathize with the perpetrator, from the *captatio benevolentiae* (Delorme 2010: 33) that opens the novel, to Aue's continuous wit, to the literary references, to the character's exhibition of culture and contrition. When he exposes his rationale, it may sound reasonable for a moment, but we already know that it is false – or at least hypocritical. His excuses are not meant to persuade us, but to charm us with their wit and slyness. Aue is never entirely convinced that his reasoning can absolve him of his crimes and, unlike Orestes, he does not undergo judgement and therefore cannot expiate his crimes. Quite surprisingly, Édouard Husson criticizes *The Kindly Ones*' tendency to relativize Nazi crimes (Husson and Terestchenko 2007: 39). What he fails to notice is that it is not *The Kindly Ones* that relativizes the crimes, but Aue. By mistaking the author for the narrator, Husson misses Littell's point: to provide his narrator with preposterous excuses for his deeds. Whilst, on the one hand, these excuses remind readers that it is possible to compare the Holocaust and other more recent genocides, they insist, on the other hand, that we cannot merely accept such comparisons. Aue's relativization does not cancel out the enormity of his actions. He desperately attempts to justify himself and his anxiety as he provides excuses signals his own lack of faith in the possibility of redemption.

Max Aue's attack 'on differentiations of any kind' (Razinsky 2012a: 47) at the beginning of the book, during which he claims that Germany's only fault lies in losing the war and accuses every other Western country of committing similar crimes, may derive from credible theories and indeed helps Littell to convey a message about our contemporary world. But this reasoning does not absolve his narrator. *The Kindly Ones* portrays a deterministic world in which there is no place for individual choice. Even the language the characters speak encourages them to commit certain acts, as we have seen. However, determinism is not a justification for Max and he knows it: 'for the Greeks, chance played a part in the doings of men [...], but they did not consider that this chance diminished one's responsibility in any way' (*KO*: 592). In this sense, it is significant that Max is an unreliable narrator. In much the same way as his denial of the matricide he committed never succeeds in convincing readers of his innocence, his continuous justifications remain ineffective in suggesting his lack of guilt. But why, then, does Aue speak?

The choice of Aue as narrator is bound to the final message of *The Kindly Ones*. According to Littell's *The Dry and the Wet*, the aim of the fascist is to eliminate the Other, so that the Other will not pose a threat to the integrity of his body. It is notable then that, throughout the whole novel, Aue cannot help seeing himself in others. We now understand the importance of the appearance of Aue's two doubles, Una and Thomas, who constantly remind him, through their presence and distance, of the existence of contradictory parts of his character. He understands from the beginning of the genocide that the presence of the Other cannot be erased, no matter how inhuman the methods and how scrupulous the artificial distinctions between human beings may be:

> I came to the conclusion that the SS guard doesn't become violent or sadistic because he thinks the inmate is not a human being; on the contrary, his rage increases and turns into sadism when he sees that the inmate, far from being a subhuman as he was taught, is actually at bottom a man, like him, after all, and it's this resistance, you see, that the guard finds unbearable, this silent persistence of the other, and so the guard beats him to try to make their shared humanity disappear. Of course, that doesn't work: the more the guard strikes, the more he's forced to see that the inmate refuses to recognize himself as non-human. In the end, no other solution remains for him than to kill him, which is an acknowledgement of complete failure. (*KO*: 624)

Littell's idea, also expressed also in *The Dry and the Wet*, is that the Nazi hatred of Jews derives from them seeing in Jews some part of themselves that they want to hide (*KO*: 691–692). During hallucinations, Aue sees Hitler wearing the typical Jewish shawl (*KO*: 466–467) and sees his hated mother when he looks at himself in the mirror (*KO*: 514–515). We also learn that he is circumcised, as Jewish people traditionally are. Murder and death do not eliminate the presence of the Other. After having killed Thomas, Aue is forced to lose his own identity (Compagnon 2012: 125).

It is worth emphasizing Littell's point that the Nazis hated the Jews because they saw in them something they were trying to hide in themselves. But we, likewise, hate the Nazis because they incarnate the perversion of the allegedly positive ideals that regulate our modern society. We hate them not because they are necessarily different from us, but because we share the same roots and belong to the same cultural landscape. The unavoidability of the encounter with the Other, then, is also evident in another manner. In much the same way as Aue cannot help identifying with others, readers cannot help sympathizing and identifying with Aue. Laurent Binet, whom I will discuss in further detail later in this chapter, ironically suggests that Max is not the mirror of his time, but of ours. This is exact as Littell intended. Max's public, his 'human brothers' (*KO*: 3), are not the men who fought with him in Russia or other SS officers, but contemporary readers who are not asked to accept Aue's reasoning and ideas, but to be fascinated by them and, in the end, identify with him. This is clear in Aue's words on the opening page of the book: 'don't think I am trying to convince you of anything [...], your opinions are your own business' (*KO*: 11). In other words, Aue's opinions are not as important as Littell giving him a space in which to speak. For Littell, like Vollmann, the exhibition of moral problems and ambiguity is more important than explicit moral judgement.

Alongside the mimetic effort, the validatory means and the persuasiveness of Aue's speech, the decision to allow a perpetrator to speak and the decision to make him the protagonist of the most symbolic massacre in European history encourage the banal notion that Nazis are humans just like us and, even more terrifyingly, that we are men just like Nazis. We could have behaved like them in the same circumstances. In this sense, the value of Littell's novel is that it forces us to face what we are not willing to see on our own initiative. For this reason, it is significant that the author chooses to make the protagonist and the narrator coincide, thereby depriving himself of the opportunity to explicitly judge the actions and ideas in the novel. Littell deems his judgement as unimportant. What is important is that actions and ideas are respectively taking place and being expressed.

Comparisons and Oppositions

Since its publication, the problematic content and style of *The Kindly Ones* have caused controversy amongst literary critics and historians. Littell's choice to narrate from the perspective of a perpetrator has often been denounced, either because its implications have not been fully understood or because it is considered unacceptable. I have already mentioned that there are entire books dedicated to criticizing Littell's novel. However, it is more interesting to note that Littell's approach has influenced other writers, encouraging both imitation and repudiation. In this section of the chapter, I discuss two books, Laurent Binet's *HHhH* (*HHhH*) and Giorgio Falco's *The H Twin* (*HT*), whose approaches could be considered the opposite of Littell's approach in the sense that the authors challenge the sensational and sometimes kitsch fictionality of *The Kindly Ones*. These authors prioritize strict historical accuracy (Binet) and detachment (Falco). Although their books were not written as responses to *The Kindly Ones*, they interact with Littell's novel (which is even mentioned in *HHhH*). It is useful to compare Littell's novel with

Falco's and Binet's books in order to highlight an alternative approach and its potential flaws.

'What Could Be More Vulgar Than an Invented Character?' Laurent Binet's Metafiction

Laurent Binet's *HHhH* (an acronym for the German *Himmlers Hirn heißt Heydrich* [Himmler's brain is called Heydrich]) is an account of Operation Anthropoid, which involved the assassination of Reinhard Heydrich, who was head of the RSHA, the SS secret service, and Reichsprotektor of Bohemia and Moravia, by Jozef Gabčík and Jan Kubiš. It is a metafictional account, as the narrator[10] pieces together the history of the operation, the biographies of its protagonists and his own attempt to write it – indeed, the novel *is* this attempt, containing sections of narration, enumerations of historical sources, a critique of other fictional texts (including Littell's) that deal with this event and progressive corrections of information provided earlier in the text. As Carrard sums up, the narrator's intrusions are autobiographical, scholarly, metafictional, metanarrative, meta-novelistic, polemical and they serve to 'formulate hypotheses and acknowledge lacks' (2014: 188–190).

HHhH, in other words, is not simply a mixture of literary elements. It illustrates, instead, the process of constructing a novel through a narrator that reveals its construction and provides corrections to his own text during the process. It is clear, then, that the real subject of Binet's book is

10 I refer to a non-specified narrator to differentiate from the author because the novel never explicitly suggests there are coincidences between the two. Nevertheless, there are some biographical similarities between them, such as certain details of Binet's biography on the cover of the book that are reprised in the text: 'He completed his military service in Slovakia' ('Il a effectué son service militaire en Slovaquie'), the back of the French cover says. Van Kelly has written about an 'autofictional aura' ('aura autofictive') (Kelly 2013). I find this expression satisfactory since the author does not deny a possible coincidence with the narrator, nor does he insist on it, and as autofiction does not play a pivotal role in the novel. Binet himself simply refers to a 'fictional narrator' ('narrateur fictif') (2013).

not Operation Anthropoid, but rather the struggle of writing a truthful historical novel. For instance, the narrator of *HHhH* criticizes the film *Conspiracy* (*HHhH*: 7)[11] and explains how and where he collects his information, offering a biographical account of a visit to a museum (*HHhH*: 8). Again, instead of presenting a fixed fictional text, he offers different versions of events, correcting himself in his writing. Whilst Chapter 83 ends with the sentence 'at 9:00 a.m., the first German tank enters the city' (*HHhH*: 83), Chapter 84 opens with this remark: 'Actually I don't know if it was a tank that first entered Prague. The most advanced troops seem largely to have driven motorbikes with sidecars. So: at 9:00 a.m., German soldiers on motorbikes enter the Czech capital' (*HHhH*: 84). Such observations are a constant in the book:

> I have no evidence that Gabčík and Kubiš's clothes were provided by the British SOE (Special Operations Executive). In fact, it's more likely that this was dealt with by Moravec's Czech services. So there's no reason why the NCO who looks after them should be British. Oh, what a pain … (*HHhH*: 144)

This extract shows that Binet is not writing a historical novel ('if this were a novel …', *HHhH*: 176), but a metafictional one or, as he defines it, an *infranovel* (*HHhH*: 205).[12] His refusal to write a historical novel is motivated by a concern about the dangers of historical fiction about as complex matter as the resistance against Nazism. Binet attributes significant importance to realism, but it is not the same kind of realism as Littell's mimetic realism. Whereas Littell aims for plausibility, Binet claims to be aiming for truth. The narrator of *HHhH* is constantly worried about the risk of sounding fictional, and therefore false, since literary fiction – however effective and entertaining – cannot succeed in accurately rendering the truth of an event:

> Kundera implies that he feels a bit ashamed at having to name his characters. […] What could be more vulgar than to arbitrarily give – from a childish desire for

11 When referring to *HHhH*, the numbers will not indicate the pages but the chapters, because the pages of the British edition I am consulting are not numbered.

12 It is not clear what this term means. However, as 'roman' means 'novel' in French and 'infra' means 'between' in Latin/English, I assume that it is a variation on 'meta-novel'.

> verisimilitude or, at best, mere convenience – an invented name to an invented character? In my opinion, Kundera should have gone further: what could be more vulgar than an invented character? (*HHhH*: 1)

Not only is the invention of a character vulgar, but the use of a historical figure in a fictional novel enacts violence against historical truth (*HHhH*: 91).

This lack of faith in literature leads Binet to the creation of a sophisticated work of historiographic metafiction. This solution allows him to retain the reality of data and sources and the fictional narration, whilst the use of the narrator consistently signals the distance between reality and its reconstruction:

> There is nothing more artificial in a historical narrative than this kind of dialogue – reconstructed from more or less firsthand accounts with the idea of breathing life into the dead pages of history. [...] If my dialogues can't be based on precise, faithful, word-perfect sources, they will be invented. However, if that's the case, they will function not as a hypotyposis but as a parable. And just so there's no confusion, all the dialogues I invent (there won't be many) will be written like scenes from a play. A stylistic drop in an ocean of reality. (*HHhH*: 15)

Realism in *HHhH* is not synonymous with the ability to imitate another historical period and the actions of other people. Rather, it attempts to offer a precise account of historical sources, without literary invention. Binet explicitly refuses to use the mimetic model of the nineteenth-century historical novel, a model that is so pivotal in *The Kindly Ones* (*HHhH*: 13).

Curiously, Binet chooses historiographic metafiction not to undermine the truthfulness of historiography and counter the official narrations of the past, but to investigate whether literature is authoritative in its reconstruction of history. In postmodern historiographic metafiction, by contrast, literature is used to fill the gaps in official historical reconstructions and open new spaces for minority and marginal identities. Binet trusts his historical sources and when he contradicts them, he always does so on the basis of another source that he considers more reliable. History, for Binet, is knowable. It is literature that is put on trial. The meta-narrator is exploited precisely in order to signal the separation of invention and facts. Contrary to how it is viewed in postmodern historiographic metafiction, history is not a discourse, but a set of precise information and data, according to a positivist model (Bracher 2015: 100). Moreover, in Littell's novel (and also in Falco's), history is presented as an uncontrollable flow of events that involves masses of human beings on a vast stage, comparable in its uncontrollability to fate in Greek tragedy. Binet's narrator's obsession with Operation Anthropoid, on the other hand, reveals an idea of history that still, to an extent, adheres to the Rankean model of great men and decisive situations.

Although it does not share the ideological framework of historiographic metafiction, *HHhH* shares its hermeneutic limits and the metafictional frame is perhaps more interesting than its content. That is not to say that the story told is not fascinating or that Binet is unable to create narrative tension through his descriptions of the actions of the Czechoslovak agents. At the novel's climax, the narrator almost enters the story by relaying the events of the night using the chronological details of his own actions: 'Today is May 27, 2008. When the firemen arrive, about 8:00 a.m., they see SS everywhere and a corpse on the pavement' (*HHhH*: 250). The main flaw of Binet's historiographic metafiction is that the pre-eminent role of the narrator has the effect of distracting readers from the story of Operation Anthropoid, as the focus is constantly shifted towards how the novel is being written. At the same time, his obsession with reality (and not simply plausibility) prevents the creation of a realistic psychological portrait with which readers can interact, creating distance between characters and readers that inhibits sympathy. As Peter Tame argues, 'un des problèmes […] de l'approche de Binet, c'est l'importance accordée aux interrogations du narrateur, à la première personne du singulier' [one of the problems […] of Binet's approach is the importance given to the narrator's questions, in the first person] (Tame 2013). Littell, Tame continues, enacts something similar through his first-person narrator, but nevertheless creates a character and a narrative that fascinate readers. Binet, meanwhile, 'plus neutre et fade, risque de l'ennuyer avec ses tergiversations, ses spéculations et ses délibérations qui tournent principalement autour de faits historiques' [more neutral and bland, risks boring the reader with his procrastination, speculations, and discussion, which mainly concern historical facts] (Tame 2013).

Littell is directly critiqued in *HHhH* for the liberties he takes in his fictional reconstruction of the Second World War and the kitsch excesses of certain parts of it, a matter I have already discussed. Littell becomes representative of the lack of precision of the historical novel:

> I wonder how Jonathan Littell, in his novel *The Kindly Ones*, knows that Blobel had an Opel. If Blobel really drove an Opel, then I bow before his superior research. But if it's a bluff, that weakens the whole book. Of course it does! It's true that the Nazis were supplied in bulk by Opel, and so it's perfectly *plausible* that Blobel possessed, or used, a vehicle of that make. But *plausible* is not *known*. I'm drivelling, aren't I? When I tell people that, they think I'm mental. They don't see the problem. (*HHhH*: 189)

Such imprecision, in Binet's opinion, makes all the difference between his novel and Littell's as it signals a liberty of approach that undermines the fictional construction as a whole and its ambition to describe history truthfully.

Moreover, Binet's narrator also finds Littell guilty of having created a fictional account of the Holocaust, innerved with morbid details and hyper-literary references:

> A poster on an Internet forum expresses the opinion that Max Aue, Jonathan Littell's protagonist in *The Kindly Ones*, 'rings true because he is the mirror of his age.' What? No! He rings true (for certain, easily duped readers) because he is the mirror of *our* age: a postmodern nihilist, essentially. At no moment in the novel it is suggested that this character believes in Nazism. On the contrary, he displays an often critical detachment towards National Socialist doctrine – and in that sense, he can hardly be said to reflect the delirious fanaticism prevalent in *his* time. On the other hand, this detachment, this blasé attitude towards everything, this permanent malaise, this taste for philosophizing, this unspoken amorality, this morose sadism, and this terrible sexual frustration that constantly twists his guts ... but of course! How did I not see it before? Suddenly, everything is clear. *The Kindly Ones* is simply 'Houellebecq does Nazism'. (*HHhH*, 204)

I detailed earlier why an interpretation of Aue as an *impossible* Nazi is inaccurate. Binet, despite the vastness of his historical documentation, cannot escape the very naïve paradigm according to which the Nazis were all bloodthirsty idiots or ruthless animals. While Heydrich indeed fits this model, not all the men involved with the Nazi party, and not all members of the SS, do and I do not think it is particularly useful to falsify their character. A man such as Albert Speer, cultivated, doubtful regarding the purposes of the Reich and at the same time devoted to them, who also often appears in *HHhH*, has much more in common with Aue than with Heydrich. Moreover, the narrator's statement that nothing in the novel suggests that Aue truly believes in National Socialism is an utter misunderstanding of the text. Aue is not a fanatical Nazi (it is worth remembering that he joined the SS in order to avoid a scandal about his homosexuality), but he does believe in the propaganda of the Reich, as he shows in his conversations with Voss. He has doubts about the cultural processes of the Reich, but he also has faith in their purpose, as the whole episode of the Bergjuden demonstrates. Moreover, his psychological structure is coherent (up to a certain point) with that of the fascist, as outlined by Theweleit. In other words, Aue is not a likely Nazi (this is what allows him to work 'as a scanner'), but he is not implausible.

Nevertheless, it is true that Littell creates a character that, whether a likely Nazi or not, is most certainly not an everyman. It is precisely this choice, together with the notion that he is 'a mirror of our times', that allows Littell's readers to empathize with Aue and admire him and therefore be disturbed by this feeling of empathy. Binet's aim, on the other hand, is less subtle. His motivation in writing the book, as stated by the narrator, derives from his admiration of the two men who carried out Operation Anthropoid and his hatred towards Heydrich – a hatred often expressed through an abundance of insults and mockery. Binet opposes his admiration of Jan Kubiš and Jozef Gabčík with the 'decadence, mediocrity and superficial concerns of his own time' (Bracher 2016: 14). This mediocrity is encapsulated by the sensationalist murder of the collaborationist René Bousquet and, indeed, by the very success of *The Kindly Ones* (19). 'Those finding themselves adrift in an era devoid of substance and meaning naturally gravitate toward its drama and intensity', Nathan Bracher writes (2016: 19); such is the case for Binet.

I would argue that the main flaw of Binet's novel lies in this stylization. Readers know from the first page that the heroes are some of the most admirable people who ever lived and that the villains are despicable human beings. Their knowledge and understanding of the war, in relation to heroes and villains or victims and perpetrators, does not evolve throughout the novel. On the other hand, Littell has no interest in disapproving of the Holocaust, as he nevertheless obviously does. According to Walter Benn Michaels, 'Littell doesn't tell the reader what he already knows and doesn't seek to make him feel what he already feels' (Benn Michaels 2013: 923). Binet, by refusing to provide readers with a psychological recreation of some of his characters' thoughts, obtained through an imaginative effort, abandons the opportunity to say something more than what motivated readers could have found in a history book. In other words, while Littell *shows* the readers a disturbing and seductive portrait of someone they *could* have been, had they been born in a particular time and place, Binet simply *states* something that they already know and produces a distancing effect.

Although it is clever and entertaining, I would argue that Binet's novel fails to say anything significant about the Second World War or encourage readers to experience empathy and understanding. I stated above that *HHhH* is a novel that is more concerned with novel writing than with being a novel about the Second World War. It is precisely Binet's metafictional framework that prevents him from saying anything new or interesting about the war. Binet's choice of historiographic metafiction ultimately employs a problematic yet highly fertile literary device as an excuse not to reconstruct psychological portraits of his heroes insofar as the narrator does not even interact with his material by problematizing it. In the story of Operation Anthropoid, as told in *HHhH*, there are no ambiguities, nor are there any experiences that can be (re)made, and the novel simply provides a testimony of heroism that is already contained in history books.

Giorgio Falco's 'Objective Piety'

Giorgio Falco's approach to the historical novel is different from Binet's and lacks Binet's polemic intent. Nevertheless, I argue that there are similarities between the two, especially when considered in opposition to the model of *The Kindly Ones*. Specifically, just as Binet avoids empathy and identification by using a metafictional narrator, Falco chooses distancing and alienating textual strategies in order to prevent readers from participating in the drama of the protagonists (mediocre everymen) and to expose how fascism was in line with the goals of capitalism by focusing mainly on objects and commercial goods.

Before I proceed to analyse *The H Twin*, it is worth devoting some space to an explanation of why I chose this novel, of the many novels on the Second World War published in Italy, and, more generally, why I have not included a wider perspective on Italian narratives in this book. In Italy, narratives of the Second World War have peculiar features compared to the novels I have discussed so far. Seventy years after its end, the narration of the Second World War in Italy still predominantly coincides with the narration of anti-fascism, the occupation and the Resistance. It comes as no surprise that the Resistance continues to play such a pivotal role in Italian public memory. As a historical phenomenon, it has been read as a moment of revenge for a people oppressed by a twenty-year-long dictatorship and as a moment of atonement for that dictatorship's crimes.

Furthermore, since the aftermath of the war, the Resistance has been at the heart of the majority of the narrations of the war, although the partisan war was fought by a very small fraction of those who took part in the conflict. Specifically, the narration of the Resistance gained pre-eminence over the experience of fascist fighters of the RSI (Italian Social Republic, the collaborationist northern Italy) and, less obviously, that of the Italian soldiers abandoned by the government after the 8 September 1943 armistice (Foot 2011: 111–114). The canon of postwar Italian literature centres on Resistance novels such as Elio Vittorini's *Uomini e no* [*Men and Not Men*] (1945), Italo Calvino's *Il sentiero dei nidi di ragno* [*The Path to the Nest of Spiders*] (1946), Cesare Pavese's *La casa in collina* [*The House on the Hill*] (1948), Renata Viganò's *L'Agnese va a morire* [*And Agnese Chose to Die*] (1949), and Beppe Fenoglio's *I ventitrè giorni della città di Alba* [*The Twenty-Three Days of the City of Alba*] (1952) and the posthumous *Il partigiano Johnny* [*Johnny the Partisan*] (1968) (Cooke 2011: 31–34 and 49–52). On the contrary, a memoir dedicated to the experience of a deported Italian Jewish writer, *Se questo è un uomo* [*If This Is a Man*] by Primo Levi (1947), initially met with a rather cold reception, while the first major literary work on the withdrawal of Italian soldiers was published only thirty years after the war (Stefano D'Arrigo's *Horcynus Orca*, 1975; Alfano 2000: 10–15).

More than other European countries, Italy's memory of the war is a peculiar 'divided memory', to quote the suggestive title of John Foot's essay (2011). The Resistance functions as an essential space for the country's symbolic reconstruction after twenty years of dictatorship and thus it has been variously reclaimed and diminished for political purposes. Nevertheless, despite some controversial moments[13] and the quarrel between the various movements of the anti-fascist fight (socialist, communist, Christian), the Resistance was the pivotal moment in Italian public memory of the Second World War during the First Republic (1948–1992), especially in light of the presidential election of the anti-fascist and former partisan Sandro Pertini (1978). However, this Resistance literary tradition began to change, both culturally and politically, in the early 1990s. In 1991 and 1992, two books were published which challenged the conventional reading of the Resistance, Claudio Pavone's *Una guerra civile* [*A Civil War*] (1991) and Romolo Gobbi's *Il mito della Resistenza* [*The Resistance Myth*] (1992). While the first is a reading of the Resistance as a series of wars (a patriotic war against the Germans, a civil war between North and South and between different political ideologies and a class war), rather than a single, coherent one, the latter is a controversial attempt to debunk the 'mythological' axioms of the public memory of the Resistance. Moreover, the action of right-wing governments and indeed the rise to power of Alleanza Nazionale [National Alliance] (a direct heir of the Fascist Party) in the 1990s and 2000s were perceived by many as undermining the values of the Resistance.[14] Nowadays, the post-ideological nature of the Movimento 5 Stelle [Five-Star Movement] often leads its members to equate fascism and anti-fascism.

13 The most notable of which were the arrest and trial of 3,500 communist partisans in 1949 and the Tambroni affair in 1960 (the attempt of the Christian Democracy party to form a government with the Neo-Fascist Party). See Cooke 2011: 42–44 and 84–86.

14 It is worth mentioning, on this subject, the controversial revisionist work of Giampaolo Pansa, who was widely supported and sponsored by right-wing newspapers (Cooke 2011: 177–186).

In a national literature in which the concept of *impegno* [political and social commitment][15] is so historically pre-eminent, the vast majority of recent Italian literature about the Second World War still focuses on the centrality of the anti-fascist experience. Such is the case in novels like *Storie di uno scemo di guerra* [*Memories of a Madman at War*] (2005) by Ascanio Celestini, *Dove finisce Roma* [*Where Rome Ends*] (2012) by Paola Soriga, *Partigiano inverno* [*Partisan Winter*] (2012) by Giacomo Verri, *In territorio nemico* [*In Enemy Territory*] (2013) by the SIC group (Scrittura Industriale Collettiva), *Il tempo migliore della nostra vita* [*The Best Time of Our Life*] (2015) by Antonio Scurati and *Rosso nella notte bianca* [*Red in the White Night*] (2016) by Stefano Valente, to mention only a few prominent recent Italian narratives about the Second World War. To a certain extent, this is also true of thematically and narratively more elaborate texts, such as *Le rondini di Montecassino* [*The Swallows of Montecassino*] (2010) by Helena Janeczek and *Point Lenana* (2013) by Wu Ming 1 and Roberto Santachiara, that make strong use of meta- and autofictional devices, as well as a complex narrative framework. These novels attempt, emphatically and often by directly referring to the literary tradition of the Resistance, to create a parallel between the anti-fascist experience and the present political struggles.

Contemporary Italian literature appears to still depend on a national literary model and state-specific political controversy. Such dependence has led me to exclude these kinds of texts from this book on the grounds that they are not coherent with the working framework of a global dimension of the novelistic form and the representation of the Second World War. Moreover, even the attempts of certain novels to situate the Italian national experience in a transnational framework tend to result in a kitsch exploitation of the Second World War. In Janeczek's novel, for instance, the transnational Allied effort in the Battle of Montecassino is paralleled with the present-day protests against Silvio Berlusconi. Indeed, those novels that avoid focusing on the Resistance are not worthy of extensive

15 On this topic, see Burns 2001. As Burns shows, the seminal concept of *impegno* was still very much present in the apparently politically and socially detached 1980s and 1990s.

consideration. Giuseppe Genna's *Hitler* (2008) is a fictional biography of the Führer, innerved with mythological elements and literary references that ultimately result in the creation an inadvertent parody of Vollmann's *Europe Central*. Enrico Brizzi's mainstream alternate history, *L'inattesa piega degli eventi* [*The Unexpected Turn of the Events*] (2008) – the first novel in a trilogy, followed by *La nostra guerra* [*Our War*] (2009) and *Lorenzo Pellegrini e le donne* [*Lorenzo Pellegrini and Women*] (2010) – reprises the postmodern and science-fictional device of uchronia. Despite Brizzi's ambition to create a portrait of contemporary fascist Italy that mirrors the real republican history (full of references to Berlusconi's Italy; see Brioni 2015: 305–318 and Brioni and Comberiati 2019: 205–231) and thus to reveal the continuity of fascism in the present age, the result is rather stereotypical and stylistically shallow.

The one exception that I have been struck by in this literary landscape is *The H Twin* by Giorgio Falco (2014), one of the few contemporary Italian novels that evades the paradigm of the Resistance and the most accomplished of them. Falco's novel is even more interesting as the requirement of sociopolitical commitment (so typical of Italian literature) is present not only thematically, but also stylistically. Falco exploits the formal expedients of the Italian *neo-avanguardia* in order to create a sense of detachment in readers and to provide them with a critical reading of their present. This sense of detachment is what distinguishes it from Littell's *The Kindly Ones* and allows me to compare it with Binet's *HHhH*.

In *The H Twin*, Falco extends the focus of the traditional paradigm of the Resistance thematically and geographically, drawing a parallel between the Nazi dictatorship and contemporary consumerist society. Falco locates the origins of contemporary neo-capitalist economies in the mass policies of twentieth-century dictatorships, as evidenced by Leo Longanesi's epigraph to the book, 'Il fascismo era lo spirito, UPIM era il corpo' [fascism was the spirit, UPIM was the body] (UPIM was one of the first Italian department stores and was part of the Rinascente group). The protagonists of the novel are the Hinner family from Bockburg, a fictional Bavarian town north of Munich. The family consists of Maria and Hans, the parents, and twin sisters Hilde and Helga. Hans Hinner, a journalist, is an early member of the Nazi party. The novel follows him from Bavaria to Merano (Alto

Adige), where he buys a house for his terminally ill wife, and then onto Milan, where he escapes to after the war, and finally to the Adriatic riviera, where he buys and runs a small hotel named the Hotel Sand.

The fortune of the Hinners is intertwined with the fortune of the Nazi party. Hans Hinner, 'un nazista piccolo piccolo' [a petty Nazi], as Roberto Saviano defines him (2014), who has occupied his profession and role in the party since 1929, benefits from Adolf Hitler's rise to power. Moreover, the true cause of his economic prosperity lies in his purchase of the house of his Jewish neighbours after the establishment of the Nuremberg Laws. The Hinner family witness the violence the Kaumann family (their neighbours) are subjected to by the SS without objection and then buy their heavily underpriced house and car. The properties that the Hinners buy increase in value because of the German success in the war. At the same time, the low price at which Hans buys a house in Merano is justified by the disproportionate success of the Italian and German military operations (Merano being in a German-speaking part of Italy that Germany aimed at annexing).

Traditionally, the family novel is geographically stable and chronologically various and the insistence on a precise and meaningful place, such as the family home or a town, balances the temporal vastness of the narration. In *The H Twin*, however, the continuous peregrinations of the Hinners signal both the transnational (and super-national) nature of capitalism and the evolution of one cultural and commercial system into another. As the writer Giorgio Vasta argues, *The H Twin* suggests that our way of living and thinking is a direct consequence of a totalitarian system (2014). Indeed, after the war, the rituals of mass consumerism substitute those of the mass party and the totalitarian state. National Socialism and its desire for alleged racial purity evolve into the models of the Rinascente, the first Italian chain of department stores and 'the new, great mother' ('la nuova grande madre') for whom Hilde works (*HT*: 179). Hilde is hired after passing medical exams and aesthetical evaluations, wears a uniform and is invited to suppress her German accent and speak 'un italiano sorridente e radiofonico' [a smiling, radio-like Italian] (*HT*: 180). In other words, the world of mass consumerism continues those processes of selection and uniformity that began during the fascist era. As Falco writes:

> Ci aiuta l'insorgenza di un anomalo disturbo della memoria. Il motto collettivo è qualcosa di simile a dimenticate in memoria di me. Le nostre azioni passate svaniscono, seppellite dagli stereotipi. Il Grande Male. La Belva Umana. Il Criminale Assoluto. Milioni di morti e siamo ancora qui, pronti a nuovi oggetti, a criteri di comportamento volti alla concupiscenza delle cose. Ridimensionata la visibilità dell'ideologia – ora diluita sotto ogni traccia – resta la volontà di vivere secondo quelle stesse dinamiche totalitarie applicate ai rapporti lavorativi e familiari. Possiamo fare e subire tutto, purché rimaniamo in una sfera economica, finanziaria. (*HT*: 215)
>
> [The rising of an anomalous memory problem proves helpful. The collective motto is, more or less, forget in remembrance of me. Our past actions disappear, submerged by stereotypes. The Great Evil. The Human Beast. The Absolute Criminal. Millions of people died and we are still here, ready for new products, for ways of behaving aiming at the lust for things. Despite the reduced visibility of ideology, which has been diluted in every respect, there is still the will to live according to the same totalitarian dynamics as they apply to work and family relationships. We can do and endure anything, as long as we remain in an economic, financial sphere.]

The character of Franco, Helga's boyfriend and later husband, suggests that entrepreneurship is intertwined with the abuse of others. Franco, who is compared to Mussolini when he first appears because of his emphatic gesturality (*HT*: 229), is a young and resourceful cook who convinces Helga that he should be hired in her father's hotel because he would be able to greatly improve the service. This is indeed what happens, since, once hired, Franco continuously demonstrates his economic shrewdness by inventing ways of saving on food whilst simultaneously creating the impression of higher-quality dishes, thus deceiving customers. In order for Franco to be hired, however, he and Helga have to get rid of the previous cook, so Helga hides three apples in her purse (it is these apples that appear on the cover of the novel) and informs her father of the cook's 'theft'. Hilda, who witnesses the misdeed, does not interfere with her sister's plan. Hans fires the woman and hires Franco and their collaboration improves the fortune of the hotel, showing how, once again, the Hinners' economic success is intrinsically wedded to deception and violence.

The evolution of National Socialism into capitalism and the continuity of two goods-oriented systems are also underlined by Falco's style, which maintains the formal experimentalism that characterized his previous books and collections of short stories, *Pausa caffè* [*Coffee Break*] (2004) and *L'ubicazione del bene* [*The Location of the Propriety*] (2009). *The H Twin* is stylistically characterized by its distancing effects and its insistence on the focalization of objects. Thus, the text enacts a *lateral* dislocation of the point of view (I will return to this term later). The distancing effects are mainly generated by the narrator's lack of emotional participation in the events of the plot, the neutral and unemphatic tone of the language, and the variety of the narrators.[16] Whilst a third-person perspective is adopted in the second part and the intermezzo, the first part is narrated from Hilde's point of view, though Hilde also reports events that she could not have witnessed, such as her birth. Moreover, the story of the Hinner family is interrupted by the insertion of exchanges by letter, pages of diaries and essays. Similarly, the focalization is always varied in order to disorientate readers and prevent them from getting attached to the characters and story. For instance, after the arrival of the Hinners in Merano, Falco devotes some pages to a digression on the work of Franz Lenhart, a commercial illustrator whose work depicts the satisfying happiness of a lively tourist resort. Thereafter, Falco moves the focalization of the story to a new, anonymous character inspired by Lenhart's work, simply introducing him with the words: 'abbiamo i tagliandi delle scommesse in tasca. Siamo l'uomo di Lenhart' [we have the betting slips in our pockets. We are the Lenhart man] (*HT*: 96). This approach shares similarities with Binet's metafictional framework, which creates a distance between readers and the characters of the story, and indeed opposes the seductive and philosophizing first-person narrator of Littell's text.

This distancing effect is augmented by the overwhelming presence of objects in the novel. Falco's attention is always focused on the inanimate goods that crowd the Hinner family's life. Not only is this focus intended to create a sense of realism in the story, as Falco carefully recreates the objects and their social function, but it distracts readers from the interior life of the characters. Indeed, objects are a central character in *The H Twin*. However, the opposite is also true. Characters are reduced to objects and deprived of interiority. Objects that are central in the novel include the properties

16 For further information on Falco's use of different narratorial voices, see Pennacchio 2020: 141–160.

bought and sold by the Hinners and the automobiles that signal the social and economic accomplishments and the progression of the family history. Hans buys an Opel Olympia out of envy of his Jewish neighbours, then, after they have been forced to leave, acquires their own Mercedes at a fraction of its value and, after the war, purchases a Volkswagen Beetle (Marsilio 2016). Similarly, the Rinascente where Hilde works is filled with objects, making it seem like a temple of contemporary consumerism. The Rinascente plays a pivotal role in the novel. It represents the first step towards Hilde's economic independence from her family and the beginning of a new life for the Hinners. At the same time, it constitutes a symbol of the continuing influence of fascism and consumerism. Not only was its name coined by Gabriele D'Annunzio, the proto-fascist intellectual, but the franchise continues to pursue the same social policies the regime initiated, including 'attività dopolavoristiche [...] iniziate durante il fascismo e pervenute intatte in questi anni italiani' [post-work activities [...] that began during Fascism and continued unchanged into those years] (*HT*: 186).

There is neither a personal nor an emotional bond between these objects and the protagonists. The food served to the patrons of Hotel Sand is not treated as a delicious product of shared human labour that is capable of providing joy and bringing people together. Instead, it is represented as an economic resource with which to generate maximum profit. In the pages in which we are introduced Franco, for example, his daily work of cleaning and cutting eighty chickens is described as being reminiscent of an assembly line due to its precision and rapidity (*HT*: 235–236). Similarly, the policies of the Rinascente metaphorically transform Hilde into a serialized object. Through capitalist labour, she becomes an unproblematic and standardized image of femininity, deprived of individual meaning and agency:

> Potrei essere la figlia, la sorella, la cugina, la nipote, la bambinaia di molte clienti, potrei essere la fidanzata, la compagna di banco, la giovane amante di molti clienti. Sono una commessa della Rinascente, la somma potenziale di tutto, e in verità niente di tutto questo. (*HT*: 179)
>
> [I could be the daughter, the sister, the cousin, the niece, the babysitter of many of my female clients, I could be the girlfriend, the classmate, the young lover of many of my male clients. I am a salesgirl at the Rinascente, the potential sum of everything, but in reality none of these things.]

Moreover, the houses that the Hinners possess are not homes, but spaces full of objects, ready to be sold for money or better properties. As Hans argues when his wife claims to already be in love with the house they want to buy in Merano, 'com'è possibile innamorarsi di una casa?' [how can you fall in love with a house?] (*HT*: 129). Even Hotel Sand, the building where half of the narrative takes place and which influences Hans's fortune, is a nondescript hotel like any other – as Hans himself underlines when he buys it (*HT*: 198). This anonymity and meaninglessness are also expressed in its name: 'Hilde, come lo chiameresti? Lo chiamerei Hotel Sand. Sand è la sabbia. Per i tedeschi e gli anglosassoni. Anche gli italiani sanno pronunciare Sand. Tutti possono dire Sand. In fondo, Sand non significa nulla. Potrebbe essere qualsiasi cosa' [Hilde, how would you call it? I'd call it Hotel Sand. For Germans and the British, Sand means beach. Even Italians can pronounce Sand. Everyone can say Sand. After all, Sand means nothing. It could be anything] (*HT*: 199).

The text's narrative prioritization of objects is rooted in the culture of material welfare promoted by Mussolini's and Hitler's regimes, which placed great emphasis on the wellness of the middle class and used this as a political propaganda tool (Hobsbawm 1994: 122–124). In the novel, Falco often suggests what his characters do not (or refuse to) realize – that their economic wealth is intimately tied to abuse and violence:

> Abbiamo il frigorifero elettrico, il refrigerante è al freon, non all'ammoniaca come quello di nonna Christa, che ha il difetto di un accumulo di brina. Sembra un miracolo la trasformazione del freon da gassoso a liquido e il passaggio al freddo. Abbiamo l'aspirapolvere, risucchiamo briciole, capelli, insetti, i rifiuti delle bambole, i peli di Blondi, i petali dei fiori morti. Abbiamo il ferro da stiro a vapore, l'asciugacapelli che mi sorprende ancora, lancia un getto di aria calda sui capelli bagnati, lo agito come uno strumento musicale, chiudo gli occhi, ho i capelli asciutti e lucenti in tre minuti. Abbiamo la lavatrice e la lavastoviglie, il tostapane automatico per il pane caldo e croccante, e tutto quello che ci serve, la credenza piena di provviste, potremmo resistere settimane senza uscire di casa, ne sarei contenta, eviterei di andare a scuola, dimenticherei il dettato, la guerra in Polonia, nell'angolo destro della cartina appesa in classe. (*HT*: 74)
>
> [We have an electric refrigerator, with a Freon cooler instead of an ammoniac one, like at Grandma Christa's, which lets frost accumulate. Freon's transformation from gas to liquid and the way it cools seem miraculous to us. We have a vacuum cleaner,

> we suck crumbs, hairs, insects, the remains of dolls, Blondie's hairs, petals of dead flowers. We have a steam iron, a hairdryer that keeps surprising me, it blows hot air on wet hair, I move it like a musical instrument, I close my eyes, my hair is dry and glossy in three minutes. We have a washing machine and a dishwasher, an automatic toaster to make bread hot and crispy, and everything we need, the cupboard is full of food, we could hold up for weeks without leaving the house, I would like it, I could skip school, I would forget the dictation exercise, the war in Poland, in the right corner of the map in our classroom.]

Despite the recognition of the luxury and convenience provided by the objects, the characters do not show love or affection for them or their cars, houses and food. Rather, they are represented merely as objects that incite envy and jealousy and affirm one's social position. Similarly, this relationship with objects and goods is represented in fascist Italy by the protagonist of a digression of the novel, the anonymous banker of Merano, simply called 'uomo di Lenhart' [Lenhart man]. This descriptive strategy, evidently modelled on taxonomic categories such as 'Neanderthal man' or 'Cro Magnon man', together with the man's namelessness, forms part of Falco's toolbox of distancing effects. It suggests that readers should perceive the Lenhart man as an anthropological type rather than a character. Indeed, the man of Lenhart is the prototype of an Italian, superficially and conveniently fascist and obsessed by his salary and what it can grant him.

Andrea Cortellessa suggests that this attention to the interaction between the material and the human, and indeed to the way in which the material determines the human, together with the absence of pathos in the narration, is influenced by texts of the *neo-avanguardia* such as *La ragazza Carla* [*The Girl Carla*] (1959) by Elio Pagliarani. The *neo-avanguardia* was an Italian poetic movement of the 1960s characterized by formal experimentalism and political commitment (and not too dissimilar from American postmodernism). By focusing his gaze on inanimate objects, Falco isolates them from their context, as a result of which they gain an epiphanic value (Cortellessa 2015). Cortellessa attributes to Falco what Pagliarani calls, in a poem, 'objective piety'. The absence from the page of the pathetic effect of the narrative 'I' allows for the creation of a collective point of view (2015). This stylistic choice is also expressed by Falco in a passage of *The H Twin* in which he contrasts this detachment with the emphasis and sensationalism that characterize the narration of the Second World War, which is often based on easily narratable structures and reduced to clichés:

> I giornali celebrano gli anniversari della guerra per farla scomparire nella memoria affollata da decine di altre commemorazioni alternate a curiosità belliche e inezie quotidiane: rievocazioni del processo di Norimberga scritte come i dialoghi di un romanzo poliziesco, le condanne a morte, la dispersione delle ceneri in una puntualissima alba piovosa d'autunno; gerarchi trasformati in rappresentanti di commercio; rivelazioni improvvise del cameriere o dell'autista di Hitler, tutti pronti a svelare lo scoop, il segreto banale che dovrebbe spiegare la Storia: quanti litri occorrono per bruciare un cadavere? Non sarebbe meglio domandare all'autista, scusi, cosa provava a guidare in autostrada, in corsia di sorpasso, con Hitler sul sedile posteriore? (*HT*: 273–274)
>
> [The newspapers celebrate the anniversaries of the war in order to make it disappear from memory, which is packed with dozens of other commemorations, war trivia, and everyday things of no importance: representations of the Nuremberg trial written like the dialogues of a crime fiction novel, death sentences, the scattering of ashes during a timely, rainy autumnal dawn; party officials transformed into salesmen; sudden revelations of Hitler's butler or drivers, ready to reveal the scoop, the banal secret that's supposed to explain History: how many litres do you need to burn a corpse? Would it be better to ask the driver, excuse me, what did you feel when you drove in the overtaking lane of the highway with Hitler in your back seat?]

This extract allows me to highlight the lateral dislocation of the point of view of the narrator, which is reinforced by continuous variation and the attention paid to seemingly unimportant details. I use the word 'lateral' not arbitrarily but in reference Falco's self-description of his writing, detailed in his contribution to the *Dizionario affettivo della lingua italiana* [*Italian Sentimental Dictionary*], edited by Matteo Bianchi and Giorgio Vasta:

> La mia parola è *laterale*. Sono a mio agio quando non sto in ciò che è considerato il centro. Preferisco stare defilato, non completamente fuori dal centro ma nemmeno inglobato. Non significa mettersi in disparte. [...]. Il fotografo Guido Guidi, per spiegare la sua idea di fotografia, cita, tra le altre cose, Ruggero Pierantoni quando parla delle icone, le madonne al centro e la mobilità degli angeli sui bordi. Non a caso,

> mentre sorseggiamo un the caldo a cento metri dall'autostrada A14, Guido dice, il prete al centro dell'altare rappresenta Dio, ma appena si sposta anche solo di un paio di metri, appena diviene *laterale* vicino al leggio da cui predica, il prete ritorna uomo. Il *laterale* per me è come un messaggero tra l'immagine centrale e ciò che è marginale, anche sfuocato, ciò non si vede chiaramente, l'ignoto che sta fuori, sul bordo. Ecco, bordo è un'altra parola che mi piace, però per me implica anche un punto da cui precipitare. Per il momento, preferisco *laterale*. (Bianchi and Vasta 2008: 110–111)
>
> [My word is *lateral*. I am at ease when I'm not at the centre. I'd rather stay at a remove, not completely outside of the centre, but not enclosed by it either. This isn't to say set apart. [...] The photographer Guido Guidi, in his explanation his idea of photography, quotes, among others, Ruggero Pierantoni on sacred icons, which have the Madonnas at the centre and the angels moving at the sides. It is not by chance that (aswhile we sip a hot tea 100 metres from the A14 highway) Guido says: 'The priest in front of the altar represents God, but as soon as he moves even a couple of metres, as soon as he becomes *lateral*, close to the lectern from which he preaches, the priest is a man again.' The *lateral*, for me, is like a messenger between the central image and that which is marginal, even blurry, that which can't be seen clearly, the unknown outside, on the border. See, border is another word I like, but it also implies a point from which to fall. So for now, I prefer *lateral*.]

In this dislocation of perspective, Falco is influenced by his interest in photography (as the previous quote illustrates) and specifically in the work of the New Topographics – the group of American photographers who participated in the eponymous exhibition in 1975 who focus on a less rhetorical and lyrical representation of the North American landscape. Falco is also considerably influenced by the work of William Eggleston, whose artistic practice aims to 'sottrarre le cose quotidiane dalla banalità dello sguardo e dalla loro stessa essenza: trasforma il familiare in anomalo, attraverso un'angolatura sbieca rispetto alla visione usuale, dominante' [subtract everyday things from the banality of the gaze and from their own essence: to transform the familiar into the strange, by employing a side angle, as opposed to the usual, dominant perspective] (Falco 2009). This definition fits the object-centred and detached poetics of *The H Twin* (Marsilio and Zinato 2015: 256). During a lecture at the Galileian School of Higher Education, Falco discussed Eggleston's famous close-up of a tricycle, shot in 1969, in which the unusual perspective transforms an everyday object into a source of anxiety. As Marsilio notes, this is comparable to Falco's prose, in which the unusual attention paid to otherwise insignificant details creates a sense of uncanniness in everyday life.[17] In the case of *The H Twin*, this disproportionate attention to detail is intended to challenge readers' perspective on the Second World War and encourage them to see a continuity between the wilful perpetrators of Nazi Germany and the enthusiastic, successful capitalists of the 1950s and 1960s.

Falco's novel does not have the heroic and emphatic dimension that characterizes the Italian Resistance narrative because it focuses on the continuity between the age of totalitarianism and the present. The narration of the war is represented as an episode in an equally disturbing and violent narration of peace. According to Cortellessa, 'col coraggio delle sue scelte, Giorgio Falco ha compiuto un miracolo che pareva impossibile. [...] Nessuno [...] aveva avuto sinora il coraggio di far proprio il punto di vista della Zona Grigia: di quell'area sdrucciolevole che non comprende solo la complicità delle vittime, come ci ha mostrato Primo Levi, ma anche il silenzio dei testimoni, il mutismo che li rende a loro volta complici' [Through his brave choices, Falco has performed a miracle that seemed impossible. [...] No one [...] had ever thought to appropriate the point of view of the Grey Area: that slippery area that not only includes the complicity of the victims, as Primo Levi showed, but also the silence of the witnesses, the mutism that make them complicit] (2014). While I would not go so far as to call Falco's novel 'a miracle' and I am not sure that Falco's attempt is unprecedented, it is true that *The H Twin* represents a different approach to the many war writings centred on decisive events and tragic heroes. In this sense, despite the similarities, Falco is equally distant from both Littell and Binet. Falco's everymen illustrate a different side of the war to that of the victims and the perpetrators: that of the willing collaborators.

As I have argued, Binet and Falco, albeit in different ways, depart from Littell's model of an emphatic character-centred historical novel, preferring a metafictional framework (Binet) and a sense of emotionless, alienating minimalism (Falco). Most notably, both authors withhold the

17 I do possess further details of this lecture, which I contributed to organizing, but Falco has not agreed to its transcription and dissemination. Nevertheless, a summary of the lecture can be found in Marsilio and Zinato, who were also present (2015: 257–258).

very possibility of identification between readers and the characters, refusing to adopt the formal means that might enable such an empathetic response. I would argue that these two novels also share some flaws, which hinge on their stylistic choices and ideological aims.

Falco and, to a lesser extent, Binet write in order to reveal a continuity between two seemingly different models: fascism and totalitarianism. However, by focusing their analyses on the purely economic side of fascism (neither Binet's Heydrich nor Falco's Hans Hinner seem to believe in the ideology they support, but rather merely seek its advantages), they leave out the key irrational aspects of fascist ideology. This choice significantly limits their interpretations of fascism; according to them, the supporters of fascism *must be* hypocritical. In contrast, by referring to Theweleit's theory, Littell chooses a psychological interpretation that creates empathy in readers and highlights the continuity between the two systems (or, rather, their common roots) through Aue's excuses and mythical symbolism.

Furthermore, Binet's and Falco's stylistic choices signal that they do not necessarily seek the participation or empathy of readers. Readers are placed at a psychological distance and are not encouraged to interact emotionally with the characters. In other words, despite apparently straightforward attitudes, these novels present forms of intellectualism – postmodern in Binet's case and derived from the *neo-avanguardia* in Falco's. I say 'postmodern' because Binet retains the postmodernist scepticism towards the dangers of fiction, even if he does not use it as a grounding principle of his narration. Contrastingly, it is precisely Littell's use of fiction (and, indeed, midcult resources) that makes his novel an *experience* for readers and not simply a statement about a series of ideological contents.

Conclusion

The Second World War and the Post-Postmodern Novel

By way of beginning this conclusion, I once again evoke Jorge Luis Borges's paradox of the map, which provided a useful point of reflection in the chapter on Bolaño. According to Borges, in order to faithfully represent the territory to which it refers, the map should be on a 1:1 scale. Of course, if it respected this proportion, the map would no longer be a map – a schematization of the world meant to make its comprehension easier – but rather a useless copy. The map, as Baudrillard and Houellebecq remind us, is not the territory. Similarly, conclusions, especially those based on textual analysis, often repeat arguments already clear in the analysis of the books.

Nevertheless, by summing up and recapitulating the common traits of the novels discussed so far, I aim to show how my focus on these texts allows us to identify important characteristics of the post-postmodern novel and its approach to historical writing. My attention to these texts illuminates their stylistic coherence and their treatment of the Second World War as the subject of historical novels – a treatment that is congruent with post-postmodernism's interest in realism and great narratives that contemporary warfare is unable to provide. If we consider two apparently similar events, the assassinations of Reinhard Heydrich and Qasem Soleimani, the drastic differences in warfare between the Second World War and today become evident. Regardless of the historical and cultural circumstances and focusing solely on the dynamics of their assassinations, we note that while Heydrich's assassination required the action of selected individuals who sacrificed their lives to achieve their mission, Soleimani's assassination was carried out by a drone, an impersonal technological weapon that allows US soldiers to avoid directly risking their lives. The assassination of Heydrich and the heroism of those who perpetrated it was a concern of

Binet's *HHhH*, which focuses on the lives of the killer and the risks they faced. It is difficult to imagine a similar novel about Soleimani's killing. Therefore, we can understand the narrative pre-eminence of the Second World War as opposed to contemporary conflicts, which are much more difficult to narrate because they are so often unmanned.

Since this book concerns only a select number of case studies, further research could be conducted on the global dimension of contemporary literature, through case studies of national literatures I have not considered, such as German, Russian or Japanese national literatures. Several other novels about the Second World War could have been taken into account (for instance, Philip Roth's *The Plot Against America*, Richard Flanagan's *The Narrow Road to the Deep North*, Kate Atkinson's *Life after Life* or Jennifer Egan's *Manhattan Beach*). Broadening the scope of the analysis to the contemporary novel in general, further examples of post-postmodern novels include David Foster Wallace's *Infinite Jest*, Vollmann's *Seven Dreams* series, Mark Danielewski's metafictional *The House of Leaves* and Hilary Mantel's remarkable Thomas Cromwell trilogy. Other studies will hopefully continue mapping the ever-changing pattern of contemporary literature.

Further research could also be done on post-postmodernism as a distinct literary phenomenon. While the debate is broad and general agreement can be identified amongst many different and sometimes opposing critical voices, a definitive and unambiguous theorization of the inchoate concept of post-postmodernism as a coherent poetics has yet to be proposed. Furthermore, other scholars could investigate the relationship between the use of mimetic devices and the development of empathy towards the perpetrators, as well as the hermeneutical scope of this empathy.[1] Although I have developed this aspect of post-postmodern novels on the Second World War, more research will hopefully be done on the authors I have focused on or, indeed, different writers.

In her essay *Literature after Postmodernism*, Irmtraud Huber describes the current literary climate as a season of reconstruction, as opposed to postmodern deconstructivism (2014). This opposition is relevant to the

1 The topic of empathy in literature is vast and complex and has elicited a growing amount of studies in recent years. See Bortolussi and Dixon 2003; Keen 2007; Hammond and Kim 2014; and Ercolino 2018.

results of this research since the novels I have examined are characterized by a non-ironic reprisal of plot, characters, causality and narratorial authorship. They also lean towards realism, however challenged this realism might be by non-realistic devices. I have highlighted a generic recovery of those characteristics of the traditional novel that had been abandoned or parodied by postmodernism. Postmodernism typically depicted a fragmentary, unknowable world reduced to its own textuality and representation. On the contrary, post-postmodernism, through its non-ironic reprise of the formal tools of the traditional Western novel, distances itself from this hermeneutic nihilism and displays renewed faith in the capability of literature to respond to and represent reality.

The recovery of these characteristics of the traditional novel has led me to define the post-postmodern novel as realistic in comparison to postmodern texts. Nevertheless, I have also noted that post-postmodern realism presents problematic traits, being at the same time rich in mimetic and anti-mimetic features. In this sense, post-postmodernism is not a set of techniques, but rather an attitude of literature towards reality – an attitude that critic Adam Kelly, discussing David Foster Wallace, eloquently labelled New Sincerity (Kelly 2010). Specifically, I have highlighted that a general unlikeliness characterizes *Europe Central* and *2666*. But I have also noted that this hybridization of realism with the grotesque and the supernatural needs to be contextualized within the context of a renewed attention to the real, rather than to the textual; to the object, rather than to the sign. On the contrary, postmodernism is an anti-mimetic style not because of the presence of unrealistic elements, but because of its representation of the world as a text.

The recovery of specific features of the postmodern novel, such as autofiction and metafiction, also needs to be understood in this sense. While metafiction and especially autofiction were employed in postmodern literature to comment on the erosion of the borders between reality and fiction, I have shown that this is no longer their function in post-postmodern literature. In *HHhH*, Binet uses metafiction not to undervalue the knowability of history, but rather to remark on the truthfulness of historiographic sources and distinguish meticulously between historical accuracy and novelistic invention. In McEwan's *Atonement*, the metafictional frame serves to debunk the diffused memorialization and monumentalization of a historical event.

However, the counter-history that is proposed is founded on historical documents that are not only exhibited in the text, but derive from institutional sources such as the Imperial War Museum.

The stylistic traits employed by the authors I have considered cross global borders in that the texts originate from different nations and literary traditions. In response to the stylistic consonance of the texts despite their geographical and cultural variety, I insist that we consider the post-postmodern novel as a form of global literature. The contemporary post-postmodern novel does not happen sporadically or within a strictly national environment, but is rather conceived in a global cultural landscape within which, despite singularities, a communality of postures and praxes exists. The global dimension of the contemporary novel is not a consequence of post-postmodern poetics; rather, it depends on the global editorial market and the complex net of cultural influences, which often favour countries that are more economically powerful. Nevertheless, the global diffusion of post-postmodernism as a literary phenomenon suggests the coherence between different narrative cultures and the attention to realism that characterizes post-postmodern poetics. Postmodernism, on the contrary, did not have the same uniformity in its diffusion. It manifested, especially in Europe, in a plurality of currents and idiolects that were, at times, contradictory.

The three authors to whom I have dedicated my chapters are characterized by another similarity in their representations of the Second World War: the problematic, but not insistently polemic, portrayal of the perpetrators. Whereas in Binet's and Falco's texts we observe a clear separation between positive and negative characters that coincides with the separation of victims and perpetrators (in other words, anti-fascist and fascist characters), in Bolaño's, Vollmann's and Littell's texts (and also Seiffert's, to an extent) this separation is more ambiguous. Such an ambiguity does not suggest that these authors sympathize with fascism. It is, on the contrary, a *voluntary* ambiguity in their representations that is intended to enrich and complicate readers' understanding of the Second World War. It is not by chance that these authors insist on the mediumistic nature of fascism, albeit in different ways, and on the fascination that the deliberately irrational system of ideas that constitutes fascism can inspire. In this sense, these authors distance themselves from a purely economic Marxist interpretation of fascism, which can be found in Falco's and Binet's representations of the fascists as either sociopaths, cheaters or idiots. Bolaño presents Wieder as a distant star, a seductive and all-absorbing black hole. Vollmann uses myth to render the orotund and insistent language of the Third Reich. Littell makes an analogy between Aue and the figure of the sleepwalker (which, as we have seen, derives directly from a speech by Hitler and is also common to the other novels) to highlight the deliberate irrationality of fascist actions. While other authors in this book ridicule the self-mythology of fascism, Bolaño, Vollmann and Littell use it to lend credibility to their characters instead of straightforwardly passing judgement on them from the outside.

Indeed, the moral ambiguity of these texts is connected to each author's refusal to express an explicit opinion about his or her characters. In the case of Bolaño, I noted that the genocidal Sammer is killed in retaliation for his actions, but no explicit explanation is given by his assassin. In Littell's novel, Aue is animated by a persuasive intent and his narrative perspective is not contradicted. Vollmann, meanwhile, is open to recognizing intellectual honesty even in those characters who would not normally be labelled heroes (Paulus, Vlasov) and to elevating Gerstein as a model whose purity derives from his willingness to accept ambiguity in order to perform a greater good.

The profound ambiguity of the literary works I have analysed allows us to understand how they principally aim to provide an engaging experience for readers by challenging commonly held views and perceptions of the Second World War. The parallels with religious texts in Vollmann's work allude to experiential function of these texts. I have argued that the Second World War is evoked due to its paradigmatic nature, which allows it to function as a scenario that is unparalleled in terms of its iconicity and the radicality of the moral problems it throws up. It therefore comes as no surprise that attention is paid to the reasoning of the war's perpetrators, which was excluded from twentieth-century novels about the war, especially postmemorial ones. The focus on perpetrators represents an opportunity to further immortalize the memory of the Second World War and its exceptional place in history. And yet, this is not what these texts enact. The renewed attention to reality in post-postmodern literature, which manifests itself in the recovery of the mimetic techniques associated with the traditional novel, invites a reassessment of the victim–perpetrator paradigm. These texts function as spaces in which a problematic encounter with a disturbing other can happen.

What we have outlined so far about these contradictions and the return to (a kind of) realism signals a renewed faith in the possibility of fiction not only to describe and address reality, but also to change it by challenging the readers' preconceptions and ideas. Literature, as I noted in relation to Vollmann's work, turns into an experience rather than an intellectual calculus – or, better, literature is the space where the intellectual calculus can be experienced. Unlike their predecessors, post-postmodernist authors recover the idea that fiction can be used to influence reality, rather than simply facilitating escapism or providing reflections on the unattainability of the real. As Vollmann himself commented in a compelling passage in *Europe Central*:

> Most literary critics agree that fiction cannot be reduced to mere falsehood. Well-crafted protagonists come to life, pornography causes orgasms, and the pretense that life is what we want it to be may conceivably bring about the desired condition. Hence religious parables, socialist realism, Nazi propaganda. And if this story likewise crawls with reactionary supernaturalism, that might be because its author longs to see letters scuttling across ceilings, cautiously beginning to reify themselves into angels. For if they could only do that, then why not us? (*EC*: 27)

Why not us indeed?

Bibliography

Aeschylus, *The Oresteia*, trans. Hugh Lloyd-Jones (London: Bloomsbury, 2014).

Agamben, Giorgio, *Quel che resta di Auschwitz* (Torino: Bollati Boringhieri, 1998).

Alden, Natasha, '"Accompanied by Ghosts": The Changing Uses of the Past in Sarah Waters's Lesbian Fiction', in Adele Jones and Claire O'Callaghan, eds, *Sarah Waters and Contemporary Feminism* (Basingstoke: Palgrave Macmillan, 2016), 61–78.

——, '"Possibility, Pleasure and Peril": *The Night Watch* as a Very Literary Story', in Kaye Mitchell, ed., *Sarah Waters. Contemporary Critical Perspectives* (Basingstoke: Palgrave Macmillan, 2013), 70–83.

——, *Reading Between the Lines. Postmemory in Contemporary British War Fiction* (Manchester: Manchester University Press, 2014).

Alfano, Giancarlo, *Gli effetti della guerra. Su* Horcynus Orca *di Stefano D'Arrigo* (Naples: Luca Sossella Editore, 2000).

Andrews, Chris, *Roberto Bolaño's Fiction: An Expanding Universe* (New York: Columbia University Press, 2014).

Apter, Emily, *Against World Literature: On the Politics of Untranslatability* (London: Verso, 2013).

Arendt, Hannah, *Eichmann in Jerusalem. A Report on the Banality of Evil* (London: Penguin, 1979 [1963]).

Asensi Pérez, Manuel, 'Atreverse a mirar por el agujero: lo real y lo político en *2666* de Roberto Bolaño', in Felipe A. Ríos Baeza, ed., *Roberto Bolaño. Ruptura y violencia en la literatura finisecular* (México D. F.: Eón, 2010), 342–368.

Asholt, Wolfgang, 'A German Reading of the German Reception of *The Kindly Ones*', in Aurélie Barjonet and Lirian Razinsky, eds, *Writing the Holocaust Today. Critical Perspectives on Jonathan Littell's The Kindly Ones* (Amsterdam: Rodopi, 2012), 221–238.

Baackmann, Susanne, 'Lore, or the Implicated Witness: Rachel Seiffert's Postmemory Work', in María Jesús Martínez-Alfar and Silvia Pellicer-Ortín, eds, *Memory Frictions in Contemporary Literature* (Basingstoke: Palgrave-Macmillan, 2017), 165–186.

Barberán Reinares, Laura, 'Globalized Philomels: State Patriarchy, Transnational Capital, and the Femicides on the US–Mexican Border in Roberto Bolaño's *2666*', *South Atlantic Review*, 75/4 (2010), 51–72.

Barthes, Roland, 'La mort de l'auteur', in *Le bruissement de la langue* (Paris: Éditions du Seuil, 1984), 61–67; trans. Stephen Heath as 'The Death of the Author', in *Image, Music, Text* (New York: Hill and Wang, 1997), 128–142.

Battini, Michele, *Il socialismo degli imbecilli. Propaganda, falsificazione, persecuzione degli ebrei* (Torino: Bollati Boringhieri, 2010); trans. Noor Mazhar and Isabella Vergnano as *Socialism of Fools. Capitalism and Modern Anti-Semitism* (New York: Columbia University Press, 2016).

Baudrillard, Jean, *La guerre du Golfe n'a pas eu lieu* (Paris: Editions Galilée, 1991); trans. Paul Patton as *The Gulf War Did Not Take Place* (Bloomington: Indiana University Press, 1995).

——, *L'esprit du terrorism* (Paris: Galilée, 2002); trans. Chris Turner as *The Spirit of Terrorism* (New York: Verso, 2002).

——, *Simulacres et simulation* (Paris: Editions Galilée, 1980); trans. Sheila Faria Glaser as *Simulacra and Simulations* (Ann Arbor: University of Michigan Press, 1994).

Bauman, Zygmunt, *Modernity and the Holocaust* (Cambridge: Polity, 1989).

Bellamy, Chris, *Absolute War. Soviet Russia in the Second World War: A Modern History* (London: Pan, 2009).

Benbassa, Esther, *La souffrance comme identité* (Paris: Librairie Arthème Fayard, 2007).

Benn Michaels, Walter, 'Forgetting Auschwitz: Jonathan Littell and the Death of a Beautiful Woman', *American Literary History*, 25/4 (2013), 915–930.

Bentley, Nick, '"Who Do You Think You Are Kidding?": The Retrieval of the Second World War in Kazuo Ishiguro's *The Remains of the Day* and Ian McEwan's *Atonement*', in Elodie Rousselot, ed., *Exoticizing the Past in Contemporary Neo-Historical Fiction* (Basingstoke: Palgrave Macmillan, 2014), 138–159.

Berberich, Christine, '"We Shall Be Punished": Positionality and Postmemory in Rachel Seiffert's *The Dark Room* and Uwe Timm's *In My Brother's Shadow*', *Holocaust Studies: A Journal of Culture and History*, 17/2–3 (2011), 261–281.

Berman, Marshall, *All that is Solid Melts into Air. An Experience of Modernity* (New York: Simon and Schuster, 1982).

Binet, Laurent, *HHhH* (Paris: Bernard Grasset, 2009); trans. Sam Taylor as *HHhH* (London: Vintage Books, 2013).

Birns, Nicholas, 'Black Dawn: Roberto Bolaño as (North) American Writer', in Nicholas Birns and Juan E. De Castro, eds, *Roberto Bolaño as World Literature* (New York: Bloomsbury, 2016), 220–243.

Bizzarri, Gabriele, 'Lo propio y lo alienígena: ciencia ficción y identidad en la construcción imaginaria de Santa Teresa', *Orillas*, 2 (2017), 171–183.

Blanchot, Maurice, *Faux Pas* (Paris: Gallimard, 1943); trans. Charlotte Mandel as *Faux Pas* (Stanford, CA: Stanford University Press, 2011).

Blanrue, Paul-Éric, *Les Malveillantes. Enquête sul le case Jonathan Littell* (Paris: Éditions Scali, 2006).

Blejer, Daniella 'Pensar/clasificar/denunciar: las resignificaciones del archivio en *2666*', in Felipe A. Ríos Baeza, ed., *Roberto Bolaño. Ruptura y violencia en la literatura finisecular* (México D. F.: Eón, 2010), 253–280.

Boe Birns, Margaret, '666 Twinned and Told Twice: Roberto Bolaño's Double Time Frame in *2666*', in Ignacio López-Calvo, ed., *Roberto Bolaño, A Less Distant Star. Critical Essays* (New York: Palgrave Macmillan, 2015), 67–84.

Boehm, Katharina, 'Historiography and the Material Imagination in the Novels of Sarah Waters', *Studies in the Novel*, 43/2 (2011), 237–257.

Boisseleau, Yves, '*Les Bienveillantes* : une position ironique', in Murielle Lucie Clément, ed., *Les Bienveillantes de Jonathan Littell* (Cambridge: Open Book Publishers, 2010), 277–298.

Bolaño, Roberto, *2666* (Barcelona: Editorial Anagrama, 2009); trans. Natasha Wimmer as *2666* (New York: Farrar, Straus and Giroux, 2008).

——, *El Tercer Reich* (Barcelona: Editorial Anagrama, 2010); trans. Natasha Wimmer as *The Third Reich* (London: Picador, 2011).

——, *Estrella distante* (Barcelona: Editorial Anagrama, 1996); trans. Chris Andrews as *Distant Star* (New York: New Directions Books, 2004).

——, *La literatura nazi en América* (Barcelona: Editorial Seix Barral, 2008); trans. Chris Andrews as *Nazi Literature in the Americas* (New York: New Directions Books, 2008).

——, *Los sinsabores del verdadero policía* (Barcelona: Editorial Anagrama, 2011); trans. Natasha Wimmer as *The Woes of the True Policeman* (New York: Farrar, Straus and Giroux, 2012).

Borges, Jorge Luis, *Collected Fictions*, trans. Andrew Hurley (New York: Viking, 1998).

——, *The Total Library. Non-Fiction 1922–1986*, ed. Eliot Weinberger (London: Penguin, 2001).

Bortolussi, Marisa, and Peter Dixon, *Psychonarratology: Foundations for the Empirical Study of Literary Response* (Cambridge: Cambridge University Press, 2003).

Bougnoux, Daniel, 'Max Aue, personnage de roman', *Le Débat*, 144 (2007), 66–69.

Bourke, Joanna, *An Intimate History of Killing: Face-to-face Killing in Twentieth Century Warfare* (London: Granta Books, 1999).

Bourmeau, Sylvain, 'Bête à Goncourt', *Les Inrockuptibles* 569 (24 October 2006).

Bracher, Nathan, 'L'Histoire à l'épreuve de l'affabulation romanesque: *HHhH* de Laurent Binet comme cas de figure', *Symposium: A Quarterly Journal in Modern Literatures*, 69/2 (2015), 98–110.

——, 'Timely Representations. Writing the Past in the First-Person Present Imperfect', *History & Memory*, 28/1 (2016), 3–35.

Braudel, Fernand, 'Histoire et sciences sociales: la longue durée', *Annales*, 13/4 (1958), 725–753.

Brett, Laurel, *Disquiet on the Western Front. World War II and Postmodern Fiction* (Newcastle upon Tyne: Cambridge Scholars Publishing, 2016).

Briand, Denis, 'Max aux enfers. Esquisses « topographiques » …', in Murielle Lucie Clément, ed., *Les Bienveillantes de Jonathan Littell* (Cambridge: Open Book Publishers, 2010), 87–102.

Brioni, Simone, 'Fantahistorical vs. Fantafascist Epic: "Contemporary" Alternative Italian Colonial Histories', *Science Fiction Studies*, 42 (2015), 305–318.

——, and Daniele Comberiati, *Italian Science Fiction. The Other in Literature and Film* (London: Palgrave Macmillan, 2019).

Brown, Peter, *The Cult of the Saints. Its Rise and Function in Latin Christianity* (Chicago: The University of Chicago Press, 2015).

Bucher, Vincent, 'Putting Historical Inquiry to the Test', in Françoise Palleau-Papin, ed., *Under Fire. William T. Vollmann, The Rifles: A Critical Study* (Bern: Peter Lang, 2016), 55–82.

Burke, Jason, *The 9/11 Wars* (London: Penguin, 2012).

Burns, Jennifer, *Fragments of* impegno. *Interpretations of Commitment in Contemporary Italian Narrative, 1980-2000* (Leeds: Northern Universities Press, 2001).

Calabrese, Stefano, *www.letteratura.global* (Torino: Einaudi, 2005).

Calvocoressi, Peter, Guy Wint and John Pritchard, *Total War. The Causes and Courses of the Second World War, Volume II: The Greater East Asia and Pacific Conflict* (London: Penguin, 1989).

Candia, Alexis, '*2666:* la magia y el mal', *Taller de letras*, 38 (2006), 121–139.

Carrara, Giuseppe, 'Il problema (est)etico della rappresentazione: *Poor People* di William T. Vollmann', *Enthymema* 23, 2019, 6–19.

Carrard, Philippe, 'Historiographic Metafiction, French Style', *Style*, 48/2 (2014), 181–202.

Casadei, Alberto, *Romanzi di Finisterre – Narrazione della guerra e problemi del realismo* (Rome: Carocci, 2000).

Casanova, Pascale, 'Literature as a World', in David Damrosch, ed., *World Literature in Theory* (Chichester: John Wiley & Sons, 2014), 192–209.

——, *The World Republic of Letters* (Cambridge, MA: Harvard University Press 2004).

Cassata, Carlo, *A destra del fascismo. Profilo politico di Julius Evola* (Torino: Bollati Boringhieri, 2003).

Cassini Wolf, Elisabetta, 'Evola's Interpretation of Fascism and Moral Responsibility', *Patterns of Prejudice*, 50/4–5 (2016), 478–494.

Cavalié, Elsa, '"It's Like Gold Leaf, and Now It's Rising, Peeling Away": Britishness and Exoticism in Sarah Waters's *The Night Watch*', in Elodie Rousselot, ed.,

Exoticizing the Past in Contemporary Neo-Historical Fiction (Basingstoke: Palgrave Macmillan, 2014), 84–100.

Chamayou, Grégoire, *Théorie du Drone* (Paris: La Fabrique Editions, 2013); trans. Janet Lloyd as *A Theory of the Drone* (New York: The New Press, 2015).

Chatman, Seymour, 'Backwards', *Narrative*, 17/1 (2009), 31–55.

Christensen, Peter G., 'Shostakovich in Love: William T. Vollmann's *Europe Central*', *The Journal of the Midwest Modern Language Association*, 40/1 (2007), 97–108.

Christie, Agatha, *The Murder of Roger Ackroyd* (London: Harper Collins, 2016).

Ciccarello di Blasi, Maria Grazia, *Intertestualità e contaminazione: il Quijote borgesiano di Paul Auster* (Rome: Libreria Istituti Nuovi, 1995).

Cinquegrani, Alessandro, and Valentina Re, *L'innesto. Realtà e finzioni da Matrix a 1Q84* (Milan: Mimesis, 2014).

Ciocia, Stefania, 'The Last of the Romantics? The Accidental Investigator in Postmodern Detective Fiction', in Carmen Casaliggi and Paul March-Russell, eds, *Legacies of Romanticism. Literature, Culture, Aesthetics* (New York: Routledge, 2012), 198–210.

Coffman, Christopher K., 'Introduction: Lonely Atoms', in Christopher K. Coffman and Daniel Lukes, eds, *William T. Vollmann. A Critical Companion* (Newark: University of Delaware Press, 2015), 1–22.

——, and Theophilus Savvas, *After Postmodernism. The New American Fiction* (New York: Routledge, 2020).

Coker, Christopher, *Humane Warfare* (London: Routledge, 2001).

Compagnon, Antoine, 'Nazism, History, and Fantasy: Revisiting *Les Bienveillantes*', *Yale French Studies*, 121 (2012), 113–127.

Connelly, Mark, *We can take it! Britain and the Memory of the Second World War* (Harlow: Pearson/Longman, 2004).

Cooke, Philip, *The Legacy of the Italian Resistance* (Basingstoke: Palgrave Macmillan, 2011).

Cortellessa, Andrea, 'Epica e fotografia. Giorgio Falco con Sabrina Ragucci', 15 September 2015, available at <http://www.doppiozero.com/materiali/anteprime/epica-e-fotografia> [last accessed 31 March 2020].

——, 'Giorgio Falco. *La gemella H*', 15/3/2014, available at: <http://www.doppiozero.com/materiali/parole/giorgio-falco-la-gemella-h> [last accessed 31 March 2020].

Costa, Daniele, *Il perverso ritorno del reale* (Milan: Mimesis, 2016).

Cox, John K., 'Writing Europe: Death, History, and the Intersecting Intellectual Worlds of William T. Vollmann and Danilo Kiš', in Christopher K. Coffman and Daniel Lukes, eds, *William T. Vollmann. A Critical Companion* (Newark: University of Delaware Press, 2015), 123–140.

Crosthwaite, Paul, *Trauma, Postmodernism, and the Aftermath of World War II* (Basingstoke: Palgrave Macmillan, 2009).

Crownshaw, Richard, *The Afterlife of Holocaust Memory in Contemporary Literature and Culture* (Basingstoke: Palgrave Macmillan, 2010).

Dalley, Hamish, *The Postcolonial Historical Novel. Realism, Allegory, and the Representation of Contested Past* (Basingstoke: Palgrave Macmillan, 2014).

Dambre, Marc, 'The Memory of Some French Texts in *Les Bienveillantes*: The Explicit and the Implicit', *Yale French Studies*, 121 (2012), 169–184.

Davies, J. Marina, 'La Shoah en flânant?', in Murielle Lucie Clément, ed., *Les Bienveillantes de Jonathan Littell* (Cambridge: Open Book Publishers, 2010), 171–184.

Dawson, Paul, *The Return of the Omniscient Narrator. Authorship and Authority in Twenty-First Century Fiction* (Columbus: The Ohio State University Press, 2013).

de Tholozany, Pauline, 'Le « curieux exercice » : voyeurisme et conscience du meurtre dans *Les Bienveillantes*', in Murielle Lucie Clément, ed., *Les Bienveillantes de Jonathan Littell* (Cambridge: Open Book Publishers, 2010), 197–212.

Dei, Fabio, 'Il mito in Frazer e nelle poetiche del modernismo', in Giovanni Leghissa and Enrico Manera, eds, *Filosofie del mito nel Novecento* (Bologna: il Mulino, 2015), 71–80.

Delorme, Julie, '*Les Bienveillantes* : une parole qui donne la voix au bourreau', in Murielle Lucie Clément, ed., *Les Bienveillantes de Jonathan Littell* (Cambridge: Open Book Publishers, 2010), 31–46.

Dentith, Simon, *Parody* (London: Routledge, 2000).

DeVane Brown, Katherine, 'Courtly Rivalry, Loyalty Conflict, and the Figure of Hagen in the Nibelungenlied', *Monatshefte*, 107/3 (2015), 355–381.

Di Giacomo, Giuseppe, *Estetica e letteratura. Il grande romanzo tra Ottocento e Novecento* (Bari: Laterza, 1999).

Diner, Dan, *Beyond the Conceivable: Studies on Germany, Nazism, and the Holocaust* (Berkeley: University of California Press, 2000).

Donnarumma, Raffaele, *Ipermodernità. Dove va la narrativa contemporanea* (Bologna: il Mulino, 2014).

——, 'La macchina dell'oscurità', *Allegoria*, 71–72 (2015), 216–229.

Donoghue, Denis, 'Yeats, Eliot, and the Mythical Method', *The Sewanee Review*, 2 (1997), 206–226.

Dower, John W., *War Without Mercy. Race and Power in the Pacific War* (New York: Pantheon Books, 1986).

Duszat, Michael, 'Foucault's Laughter. Enumeration, Rewriting, and the Construction of the Essayist in Borges's "The analytical language of John Wilkins"', *Orbis Litterarum*, 67 (2012), 193–218.

Eaglestone, Robert, '"The age of reason was over … An age of fury was dawning": Contemporary Fiction and Terror', in Elleke Boehmer and Stephen Morton, eds, *Terror and the Postcolonial: A Concise Companion* (Hoboken, NJ: Wiley-Blakwell, 2009), 361–369.

——, *The Holocaust and the Postmodern* (Oxford: Oxford University Press, 2004).

——, *Postmodernism and Holocaust Denial* (Cambridge: Icon Books, 2001).

Echternkamp, Jörg, and Stefan Martens, 'The Meanings of the Second World War in Contemporary European History', in Jörg Echternkamp and Stefan Martens, eds, *Experience and Memory. The Second World War in Europe* (Oxford: Berghahn Books, 2010), 245–269.

Eder, Jens, Fotis Jannidis and Ralf Schneider, 'Characters in Fictional Worlds. An Introduction', in Jens Eder, Fotis Jannidis and Ralf Schneider, eds, *Characters in Fictional Worlds. Understanding Imaginary Beings in Literature, Film, and Other Media* (Berlin: De Gruyter, 2010), 3–66.

Eliot, Thomas Stearns, '*Ulysses*, Order and Myth', *The Dial*, 1923, 201.

Ercolino Stefano, *Il romanzo massimalista* (Milan: Bompiani, 2015).

——, 'Negative empathy. History, theory, criticism', *Orbis Litterarum*, 73/3 (2018), 243–262.

Eshel, Amir, *Futurity: Contemporary Literature and the Quest for the Past* (Chicago: University of Chicago Press, 2014).

Eshelman, Raoul, *Performatism, or The End of Postmodernism* (Aurora, CO: The Davies Group Publishers, 2008).

Esposito, Fernando, 'Mito e fascismi', in Giovanni Leghissa and Enrico Manera, eds, *Filosofie del mito nel Novecento* (Bologna: Carocci, 2015), 281–290.

Eve, Martin Paul, *Literature Against Criticism. University English and Contemporary Fiction in Conflict* (Cambridge: Open Book Publisher, 2016).

Evola, Julius, *Rivolta contro il mondo moderno* (Rome: Edizioni Mediterranee, 1969).

Falco, Giorgio, *La gemella H* (Torino: Einaudi, 2013).

——, 'Laterale', in Matteo Bianchi and Giorgio Vasta, eds, *Dizionario Affettivo della Lingua Italiana* (Rome: Fandango, 2008), 110–111.

——, 'William Eggleston. Lo sguardo democratico dell'America', *La Repubblica* (26 August 2009).

Farinelli, Franco, *La crisi della ragione cartografica* (Torino: Einaudi, 2009).

Ferdjani, Youssef, '*Les Bienveillantes* : Le National-socialisme comme mal métaphysique', in Murielle Lucie Clément, ed., *Les Bienveillantes de Jonathan Littell* (Cambridge: Open Book Publishers, 2010), 263–276.

Finchelstein, Federico, 'On Fascism, History, and Evil in Roberto Bolaño', in Nicholas Birns and Juan E. De Castro, eds, *Roberto Bolaño as World Literature* (New York: Bloomsbury, 2016), 32–53.

Finney, Brian, 'Briony's Stand Against Oblivion: The Making of Fiction in Ian McEwan's *Atonement*', *Journal of Modern Literature*, 27/3 (2004), 68–82.

Foot, John, *Italy's Divided Memory* (Basingstoke: Palgrave Macmillan, 2011).

Fowler, Alastair, *Kinds of Literature: An Introduction to the Theory of Genres and Modes* (Cambridge, MA: Harvard University Press, 1972).

Fragero Guerra, Carmen, 'La novela popular y *2666* de Roberto Bolaño', *Anales de Literatura Hispanoamericana*, 41 (2012), 245–264.

Friedlander, Saul, *Kurt Gerstein ou L'Ambiguité du Bien* (Paris: Casterman, 1967); trans. Charles Fullnam as *Counterfeit Nazi. The Ambiguity of Good* (London: Weidenfeld and Nicolson, 1969).

Fritz, Stefen, *Ostkrieg. Hitler's War of Extermination in the East* (Lexington: University of Kentucky Press, 2011).

Furlong, Paul, 'Riding the Tiger: Crisis and Political Strategy in the Thought of Julius Evola', *The Italianist*, 31/1 (2011a), 25–40.

——, *Social and Political Thought of Julius Evola* (London: Routledge, 2011b).

Fusillo, Massimo, *L'altro e lo stesso – Teoria e storia del doppio* (Firenze: La Nuova Italia Editrice, 1998).

Galli, Giorgio, *Hitler e il nazismo magico* (Milan: Rizzoli, 1989).

Ganguly, Debjani, *This Thing Called the World. The Contemporary Novel as Global Form* (Durham, NC: Duke University Press, 2016).

Gasparini, Philippe, *Autofiction* (Paris: Éditions du Seuil, 2008).

Gentry, Francis G., 'Key Concepts in the *Nibelungenlied*', in Winder McConnell, ed., *A Companion to the Nibelungenlied* (Rochester, NY: Camden House, 1998*), 66–78.*

Giglioli, Daniele, *Senza trauma* (Macerata: Quodlibet, 2011).

Gilroy, Paul, *After Empire. Melancholia or Convivial Culture?* (London Routledge, 2004).

Goslan, Richard J., 'The American Reception of Max Aue', *Substance*, 39/1 (2010), 174–183.

——, 'Perversion and Pulp: Reading Edgar Rice Burroughs and Figuring America in *Les Bienveillantes*', *Yale French Studies*, 121 (2012), 204–226.

Gould, Eric, *Mythical Intentions in Modern Literature* (Princeton, NJ: Princeton University Press, 1981).

Grall, Catherine, '*2666* by Roberto Bolaño: fiction as an attempt to travel between worlds', *Neohelicon*, 40/32 (2013), 475–487.

Grethlein, Jonas, 'Myth, Morals, and Metafiction in Jonathan Littell's *Les Bienveillantes*', *PMLA*, 127/1 (2012), 77–93.

Gutiérrez-Mouat, Ricardo, *Understanding Roberto Bolaño* (Columbia: University of South Carolina Press, 2016).

Hables Gray, Chris, *Postmodern War. The New Politics of Conflict* (New York: Guilford Press, 1997).

Hake, Sabina, *Screen Nazis. Cinema, History and Democracy* (Madison: The University of Wisconsin Press, 2012).

Hall, Stuart, 'The Question of Cultural Identity', in Stuart Hall, David Held, Don Hubert and Kenneth Thompson, eds, *Modernity. An Introduction to Modern Societies* (London: Blackwell, 1995), 596–632.

Hamilton, Paula, 'Contested Memories of the Pacific War in Australia', in Christina Twomey and Ernest Koh, eds, *The Pacific War: Aftermaths. Remembrance and Culture* (London: Routledge, 2015), 50–66.

Hammond, Meghan Marie, and Sue J. Kim, eds, *Rethinking Empathy through Literature* (New York: Routledge, 2014).

Hanson, Victor Davis, *The Western Way of War. Infantry Battle in Classical Greece* (Berkeley: California University Press, 1989).

Hartmann, Christian, *Operation Barbarossa. Nazi Germany's War in the East, 1941–1945* (Oxford: Oxford University Press, 2013).

Hassan, Ihab, 'Beyond Postmodernism: Toward an Aesthetic of Trust', in Klaus Stierstorfer, ed., *Beyond Postmodernism. Reassessments in Literature, Theory, and Culture* (Berlin: Walter de Gruyter, 2003), 199–212.

——, *The Postmodern Turn. Essays in Postmodern Theory and Culture* (Columbus: Ohio State University Press, 1987).

Hemmingson, Michael, *William T. Vollmann: A Critical Study and Seven Interviews* (Jefferson, NC: McFarland & Co., 2009).

Hilberg, Raul, *The Destruction of the European Jews* (New Haven, CT: Yale University Press, 2003).

Hirsch, Marianne, *Family Frames. Photography, Narrative and Postmemory* (Cambridge, MA: Harvard University Press, 2002).

——, *The Generation of Postmemory. Writing and Visual Culture After the Holocaust* (New York: Columbia University Press, 2012).

Hoberek, Andrew, 'After Postmodernism: Form and History in Contemporary American Fiction', *Twentieth Century Literature*, 53/3 (2007), 233–247.

Hobsbawm, Eric, *Age of Extremes. The Short Twentieth Century 1914–1991* (London: Michael Joseph, 1994).

Hocevar, Drina, 'Pynchon's Maas: Subversion or Polyphonic Echoing and Mirroring of Myth', in José Manuel Losada Goya and Marta Guirao Ochoa, eds, *Myth and Subversion in the Contemporary Novel* (Newcastle upon Tyne: Cambridge Scholars Publishing, 2012), 107–118.

Holland, Mary K., *Succeeding Postmodernism. Language and Humanism in Contemporary American Literature* (London: Bloomsbury, 2013).

Huber, Irmtraud, *Literature after Postmodernism. Reconstructive Fantasies* (London: Palgrave MacMillan, 2014).

Husson, Édouard, '*Les Bienveillantes*, un canular déplacé', *Le Figaro* (8 September 2006).

——, and Michel Terestchenko, *Les complaisantes. Jonathan Littell et l'écriture du mal* (Paris: Francois-Xavier de Guibert, 2007).

Hutcheon, Linda, 'Gone Forever, But Here to Stay: The Legacy of the Postmodern', in Pelagia Goulimari, ed., *Postmodernism: What Moment?* (Manchester: Manchester University Press, 2007), 16–18.

——, *The Poetics of Postmodernism* (London: Routledge, 1988).

——, *The Politics of Postmodernism* (London: Routledge, 2007).

Huyssen, Andreas, 'Monuments and Memory in a Postmodern Age', *Yale Journal of Criticism*, 6/2 (1993), 249–252.

Imbaud, Patrice, 'À propos des *Bienveillantes*. Variations autour de la perversion', in Murielle Lucie Clément, ed., *Les Bienveillantes de Jonathan Littell* (Cambridge: Open Book Publishers, 2010), 185–196.

Ingram, Forrest L., *Representative Short Story Cycles of the Twentieth Century. Studies in a Literary Genre* (The Hague: Mouton, 1971).

Ireland, Ken, 'Peeling the Onion. Outcomes to Origins in Retrograde Narrative', *Journal of Literary Studies*, 39 (2010), 29–41.

Jacobi, Martin, 'Who Killed Robbie and Cecilia? Reading and Misreading Ian McEwan's *Atonement*', *Critique: Studies in Contemporary Fiction*, 52/1 (2011), 55–73.

Jameson, Fredric, *Postmodernism, or, the Cultural Logic of Late Time Capitalism* (Durham, NC: Duke University Press, 1991).

Jamet, Pierre, 'Modernist Concerns and Greek and Latin Culture: Thomas S. Eliot's Mythical Method in Thomas C. Wolfe' s Novels', *Dialogues d'histoire ancienne*, 1 (2015), 229–244.

Jones, Adele, 'Disrupting the Continuum: Collapsing Space and Time in Sarah Waters's *The Night Watch*', *Journal of Gender Studies*, 21/3 (2014), 32–44.

Kaldor, Mary, *New and Old Wars: Organized Violence in a Global Era* (Cambridge: Polity, 2012).

Katz, Steven T., 'The Uniqueness of the Holocaust: the Historical Dimension', in Alan S. Rosenbaum, ed., *Is the Holocaust Unique? Perspectives on Comparative Genocide* (Boulder, CO: Westview Press, 1996), 19–39.

Keen, Suzanne, *Empathy and the Novel* (Oxford: Oxford University Press, 2007).

Kelly, Adam, 'David Foster Wallace and the New Sincerity in American Fiction', in David Hering, ed., *Consider David Foster Wallace: Critical Essays* (Austin, TX: SSMG Press, 2010), 131–146.

Kelly, Van, 'La rhétorique d'*HHhH*: Entrer dans le virage avec Binet, Heydrich, Gabčík et Kubiš', in Marc Dambre, ed., *Mémoires occupées* (Paris: Presses Sorbonne Nouvelle, 2013).

Kirby, Alan, *Digimodernism: How New Technologies Dismantle the Postmodern and Reconfigure Our Culture* (London: Continuum, 2009).

Kiš, Danilo, *Grobnica za Borisa Davidoviča* (1976); trans. Duska Mikic-Mitchell as *A Tomb for Boris Davidovich* (London: Faber and Faber, 1985).

Konstantinou, Lee, *Cool Characters. Irony and American Fiction* (Cambridge, MA: Harvard University Press, 2016).

Kurnick, David, 'Comparison, Allegory, and the Address of "Global" Realism (The Part about Bolaño)', *Boundary*, 42/2 (2015), 105–134.

LaCapra, Dominick, *History, Literature, Critical Theory* (Ithaca, NY: Cornell University Press, 2013).

Lainck, Arndt, *Las figuras del mal en 2666 de Roberto Bolaño* (Münster: LIT verlag, 2014).

Lamy-Rested, Élise, *Parole vraie, parole vice. Des Bienveillantes aux exécuteurs* (Paris: Classiques Garnier, 2014).

Langford, Barry, 'Globalizing the Holocaust: Fantasies of Annihilation in Contemporary Media Culture', in Axel Bangert, Robert C. S. Gordon and Libby Saxton, eds, *Holocaust Intersections. Genocide and Visual Culture at the New Millennium* (Leeds: Legenda, 2013), 98–111.

Lavender, William, 'The Novel of Critical Engagement: Paul Auster's *City of Glass*', in Harold Bloom, ed., *Paul Auster* (Broomal, PA: Chelsea House Publishers, 2004), 77–96.

Lee, Newton, *Facebook Nation. Total Information Awareness* (New York: Springer, 2013).

Lejeune, Philippe, *Le pacte autobiographique* (Paris: Éditions du Seuil, 1975).

Lermonier, Marc, *Les Bienveillantes décryptées* (Saint-Amand-Montrond: Le Pré aux Clercs, 2007).

Levéel, Éric, 'Maximilien Aue : une homosexualité de rigueur ?', in Murielle Lucie Clément, ed., *Les Bienveillantes de Jonathan Littell* (Cambridge: Open Book Publishers, 2010), 141–154.

Levin, Stephen, 'Is There a Booker Aesthetic? Iterations of the Global Novel', *Critique*, 55 (2014), 477–493.

Liang, Quiao, and Wang Xiangsui, *Unrestricted Warfare* (Brattleboro, VT: Echo Point Books & Media, 2015; 1st edn 1999).

Lionarons, Joyce Tally, 'The Otherworld and its Inhabitants in the *Nibelungenlied*', in Winder McConnell, ed., *A Companion to the Nibelungenlied* (Rochester, NY: Camden House, 1998), 153–171.

Lipovetsky, Gilles, and Sébastien Charles, *Les Temps Hypermodernes* (Paris: Grasset & Fasquelle, 2004).

Littell, Jonathan, *Le sec et l'humide* (Paris: Gallimard, 2008).

——, *Les Bienveillantes* (Paris: Gallimard, 2006); trans. Charlotte Mandell as *The Kindly Ones* (Toronto: McClelland & Stewart, 2009).

——, and Richard Millet, 'Conversation à Beyrouth', *Le Débat*, 144 (2007), 4–24.

——, and Pierre Nora, 'Conversation sur l'histoire et le roman', *Le Débat*, 144 (2007), 25–44.

Lukes, Daniel, *Conversations with William T. Vollmann* (Jackson: University Press of Mississippi, 2020).

Luperini, Romano, *L'incontro e il caso* (Bari: Laterza, 2007).

Luzzato, Sergio, 'Jonathan Littell, *Le benevole*', *Allegoria*, 38 (2008), 215–253.

Lyotard, Jean-François, *La condition postmoderne. Rapport sur le savoir* (Paris: Les Éditions de Minuit, 1979).

Mack, Michael, *Philosophy and Literature in Times of Crisis. Challenging Our Infatuation with Numbers* (New York: Bloomsbury, 2014).

Malvestio, Marco, ' "All Our Choices Will Probably Run Out". La non-fiction post-apocalittica di William T. Vollmann', *Ácoma* 17 (2019), 160–174.

Mancinelli, Laura, 'Memoria e invenzione. Introduzione alla lettura del "Nibelungenlied" ', in Laura Mancinelli, ed., *I Nibelunghi* (Torino: Einaudi, 1972), i–lxi.

Marchese, Lorenzo, *L'io possibile. L'autofiction come paradosso del romanzo contemporaneo* (Massa: Transeuropa, 2014).

Marichal, José, *Facebook Democracy. The Architect of Disclosure and the Threat to Public Life* (Farnham: Ashgate Publishing Limited, 2012).

Marsh, Huw, 'Narrative Unreliability and Metarepresentation in Ian McEwan's *Atonement*; or, Why Robbie Might Be Guilty and Why Nobody Seems to Notice', *Textual Practice*, 32/8 (2017), 1325–1343.

Marsilio, Morena, 'Un alfabetiere per la gemella', 25 November 2016, available at: <http://www.laletteraturaenoi.it/index.php/interpretazione-e-noi/586-un-alfabetiere-per-la-gemella.html> [last accessed 31 March 2020].

——, and Emanuele Zinato, 'Le idee letterarie degli anni Zero', *L'Ulisse*, 18 (2015), 244–268.

Martínez Alfaro, María Jesús, 'The Spectral Evidence of Photography in Rachel Seiffert's *The Dark Room*: An Album of Fractured Lives', *Alicante Journal of English Studies*, 26 (2013), 259–270.

Mazower, Mark, *Dark Continent: Europe's 20th Century* (London: Penguin, 1999).

Mazzoni, Guido, 'Jonathan Littell, *Le benevole*', *Allegoria*, 38 (2008), 215–253.

——, *Teoria del romanzo* (Bologna: il Mulino, 2011); trans. Zakiya Hanafi as *Theory of the Novel* (Cambridge, MA: Harvard University Press, 2017).

McCaffery, Larry, *The Metafictional Muse* (Pittsburgh, PA: The University of Pittsburgh Press, 1982).

——, 'Preface: The Chrysanthemum and the Flame Thrower', in Christopher K. Coffman and Daniel Lukes, eds, *William T. Vollmann. A Critical Companion* (Newark: University of Delaware Press, 2015), xii–xvi.

McEwan, Ian, *Atonement* (London: Jonathan Cape, 2001).

McGlathery, James M., 'Erotic Love in Chrétien's Perceval, Wolfram's Parzival, and Wagner's Parsifal', in William Kinderman and Katherine R. Syer, eds, *A Companion to Wagner's Parsifal* (Rochester, NY: Camden House, 2005), 55–79.

McHale, Brian, *Postmodernist Fiction* (London: Routledge, 2003).

Mercier-Leca, Florence, '*Les Bienveillantes* et la tragèdie grecque', *Le Débat*, 144 (2007), 45–55.

Mitchell, Kaye, '"What Does It Feel to Be an Anachronism?": Time in *The Night Watch*', in Kaye Mitchell, ed., *Sarah Waters. Contemporary Critical Perspectives* (Basingstoke: Palgrave Macmillan, 2013), 84–98.

Mitchell, Peta, *Cartographic Strategies of Postmodernity: The Figure of the Map in Contemporary Theory and Fiction* (London: Routledge, 2008).

Mitric, Ana, 'Turning Points: *Atonement*, *Horizons*, and Late Modernism', *Modernism/Modernity*, 21/3 (2014), 715–740.

Möller, Swantje, *Coming to Terms with Crisis. Disorientation and Reorientation in the Novels of Ian McEwan* (Heidelberg: Universitätsverlag Winter, 2011).

Monballieu, Aagje, 'Perseguidores de la nada: la subversion del mito de Jasòn y los Argonautas en *Los Premios* de Julio Cortàzar', in José Manuel Losada Goya and Marta Guirao Ochoa, eds, *Myth and Subversion in the Contemporary Novel* (Newcastle upon Tyne: Cambridge Scholars Publishing, 2012), 131–144.

Moretti, Franco, *Distant Reading* (London: Verso 2013).

——, *Graphs, Maps and Trees* (London: Verso, 2007).

Moura, Jean-Marc, 'French Within Europe and Beyond: the Case of "Francophone" Writers', *European Studies*, 29 (2012), 253–265.

Moyn, Samuel, 'To Wipe the Slate Clean', *Yale French Studies*, 121 (2012), 128–139.

Nagel, James, *The Contemporary Short-Story Cycle. The Ethnic Resonance of Genre* (Baton Rouge: Louisiana University Press, 2001).

Naimark, Norman M., *Stalin's Genocides* (Princeton, NJ: Princeton University Press, 2010).

Nealon, Jeffrey T., *Post-Postmodernism or, The Cultural Logic of Just in Time Capitalism* (Stanford, CA: Stanford University Press, 2012).

The Nibelungenlied, ed. and trans. Arthur Thomas Hatto (Harmondsworth: Penguin Books, 1969).

Nivat, Georges, 'Adelphic Incest in Musil, Nabokov, and Littell', in Aurélie Barjonet and Lirian Razinsky, eds, *Writing the Holocaust Today. Critical Perspectives on Jonathan Littell's* The Kindly Ones (Amsterdam: Rodopi, 2012), 19–31.

——, '*Les Bienveillantes* et les classique russes', *Le Débat*, 144 (2007), 56–65.

Noakes, Lucy, and Juliette Pattinson, 'Introduction: the Cultural Memory of the Second World War', in Lucy Noakes and Juliette Pattinson, eds, *British Cultural Memory and the Second World War* (New York: Bloomsbury, 2014), 1–25.

Novick, Peter, *The Holocaust in American Life* (New York: Mariner Books, 2000).

O'Bryen, Rory, 'Writing with the Ghost of Pierre Menard: Authorship, Responsibility, and Justice in Roberto Bolaño's *Distant Star*', in Ignacio López-Calvo, ed., *Roberto Bolaño, A Less Distant Star. Critical Essays* (New York: Palgrave Macmillan, 2015), 17–34.

O'Callaghan, Claire, '"Grisley 'L' Business": Re-valuating Female Masculinity and Butch Subjectivity in *Tipping the Velvet* and *The Night Watch*', in Adele Jones and Claire O'Callaghan, eds, *Sarah Waters and Contemporary Feminism* (Basingstoke: Palgrave Macmillan, 2016), 193–213.

——, *Sarah Waters. Gender and Sexual Politics* (London: Bloomsbury, 2017).

O'Hara, David K., 'Briony's Being-For: Metafictional Narrative Ethics in Ian McEwan's *Atonement*', *Critique: Studies in Contemporary Fiction*, 52/1 (2011), 74–100.

Özcan, Işil, *Understanding William T. Vollmann* (Columbia: University of South Carolina Press, 2019).

Palleau-Papin, Françoise, 'Composition as Infinity', in Françoise Palleau-Papin, ed., *William T. Vollmann,* The Rifles*: A Critical Study* (Bern: Peter Lang, 2016), 83–100.

Palumbo Mosca, Raffaello, *L'invenzione del vero* (Rome: Gaffi, 2014).

Panichi, Camilla, 'Narrare la guerra. Da *Vita e destino* a *Le benevole*', *TiConTre. Teoria, Testo, Traduzione*, 1 (2014), 125–140.

Parker, Geoffrey, 'Introduction. The Western Way of War', in Geoffrey Parker, ed., *The Cambridge Illustrated History of Warfare. The Triumph of the West* (Cambridge: Cambridge University Press, 2000; 1st edn 1995), 2–9.

Patterson, Annabel, *The International Novel* (New Haven, CT: Yale University Press, 2014).

Pearson, Nels, and Marc Singer, 'Introduction: Open Cases. Detection, (Post) Modernity, and the State', in Nels Pearson and Marc Singer, eds, *Detective Fiction in a Postcolonial and Transnational World* (Farnham: Ashgate Publishing Limited, 2009), 1–14.

Pennacchio, Filippo, 'Appunti per una lettura narratologica di *2666*', *Orillas*, 6 (2017), 201–212.

——, 'Autorialità *reloaded*. Qualche nota (e un'ipotesi) sul narratore del romanzo globalizzato', *TiConTre*, 2 (2014), 9–28.

——, *Autorialità* reloaded. *Qualche nota (e un'ipotesi) sul narratore del romanzo globalizzato* (2014), available at: <http://www.leparoleelecose.it/?p=16815> [last accessed 31 March 2020].

——, *Eccessi d'autore. Retoriche della voce nel romanzo italiano di oggi* (Milan: Mimesis, 2020).

——, *Il romanzo global. Uno studio narratologico* (Milan: Biblion, 2018).

Piva, Marika, 'La parte della letteratura: combinazione e trasformazione in Roberto Bolaño e Michel Houellebecq', *Orillas*, 2 (2017), 235–249.

Pividori, Cristina, 'Out of the Dark Room: Photography and Memory in Rachel Seiffert's Holocaust Tales', *Atlantis*, 30/2 (2008), 79–94.

Possamai, Donatella, 'Tracce di Russia in *2666* di Roberto Bolaño: "La parte di Arcimboldi". Per una ricognizione', *Orillas*, 2 (2017), 225–234.

Potter, Garry, and José Loperz, 'After Postmodernism: The New Millennium', in José Lopez and Garry Potter, eds, *After Postmodernism. An Introduction to Critical Realism* (London: The Athlone Press, 2001).

Qian, Cheng, *A Study of William Vollmann: Transgression in the Postmodern Context* (Xiamen: Xiamen University Press, 2012).

Quarrie, Cynthia, '"Before the Destruction Began": Interrupting Post-Imperial Melancholia in Ian McEwan's *Atonement*', *Studies in the Novel*, 47/2 (2015), 193–209.

Quílez, Luis Bagué, 'Performing Disappearance: Heaven and Sky in Roberto Bolaño and Raúl Zurita', in Ignacio López-Calvo, ed., *Roberto Bolaño, A Less Distant Star. Critical Essays* (New York: Palgrave Macmillan, 2015), 171–188.

Raciti, Giuseppe, *Ho visto Jünger nel Caucaso* (Milan: Mimesis, 2013).

Rau, Petra, 'Beyond *punctum* and *studium*. Trauma and Photography in Rachel Seiffert's *The Dark Room*', *Journal of European Studies*, 36/3 (2006), 295–325.

Razinsky, Liran, 'The Similarity of Perpetrators', in Aurélie Barjonet and Lirian Razinsky, eds, *Writing the Holocaust Today. Critical Perspectives on Jonathan Littell's The Kindly Ones* (Amsterdam: Rodopi, 2012a), 47–60.

——, 'We Are All the Same: Max Aue, Interpreter of Evil', *Yale French Studies*, 121 (2012b), 140–154.

Rebein, Robert, *Hicks, Tribes, and Dirty Realists. American Fiction after Postmodernism* (Lexington: The University Press of Kentucky, 2001).

Ríos Baeza, Felipe A., *Roberto Bolaño. Una narrativa en el margen* (Valencia: Tirant Humanidades, 2013).

Rippard, Lucy R., 'Foreword', in Lucy R. Rippard, ed., *Kathe Kollwitz. Graphics, Posters, Drawings* (London: Writers and Readers Publishing Cooperative, 1981), vi–xiii.

Robinson, Richard, 'The Modernism of Ian McEwan's *Atonement*', *MFS Modern Fiction Studies*, 56/3 (2010), 473–495.

Rose, Margaret, *Parody. Ancient, Modern, and Post-Modern* (Cambridge: Cambridge University Press, 1993).

Rosenfeld, Alvin, *The Americanization of the Holocaust* (Ann Arbor: Jean and Samuel Frankel Center for Judaic Studies, The University of Michigan, 1995).

——, *The End of the Holocaust* (Bloomington: Indiana University Press, 2011).

Rosenfeld, Gavriel, *Hi Hitler! How the Nazi Past Is Being Normalized in Contemporary Culture* (Cambridge: Cambridge University Press, 2015).

——, *The World Hitler Never Made. Alternate History and the Memory of Nazism* (Cambridge: Cambridge University Press, 2005)

Rousso, Henry, 'A New Perspective on the War', in Jörg Echternkamp and Stefan Martens, eds, *Experience and Memory. The Second World War in Europe* (New York: Berghahn Books, 2010), 1–9.

Rudrum, David, and Nicholas Stavris, 'Introduction', in David Rudrum and Nicholas Stavris, eds, *Supplanting the Postmodern: An Anthology of Writings on the Arts and Culture of the Early 21st Century* (New York: Bloomsbury Academic, 2015), xi–xxix.

——, 'Notes on the Supplanting of "post-" ', in David Rudrum and Nicholas Stavris, eds, *Supplanting the Postmodern, An Anthology of Writings on the Arts and Culture of the Early 21st Century* (New York: Bloomsbury Academic, 2015), 333–348.

Samuels, Robert, 'Auto-Modernity after Postmodernism: Autonomy and Automation in Culture, Technology, and Education', in Tara McPherson, ed., *Digital Youth, Innovation, and the Unexpected* (Cambridge, MA: The MIT Press, 2008).

Sandberg, Eric, ' "This Incomprehensible Thing": Jonathan Littell's *The Kindly Ones* and the Aesthetics of Excess', *The Cambridge Quarterly*, 43/3 (2014), 231–255.

Santin, Bryan M., 'Kurt Gerstein and the Tragic Parable of "Clean Hands": The Imaginative Role of Fiction in the Moral Calculus of William T. Vollmann', in Christopher K. Coffman and Daniel Lukes, eds, *William T. Vollmann. A Critical Companion* (Newark: University of Delaware Press, 2015), 141–166.

Saviano, Roberto, 'Un nazista piccolo piccolo dal Terzo Reich a Rimini', *La Repubblica* (20 February 2014).

Savvas, Theophilus, *American Postmodernist Fiction and the Past* (Basingstoke: Palgrave Macmillan, 2011).

Schmukler, Enrique, 'Abrir la historia: Roberto Bolaño, el "principio atlas" y los modos ficcionales de re-presentar la historia literaria', *Mitologías Hoy*, 7 (2013), 113–123.

Scholem, Gershom, *Der Name Gottes und die Sprachtheorie der Kabbala* (Frankfurt: Suhrkamp Verlag, 1970); (Italian) trans. Adriano Fabris as *Il nome di Dio e la teoria cabbalistica del linguaggio* (Milan: Adelphi, 1998).

——, *Ursprung und Anfänge der Kabbala* (Berlin: Walter de Gruyter & Co., 1962); trans. The Jewish Publication Society as *Origins of the Kabbalah* (Princeton, NJ: Princeton University Press, 1987).

Schwieger, Florina, '"Loyalty gleaming, guns screaming": William T. Vollmann's *Europe Central* and the Memory of Stalingrad', *War, Literature and the Arts. An International Journal of the Humanities*, 22 (2010).

Scurati, Antonio, *Guerra. Narrazioni e culture nella tradizione occidentale* (Rome: Donzelli, 2003).

——, 'Un sanguinoso desiderio di luce. Le forme della guerra come invenzione letteraria', in Stefano Rosso, ed., *Un fascino osceno. Guerra e violenza nella letteratura e nel cinema* (Verona: ombre corte, 2006), 17–29.

Sedgwick, Mark, *Against the Modern World: Traditionalism and the Secret Intellectual History of the Twentieth Century* (Oxford: Oxford University Press, 2004).

Seiffert, Rachel, *The Dark Room* (London: Vintage, 2002).

Singles, Kathleen, *Alternate History. Playing with Contingency and Necessity* (Berlin: Walter de Gruyter GmbH, 2013).

Smith, Rupert, *The Utility of Force. The Art of War in the Modern World* (London: Penguin Books, 2006).

Sparrow, Robert, 'Robotic Weapons and the Future of War', in Jessica Wolfendale and Paolo Tripodi, eds, *New Wars and New Soldiers: Military Ethics in the Contemporary World* (Surrey: Ashgate, 2011), 117–133.

Stein, Robert H., 'The Genre of Parables', in Richard N. Longenecker, ed., *The Challenge of Jesus' Parables* (Grand Rapids, MI: William B. Eerdmans Publishing Company, 2000), 30–50.

Stewart, Victoria, 'The Second World War in Contemporary Women's Fiction: Revisiting the Home Front', *Contemporary Women's Writing*, 9/3 (2015), 416–432.

Stierstorfer, Klaus, 'Introduction: Beyond Postmodernism – Contingent Referentiality?', in Klaus Stierstorfer, ed., *Beyond Postmodernism. Reassessments in Literature, Theory, and Culture* (Berlin: Walter de Gruyter, 2003), 1–10.

Summerfield, Penny, *Women Workers in the Second World War. Production and Patriarchy in Conflict* (London: Croom Helm, 1984).

Tame, Peter, '"Ceci n'est pas un roman". *HHhH* de Laurent Binet, en deçà ou au-delà de la fiction?', in Marc Dambre, ed., *Mémoires occupées* (Paris: Presses Sorbonne Nouvelle, 2013).

——, 'Lieux réels et lieux imaginaires dans *Les Bienveillantes*', Murielle Lucie Clément, ed., *Les Bienveillantes de Jonathan Littell* (Cambridge: Open Book Publishers, 2010), 213–230.

Testa, Enrico, *Eroi e figuranti. Il personaggio nel romanzo* (Torino: Einaudi, 2009).

Theweleit, Klaus, and Timothy Nunan, 'On the German Reaction to Jonathan Littell's *Les Bienveillantes*', *New German Critique*, 106 (2009), 21–34.

Thierry, Laurent, 'La réception des *Bienveillantes* dans les milieux intellectuels français', in Murielle Lucie Clément, ed., *Les Bienveillantes de Jonathan Littell* (Cambridge: Open Book Publishers, 2010), 11–18.

Timmer, Nicoline, *Do You Feel It Too? The Post-Postmodern Syndrome in American Fiction at the Turn of the Millennium* (Amsterdam: Rodopi, 2010).

Tirinanzi De Medici, Carlo, *Il vero e il convenzionale* (Milan: Utet, 2012).

Torres Perdigòn, Andrea, *La littérature obstinée. Le roman chez Juan José Saer, Ricardo Piglia et Roberto Bolaño* (Brussels: Peter Lang, 2015).

Toth, Josh, and Neil Brooks, 'Introduction: A Wake and Renewed?', in Neil Brooks and Josh Toth, eds, *The Mourning After: Attending the Wake of Postmodernism* (Amsterdam: Rodopi, 2007), 1–9.

Toth, Josh, 'Historioplastic Metafiction. Tarantino, Nolan, and the "Return to Hegel"', *Cultural Critique*, 99 (2018), 1–30

——, 'Toni Morrison's *Beloved* and the Rise of Historioplastic Metafiction', in Robin van den Akker, Alison Gibbons, and Timotheus Vermeulen, eds., *Metamodernism. Historicity, Affect, and Depth After Postmodernism* (Lanham: Rowman & Littlefield, 2017), 41–53

Traverso, Enzo, 'La singolarità storica di Auschwitz. Problemi e derive di un dibattito', in Marcello Flores, ed., *Nazismo, fascismo, comunismo. Totalitarismi a confronto* (Milan: Bruno Mondadori, 1998), 303–324.

——, *La violenza nazista. Una genealogia* (Bologna: Il Mulino, 2002); trans. Janet Lloyd as *The Origins of Nazi Violence* (New York: The New Press, 2003).

Troubetzkoy, Wladimir, '« Frères humains … »: *Les Bienveillantes*, une historie de familles', in Murielle Lucie Clément, ed., *Les Bienveillantes de Jonathan Littell* (Cambridge: Open Book Publishers, 2010), 19–30.

Turato, Fabio, *Eredi ingrati. Mondo germanico e tragedia greca tra nascita del II e apocalisse del III Reich (1871–1945)* (Venezia: Marsilio, 2014).

Usandizaga, Helena, 'El reverso poético de la prosa de Roberto Bolaño', in Ramón González Férriz, ed., *Jornadas Homenaje Roberto Bolaño (1953–2003). Simposio Internacional* (Barcelona: Casa Amèrica a Catalunya, 2005), 75–94.

Vaget, Hans Rudolf, 'Wagnerian Self-Fashioning: The Case of Adolf Hitler', *New German Critique*, 101 (2007), 95–114.

Van Creveld, Martin, *The Transformation of War* (New York: The Free Press, 1991).

——, *Wargames. From Gladiators to Gigabytes* (Cambridge: Cambridge University Press, 2013).

van den Akker, Robin, and Timotheus Vermeulen, 'Notes on Metamodernism', *Journal of Aesthetics and Culture*, 2/1 (2010), 2–15.

——, 'Periodising the 2000s, or, the Emergence of Metamodernism', in Robin van den Akker, Alison Gibbons and Timotheus Vermeulen, *Metamodernism.*

Historicity, Affect, and Depth after Postmodernism (London: Rowman and Littlefield International, 2017).

Vasta, Giorgio, 'Giorgio Falco e la gelida microfisica dell'impotenza', 28 April 2014, available at <http://www.minimaetmoralia.it/wp/la-gemella-h-giorgio-falco/> [last accessed 31 March 2020].

Villalobos-Ruminott, Sergio, 'A Kind of Hell: Roberto Bolaño and The Return of World Literature', *Journal of Latin American Cultural Studies*, 18/2–3 (2009), 193–205.

Vittorini, Fabio, *Raccontare oggi. Metamodernismo tra narratologia, ermeneutica e intermedialità* (Bologna: Pàtron Editore, 2018).

Vollmann, William T., 'Afterword to Danilo Kiš's *A Tomb for Boris Davidovich*', in Larry McCaffery and Michael Hemmingson, eds, *Expelled From Eden. A William T. Vollmann Reader* (New York: Thunder's Mouth Press, 2004a), 333–342.

——, *Europe Central* (New York: Viking Penguin, 2006).

——, *The Ice-Shirt* (New York: Viking, 1990).

——, 'List of "Contemporary" Books Most Admired by Vollmann', in Larry McCaffery and Michael Hemmingson, eds, *Expelled From Eden. A William T. Vollmann Reader* (New York: Thunder's Mouth Press, 2004b), 35–38.

——, *Rising Up and Rising Down. Some Thoughts on Violence, Freedom, and Urgent Means* (London: Gerald Duckworth & Co., 2005).

Wagner, Richard, *Parsifal*, ed. and trans. Guido Manacorda (Firenze: Le Lettere, 1997),

Walker, Carlos, 'El tono del horror: *2666* de Roberto Bolaño', *Taller de letras*, 46 (2010), 99–112.

Waters, Sarah, *The Night Watch* (London: Virago, 2006).

Watts, Philip, 'Remnants of Tragedy', *Yale French Studies*, 121 (2012), 155–168.

Waugh, Patricia, *Metafiction. The Theory and Practice of Self-Conscious Fiction* (London: Routledge, 2001).

Weinberg, Robert, *Stalin's Forgotten Zion* (Berkeley: University of California Press, 1998).

Weissman, Gary, *Fantasies of Witnessing. Postwar Efforts to Experience the Holocaust* (Ithaca, NY: Cornell University Press, 2004).

Werth, Nicolas, 'A State Against Its People', in Stéphane Courtois, ed., *Le Livre noir du communisme. Crimes, terreur, répression* (Paris: Robert Laffont, 1997); trans. Jonathan Murphy and Mark Kramer as *The Black Book of Communism. Crimes, Terror, Repression* (Cambridge, MA: Harvard University Press, 1999), 33–268.

White, Hayden, *Metahistory. The Historical Imagination in Nineteenth-Century Europe* (Baltimore, MD: Johns Hopkins University Press, 1975).

White, John J., *Mythology in the Modern Novel. A Study of Prefigurative Techniques* (Princeton, NJ: Princeton University Press, 1971).

Wicks, Robert, 'Literary Truth as Dreamlike Expression in Foucault's and Borges's "Chinese Encyclopedia"', in *Philosophy and Literature*, 27 (2003), 80–97.

Wieviorka, Annette, *L'Ère du Témoin* (Paris: Plon, 1998).

Willem, Bieke, '"Las palabras servían para ese fin": la literatura y el mal en *2666* de Roberto Bolaño', *Bulletin of Hispanic Studies*, 90/1 (2013), 79–91.

Wolfenson, Carolyn, 'El Tercer Reich y la historia como juego de guerra', in Edmundo Paz Soldán and Gustavo Faverón Patriau, eds, *Bolaño Salvaje* (Barcelona: Editorial Candaya, 2013), 204–228.

Wood, Rachel, '"Walking and Watching" in Queer London: Sarah Waters' *Tipping the Velvet* and *The Night Watch*', *Journal of Lesbian Studies*, 17/3–4 (2013), 305–316.

Wyatt, David, *Secret Histories. Reading Twentieth-Century American Literature* (Baltimore, MD: The Johns Hopkins University Press, 2010).

Young, James E., *At Memory's Edge. After-Images of the Holocaust in Contemporary Art and Architecture* (New Haven, CT: Yale University Press, 2000).

Zatti, Sergio, 'La novella: un genere senza teoria', *Moderna*, XII, 2 (2010), 13–24.

Zeitlin, Froma I., 'Imaginary Tales in the Land of Perpetrators', *Journal of Modern Jewish Studies*, 5/2 (2006), 213–228.

Zima, Peter V., 'Why the Postmodern Age Will Last', Klaus Stierstorfer, ed., *Beyond Postmodernism. Reassessments in Literature, Theory, and Culture* (Berlin: Walter de Gruyter, 2003), 13–28.

Žižek, Slavoj, *Welcome to the Desert of the Real. Five Essays on September 11 and Related Dates* (London: Verso, 2002).

Index

NEW COMPARATIVE CRITICISM

New Comparative Criticism is dedicated to innovative research in literary and cultural studies. It invites contributions with a comparative, cross-cultural, and interdisciplinary focus, including comparative studies of themes, genres, and periods, and research in the following fields: world literature, environmental humanities, literary and cultural theory, material and visual cultures, speculative fiction, reception studies, cultural history, comparative gender studies and performance studies, diasporas and migration studies, and transmediality. The series is especially interested in research that articulates and examines new developments in comparative literature, in the English-speaking world and beyond. It seeks to advance methodological reflection on comparative literature, and aims to encourage critical dialogue between scholars of comparative literature at an international level.

Proposals are welcome for either single-author monographs or edited collections. Please provide a detailed outline, a sample chapter, and a CV. For further information, please contact the series editor: Florian Mussgnug (f.mussgnug@ucl.ac.uk).

Published volumes

Margherita Laera
Reaching Athens: Community, Democracy and Other Mythologies in Adaptations of Greek Tragedy
2013. ISBN 978-3-0343-0807-6

Florian Mussgnug and Matthew Reza (eds)
The Good Place: Comparative Perspectives on Utopia
2014. ISBN 978-3-0343-1819-8

Marion Dalvai
Politics of Cross-Cultural Reading: Tagore, Ben Jelloun and Fo in English
2015. ISBN 978-3-0343-1881-5

Michael G. Kelly and Daragh O'Connell (eds)
Comparative Becomings: Studies in Transition
2017. ISBN 978-3-0343-1811-2

Simona Corso and Beth Guilding (eds)
Narrating the Passions: New Perspectives from Modern and Contemporary Literature
2017. ISBN 978-1-78707-121-6

Simone Brioni and Shimelis Bonsa Gulema (eds)
The Horn of Africa and Italy: Colonial, Postcolonial and Transnational Cultural Encounters
2018. ISBN: 978-1-78707-993-9

Simona Micali
Towards a Posthuman Imagination in Literature and Media: Monsters, Mutants, Aliens, Artificial Beings
2019. ISBN 978-1-78874-582-6

Laëtitia Saint-Loubert
The Caribbean in Translation: Remapping Thresholds of Dislocation
2020. ISBN 978-1-78997-198-9

Robert Cowan
Solace in Oblivion: Approaches to Transcendence in Modern Europe
2020. ISBN 978-1-78997-669-4

Marco Malvestio
The Conflict Revisited: The Second World War in Post-Postmodern Fiction
2021. ISBN 978-1-78997-209-2

www.ingramcontent.com/pod-product-compliance
Lightning Source LLC
Chambersburg PA
CBHW061919130726
47908CB00017B/2262

* 9 7 8 1 7 8 9 9 7 2 0 9 2 *